The Miniature Gardens Book

Angie Scarr

Publishing Data

First published 2017 Sliding Scale Books (SSPB06)

Plaza De Andalucia 1, Campofrio, 21668, Huelva, Spain.

Text and step-by-step photography Angie Scarr 2017
Additional photography Frank Fisher
Design by Frank Fisher and Angie Scarr

ISBN 978-1-97825-310-0

This book is dedicated to all the creative women in my close and extended family who I count myself blessed to be related to. Including but not exclusively Kira, Stephanie, Caroline, Rachel and Claire.

And, of course, to my new granddaughter Ada. I don't know if creativity is a blessing or a curse but I'll do my best to make sure you have some of the family abilities!

Contents

Introduction

Some people can fashion something with a beautiful form, using just their hands and a raw piece of clay or polymer clay. I'm not one of those people.

I'm not a sculptor. I've never learned sculpture and I kind of 'got away with' my miniatures for many years because my colours were good. And still I feel colour is the most important thing. And that's why, when it comes to shape ... I need a bit ... sometimes a lot of help. Because I'm a problem solver I've come up with a good number of tricks over the years and because I'm a hoarder with a particular 'fetish' for tools, I've built up a huge collection of tools including shapers, cutters, moulds, stampers, etc.

The number of commercially available tools moulds and cutters etc. for use with polymer clay is large and growing and getting yourself a collection of these can be fun and inspiring. However it can also be expensive and limiting. You are limited to using other peoples designs and, even if used in your own way, you will never feel that they are quite 'yours'. This book shows you it's also relatively easy to add to your bought tools with tools of your own making and thus build your own ideas and talents into your work just by keeping your mind open and occasionally borrowing and adding to 'ideas' to make them your own.

Originally intended to be the companion to my Colour Book and titled something along the lines of Book of Shapes / Forms / etc., the Gardens Book idea grew out of the fact that I naturally gravitate towards nature both in my borrowing of forms and in my love of colour. And also because wherever I saw vegetable gardens in miniature people had either made or bought and 'plonked' in their gardens, the table trimmed variety of vegetables ignoring the fact that real nature is somewhat messy and clumsy in it's presentation.

I wanted to redress the balance a bit. I also wanted to prove that polymer clay can be used for really delicate work. Many flower artists use paper or cold porcelain as they say polymer clay is too clumsy or sticky. I hope I've shown that there are tricks which can make polymer clay even more suitable for miniature plants than other materials.

My work is very much copying nature, but there are also some ideas for finding shapes and textures from other places to augment your tool kit and inspire your abstract work. I hope this book will add that extra dimension to your work by helping you, if your sculpting skills are limited like mine, to use your observation and problem solving skills to find the right tool for the job.

And even if you are an excellent sculptor already I hope it will provide you with another starting point or another direction to explore. This book is intended to be complementary to my Colour Book which you may find useful to reference when looking for a colour mix.

The making and use of the tools in this book are not by any means limited to miniature arts of course, but can also be used in jewellery and other polymer art as well as to sugarcraft (cake decorating) and the food arts.

Angie, October 2017.

Getting Started

Tools

Materials

Polymer Clay Ideas

Making Your Own Moulds

Growbag Project

Garden Bases

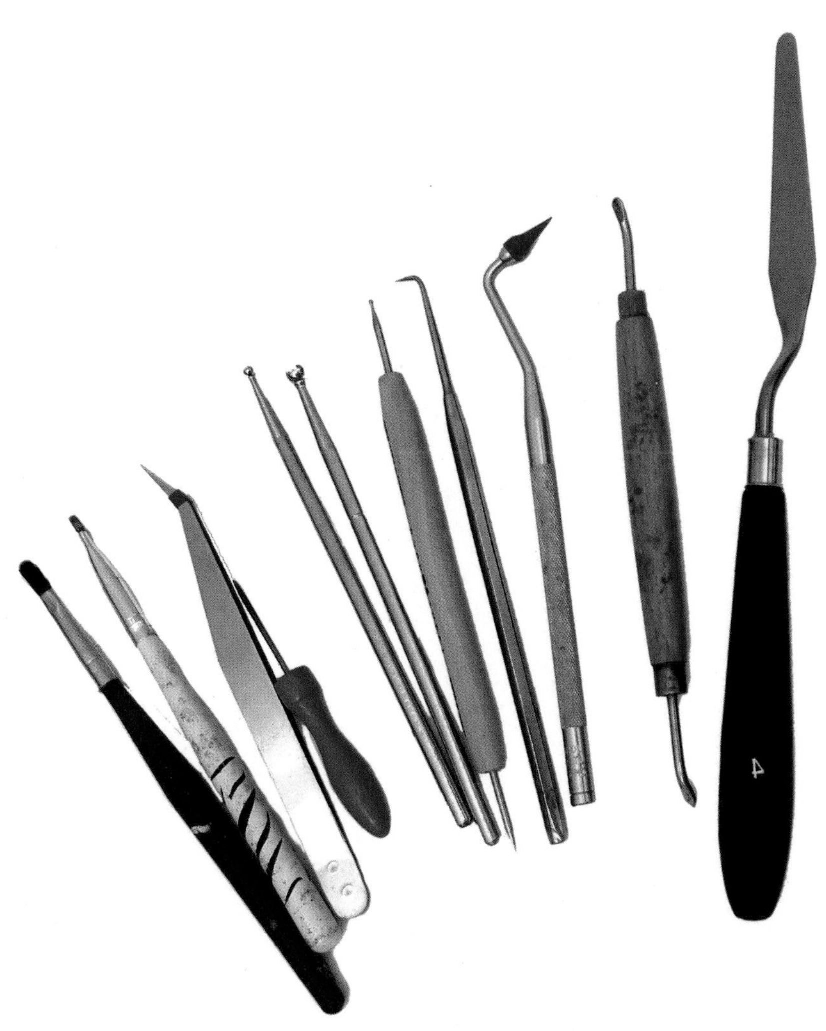

Tools

For many of my classes the tool kit is as simple as a ceramic tile, a glass bottle, a single sided blade and a cocktail stick. Apart from the clay, and lots of patience that's all you need to get started.

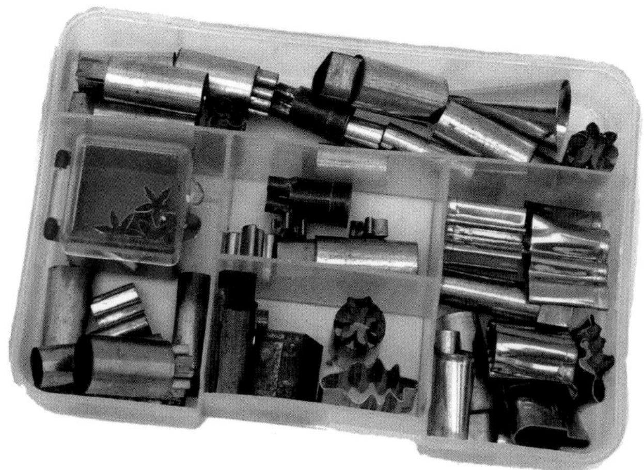

However this book isn't about getting started its about simple and more complicated tricks and short-cuts.

Over the years I have built up a huge collection of tools. Some I use all the time. some I rarely use but wouldn't be without, and others I really should get rid of but am convinced that some day I'll need them, and often that's true. When an artist wakes in the middle of the night with a new idea, it's often because the brain has finally made a connection between a vague idea and the tool required to make it a reality. More often than not it's because that tool is already in the workshop and therefore in a creative corner of the brain! Finding it in the untidy workshop ... well that's another matter because only rarely is a creative mind also a tidy mind! I'm rather envious of those who have all those skills but in some way, for me at least it's the randomness of connections which makes for inventiveness.

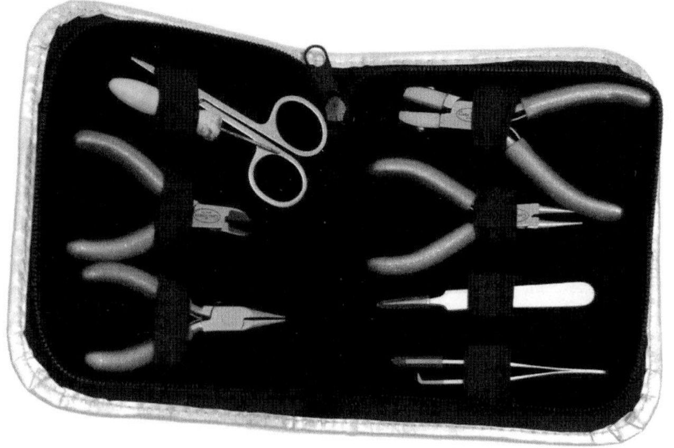

My husband says my tool kit is half the house, and he has a point as often I creep into the kitchen to steal items to do a little job. It depends if you're a hobby maker or a professional or semi professional. And I guess, how obsessive you are. I have to admit I'm 'out there'!

My tool kit in approximate order of importance (to me)

Simple tools

Single sided blade and long, inflexible blade.

Cocktail stick dental tool bent pin tool simple leaf veiner/s a ceramic tile to work and bake on and a glass bottle with straight sides for rolling with.

Medium tools

More dental tools, pergamano-hockey stick tool, flexible blade, wavy blade

Other leaf veiners some commercially available ... some not. Stem moulds and stem imprinters veiner-imprinters and texture plates.

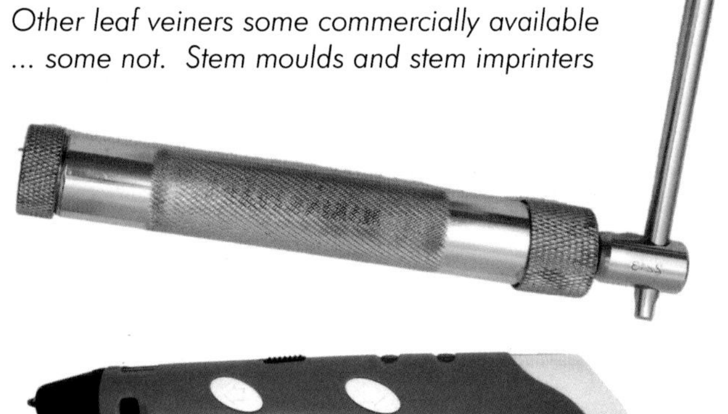

Home made moulds etc. as shown in this book. Here I need to mention silicone moulding paste which I use extensively in my work. I include this in the tools pages rather than materials because it is, or at least, it becomes part of the tool kit.

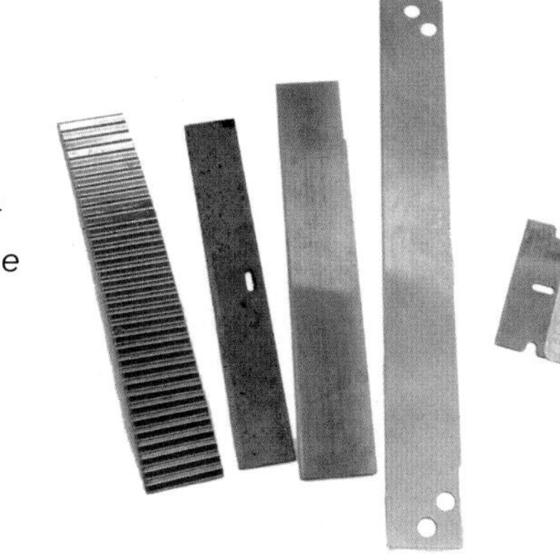

The moulds I use are dealt with separately on the project pages and how to make moulds is shown on *page 72.*

Cutters geometric, flower and leaf shapes and altered and home made cutters. See below.

Small saw (preferably a Japsaw)

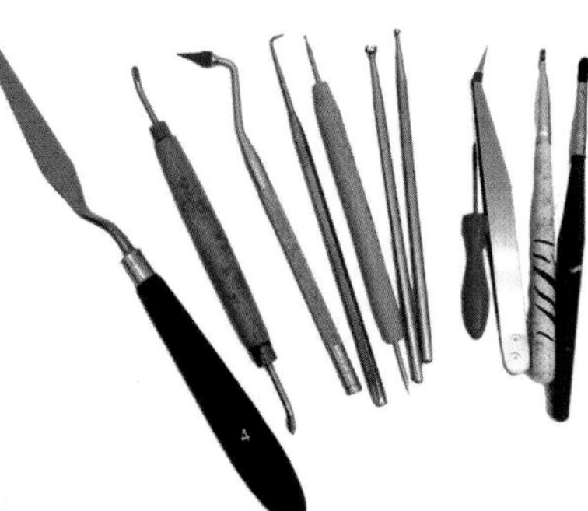

Craft drill with small bits and ball drills.

Diane Harfield cutters although I personally use these less as they are better with cold porcelain than with polymer clay. A simple pasta machine.

More advanced tools for the professional

Extruder: Makin's or Lucy Clay

Metal bowled commercial mixer.

Professional Pasta Machine such as Dream Machine.

Slicer such as Lucy Clay Slicer

My newest tool the 3d pen!

Home made tool kit

To augment your tools with tools which are specific to you and which cost maybe a little less there are some simple tricks for making your own tools.

Bent pin tool

To make a bent pin tool simply grasp the top half centimetre of an upholstery pin with a pair of pliers and bend to approximately 30 to 40 degrees off the straight.

You may wish to bang the end firmly with a hammer first. This both softens the metal in preparation for bending (by the heat generated by the shock) and also thins it out to make a more delicate end. Also hit the other end with a hammer to damage the end so that it can't simply 'slip' in it's handle. Wrap the pin in a short piece of scrap clay for a handle. Or drill a dowel and glue in with epoxy glue.

Ball tool

Take a small wooden bead. Put a little spot of glue into the hole and push a cocktail stick firmly into the hole until the point shows through. Leave to dry and then cut the tip off and sand down until smooth.

Make a zig zag sheet for baking clay

The temperatures at which you bake most polymer clays do not burn wood or even paper. This means that you can make 'formers' for your polymer clay work out of paper! Obviously it's not advisable to bake on paper in one of the smaller ovens where the clay is close to the elements or flames or in any oven with hot-spots. However for most household ovens it's perfectly possible to use paper simply as a support for items that you don't want to bake flat. For example leaves and plants. In this case fold a piece of paper into irregular gentle zig zags. The clay can then be gently draped over or between the zig zags depending on the effect you'd like to achieve. This has two functions. Adding shape, for example in the case of the grape vines and keeping the clay from getting that awful 'shiny side' effect. Remember also to cool your work on the zig zag paper or former because whenever it's still hot it will re-shape. See carrots, Radish leaves etc. I now have a silicone former which replaces my zigzag paper but the paper works just as well!

Don't forget to think about other shapes you could use as

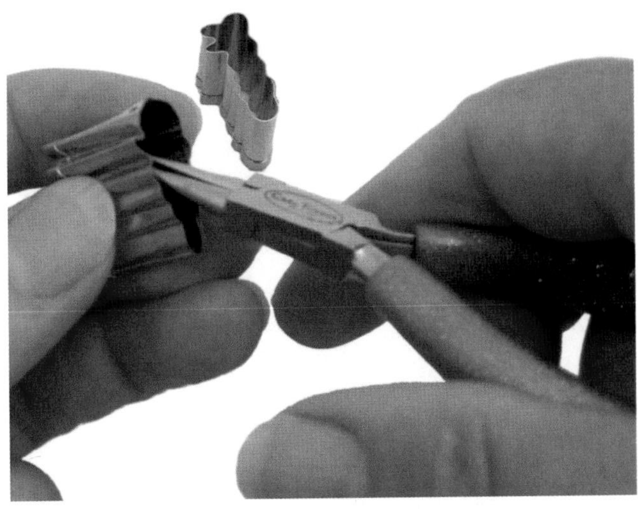

formers such as toilet rolls for curves and little bits of wood for sharp edges.

Collecting and making cutters

I've been collecting cutters for many years now and so I have an enormous collection of very small cutters. Sometimes it can be difficult to remember where I got them from but its always a good idea to keep them all in one place and sorted according to style and size. Good leaf cutters are particularly hard to find especially complex leaves like the vines and the 3 lobed cutter I use for strawberry leaves is as rare as rocking horse sh**! A couple of suppliers of micro sized cutters are listed at the back of this book but keep your eyes open in cake shops and at miniature fairs as well as watching the internet for interesting cutters. I'm still looking for a cutter maker to help me make some custom cutters. Until then I have to be inventive:-

Altering cutters and using them in unusual ways

Sometimes you can't find the cutter you need. In this case it's often a good idea to alter existing cutters that are nearly right. For example the Makin's frog cutter in the smallest size makes a very good leaf cutter for the squash family when slightly altered, Premo also has a natures cutters set which has several alterable shapes in it. I alter the little caterpillar and also the zig zag leaf into more acceptable shapes for leaves for radish and beets. The Makin's sets are cheap enough to experiment with.

Jewellers pliers are very useful for altering cutters. Don't be afraid to experiment on some of the shapes out of a cheap set to see what forms you can achieve. To make a thinner leaf you can use existing cutters twice on the same leaf.

Making your own tools and cutters

Even though I have an extensive collection of tools and cutters there are sometimes tools I just can't find. This book deals with making these tools either in mould, imprinter or cutter form.

Cutters can be altered by using pliers (see above). For

example I couldn't find the right cutter anywhere for my beets. So I took a zig zag leaf cutter from a Premo set of nature cutters and turned it upside down. Bent the stem into the upper curve of the leaf and the top of the original cutter then became the stem. A little more tweaking produces an acceptable cutter for all the beet family.

Wide cutters can also be turned into narrower cutters in 2 ways. By double cutting. That is to say, cutting one leaf out and then narrowing the leaf by cutting again to one side of the original cut.

You can also tweak a short fat leaf cutter to be a narrower longer one, or vice versa, again just using pliers.

Alternatively you can make your own cutters from scratch either using old metal can or craft metals, You'll need both straight and round pliers for this job. And some squared paper as well as an accurate ruler. Design your cutter and then 'stretch it out' to a more horizontal shape using the top middle as a point of reference and the final bend. Mark the centre of your metal so you don't use your place in the bending process. You then start at the next bend, nearest to the top middle. Assuming your cutter is symmetrical you can bend each set of two bends one after the other then move to the next bend.

Finally bend the last (top middle) bend and tape or solder the stem part together. On some leaves you'll want to make a stem in the cutter. On others you'll add the stem later.

Butter knives are very important in my work. Collect a few of those. You'll be glad you did!

Stencils

As I was working on this book I had a period of sickness when the only work I could do was cerebral. During that time I was musing on the problem of making really delicate elements in polymer clay for really delicate flowers such as poppies which were too fine to have real success with normal polymer clay or even cold porcelain. I asked my husband if perhaps he could make me a stencil for poppy flowers. The rest is history albeit very recent history as we now have a range of stencils to use with polymer clay Goo (described on page 13). You simply squeegee the semi-liquid Goo through the stencil with a palette knife and the result is then baked and later assembled into flowers and plants.

You can of course make your own stencils from light card simply by using leaf and flower cutters to cut holes in the card, or you can hand cut stencils using one of the new swivelling paper cutting blades. It takes a little practise and some of the finer elements may be too difficult using a blade.

Angie Scarr's Colour Book

I mention my colour book as a tool simply because of the number of times I even refer back to it myself when I'm lost for a colour mix. The foundation of good and realistic miniatures

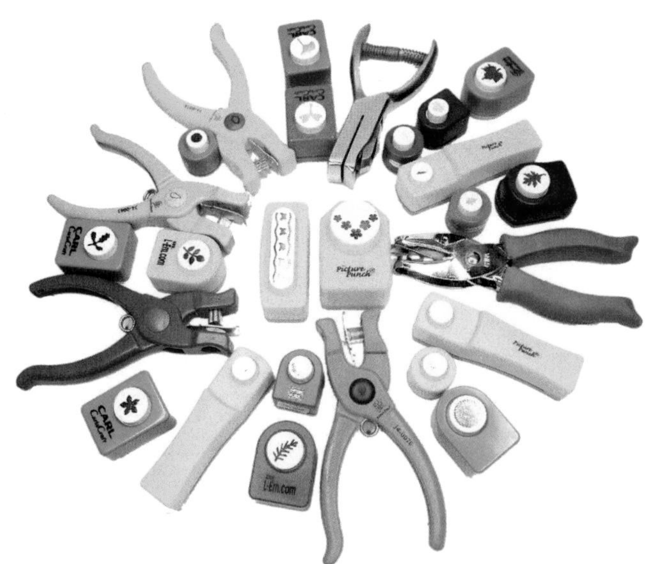

is colour more even than form or scale. A lettuce could be the wrong shape or the wrong size but if the colour looks right everything else is less noticeable. The wrong green will always look wrong and it's surprising how often we still see gaudy or

lumpen greens or even heavy varnishes in professional work just because the maker has paid more attention to shape and scale than colour and translucency.

Materials - Clay etc.

I'm assuming that the majority of readers of this book have come across polymer clay before because this is not a beginners book. So I'll get on to which polymer clay I would advise you to use? My answer is usually the same. All of them! Whatever you can get hold of, whatever you're used to whichever one or more that you like. My only advice is that you learn to mix the colours from the base colours rather than slavishly following the manufacturers version particularly of leaf greens.

Lots of advice on colour mixes for all these clays is given in my Colour Book. However for a lot of this book I've used Cernit and Premo, mostly because the manufacturers have made them easy for me to get hold of, but also because they have a certain flexibility for very fine elements and very smooth granulation. (If that's the correct term!)

If you are using Fimo I advise you to mix in a very small amount of Sculpey mould maker wherever you need a softener or an agent to make your clay more flexible. When using mixes of clays with different curing temperature advice, please check your oven for baking strength and colour. Otherwise follow the instructions on your pack and only 'tweak' the temperatures or times slightly for your oven if your work is breaking or burning.

Make sure you have lots of translucent clay and top up your supplies of yellows and get in some navy blue/marine blue and white if you haven't got any, and dig out all your leftovers which you will find very useful for making soil bases page 22.

Also make sure you have lots of liquid polymer and I do recommend Liquid Fimo as it's very strong and flexible and quite transparent in it's raw state. You especially need a good supply of liquid polymer for making Goo page 13.

Keeping your clay to hand ... and clean!

When making gardens you will often be storing sheets of clay used for leaves and flowers. For this I suggest you use cling film placed lightly between layers of work. Thin sheets of clay have a very limited life until they become a bit crumbly (rather than flexible), so I suggest you only make small sheets and use up within a week. Any left over clay from these sheets can be re-rolled and should be perfectly usable again.

I find wire letter trays really useful for storing tiles full of work in progress. Wrap your work lightly in cling film and make sure you keep the tools you are using on that tile with the work. This saves time hunting around for them later! If you have work that is 'squashable' on a tile make sure you put something on the tile to keep the cling film from squashing it. I use old silicone mould pieces as they don't slip.

Plastic boxes are useful for work in progress. Use the non rigid plastics as these don't react with the clay. Avoid clear and brittle plastics.

You'll need lots of cheap wood glue.

Other materials needed are dealt with in the garden bases section on page 21.

If you are going to have a go at the 3d pen projects you'll need black and wood coloured filaments. Plus purple and white for the wisteria flowers. And some light green filament. I recommend Rigid Ink's khaki and olive colours.

Collecting Basic Materials For Gardens

Miniature gardens can be the most fun to find materials for because most inveterate miniaturists almost always have at least half the materials you'll need already languishing in some corner of your workspace. But here's just a reminder of the kind of bits and bobs you might look out for and I advise getting a big box and labelling it "garden bits" and just putting everything in it in labelled plastic bags (since garden bits can be a bit messy)!

The cheapest bits you can gather together are pebbles, crushed slate sand and gravel for pathways and garden features.

You need soil and scenic materials. Some people use coffee grounds but I don't like organic materials which might have any kind of nutrition or moisture left in them for moulds etc. I prefer ground coconut husk as soil substitute. You can buy this in garden shops. I food process and sieve it. Anything available from the railway scenic materials range at modelling shops can be useful as well as floral display materials such as gravel, mosses and stones etc. and flower wire. I also use the powder out of the bottom of my tea bag boxes.

I also like a particular brand of railway scenic grass which comes on a thin film backing. Details in the suppliers section. Glue for attaching all these. I've found a cheap brand of wood glue works as well as anything for all these jobs. It's not clear but it's not shiny either so properly covered it disappears well.

Then you may need miniature bricks, tiles and other specialist paving materials. I advise you to buy seconds of all these materials as a preference and not just for cheapness. I think perfect materials make a garden look unrealistic. The more battered and grubby the more realistic, in my opinion. These seconds and 'perfects' too are available from British company Stacey's Miniature Masonry (address in the back of the book).

Old broken plant pots can be used in your scene as well as any other damaged item like Belfast sinks etc. Some people plant herbs in old kitchen crockery like teapots mixing bowls etc.

Remember the other items people might use in gardens and allotments such as old tyres, vegetable boxes etc. etc. Newer or more perfect pots can be sourced from miniature fairs or from my friend at MIBAKO here in Spain. You'll find details in the back of the book. Don't forget also to keep your eyes open for garden tools etc. which may enhance your scene.

Wire mesh is very useful for armatures and soil bases. You will also find paper covered floral wire and even electrical wire useful and I use a very fine wire mesh and separate the tiny wires for wiring fruits onto trees.

Paints, in muddy brown and dirty grey greens and verdigris for distressing garden pavings etc. And also any garden colours you might like for fencing and furniture. Green or brown spray paint can be useful for garden furniture. If choosing brown make sure it has a matte finish. Green is OK to be shiny.

Plant pots which can be painted any colour you like from nice muted chalky pastels for more classic scenes or tasteful patios, to vibrant majolica styles for a sunny southern European look. They don't need to be perfect!

Cheap import shops* are a great source of materials from the plastic photo frame I used for the big garden base on page 22 to wooden elements like the heat mats and bamboo table mats used for fencing and for garden stakes.

More specialist materials such as 3d filaments and polymer clays etc will be mentioned in the book where they appear in the projects.

*Wherever possible I've used the cheapest sources of materials to make these projects accessible to all, even though that often means using cheap imports which I don't necessarily like doing. Of course if you can afford materials made in your own country I would be happy to hear that you were able to do that.

A New Polymer Clay Idea

Making Goo

Polymer clay Goo is simply a mix of polymer clay and liquid polymer (like Liquid Fimo). I use it for gluing small parts of my work together in a really permanent way. It works so much better than using any form of glue. The thickness of the mix affects the 'grab', that is to say the hold of the parts before the glue is set. Of course it has to be baked. If the 'grab is not strong enough for the weight of the pieces, the parts to be glued together if pre-baked will have to be supported. You may wish to support delicate parts anyway because when re-baking polymer clay those parts can simply bend again and will set into the position they are in as they cool.

To support parts while they bake you can either use a wire support or you can use card folded or rolled into the shape you need. Don't allow the card to come into contact with a naked flame and make sure you only use the recommended baking temperature for your polymer clay.

I also use Goo with stencils to create delicate miniatures that are difficult with polymer clay alone.

To make a small quantity of Goo take a piece of polymer clay in the colour you want your Goo, some liquid polymer. A ceramic tile and a palette knife or butter knife. (1) Pressing firmly slowly and patiently work the liquid polymer into the solid. (2) (3) At a certain point you will find the mass has a 'scrambled egg' look. You need to keep working, scraping the knife really flat against the tile so that little by little the lumpiness then the graininess disappears. When you are happy with your mix use the knife to scrape the mix off the tile and scrape off the knife into a polymer clay proof container. (4) (5) Small glass jars or small flexible plastic containers will do the job. Don't use hard plastic. Most of the hard/brittle plastics will be dissolved by the solvents in liquid polymers. The mix is now ready to use. I use it to attach parts of plants together and for attaching soil and other garden materials to bases. I use a thicker mix for sculpting tree bark etc.

I have a full range of colours mixed to a fairly thick consistency. (6) I can mix colours to get exactly the shade I want at the time I need to use them. When I want a thinner mix I simply add more liquid polymer.

I also use a thick Goo when I am making wired stalks to cover the joins and, as you will see with the ancient olive tree on page 105, as a semi solid material over natural materials used as natural armatures.

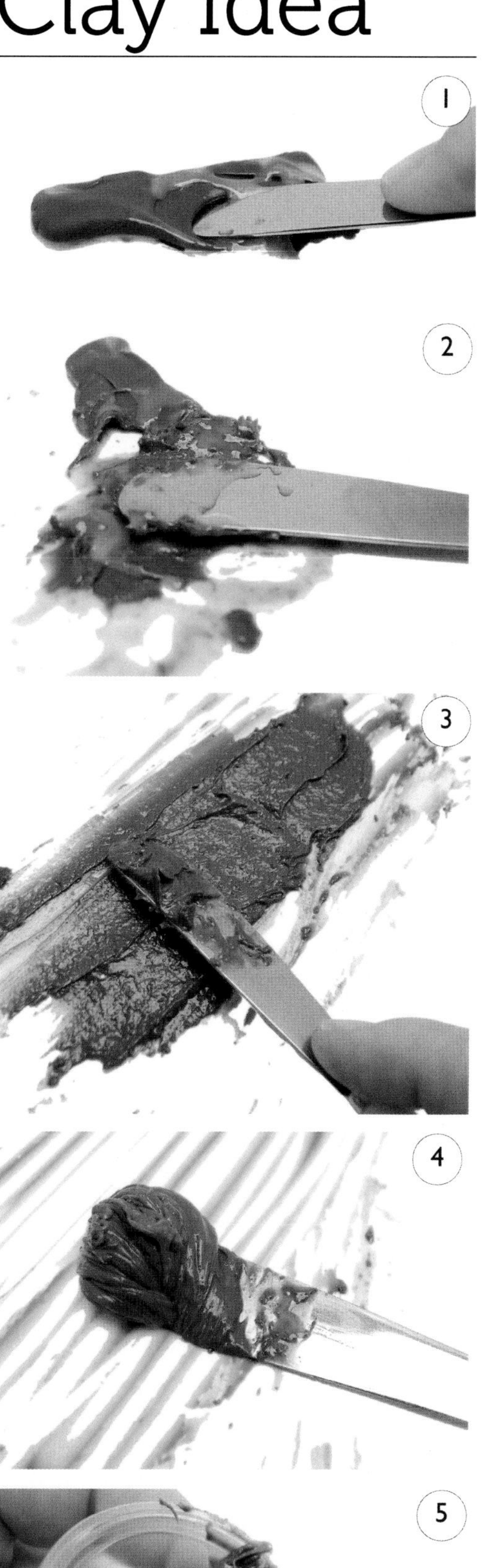

Making Your Own Silicone Moulds

You will need

Silicone moulding material

Why make Silicone moulds?

Multiple reproduction

Imagine you want to make a whole crate full of bananas, But bananas are a difficult shape for you to get right. Well you can spend a lot of time making your first few bunches, for the top of the crate and then you can make a mould for the less visible bananas at the bottom of the crate.

Saving modelling time

Miniature grapes can be tedious and time consuming to make but once you have made a bunch you can copy it by using a silicone mould. Even smaller fruit made up of tinier bead shapes, for example raspberries and blackberries (brambles) can be simulated by using glass or plastic beads on a cocktail stick to make the original. A mould is then made from this original and the fruit can then be made in large numbers using your preferred material.

Moulds for difficult shapes

by preserving stages of work. My false teeth are an example of something which was so difficult to make I had to take several attempts. I made a first model which I felt was clumsy, I took a mould from this, then started again the next day, working on the products from the first mould until I got a set I was happy with. So I could then make a second mould from that new master.

Facilitating use of liquid materials for 3 dimensional forms.

With a mould you can make a realistic jellies or blancmange etc. Make silicone jelly moulds from the metal originals as the gels and liquid polymers are easier to get out and less likely to stain. Or you can make moulds for water (Liquid Fimo or resin) or anything which is easier to get the shape or a translucency that you want in liquid materials. And making multiple layer moulds by using liquids and setting between colour stages

To take up really fine details

Moulds can hold really fine details which can otherwise be lost when copying and transferring textures and decorative motifs. The silicone moulds are particularly good at this.

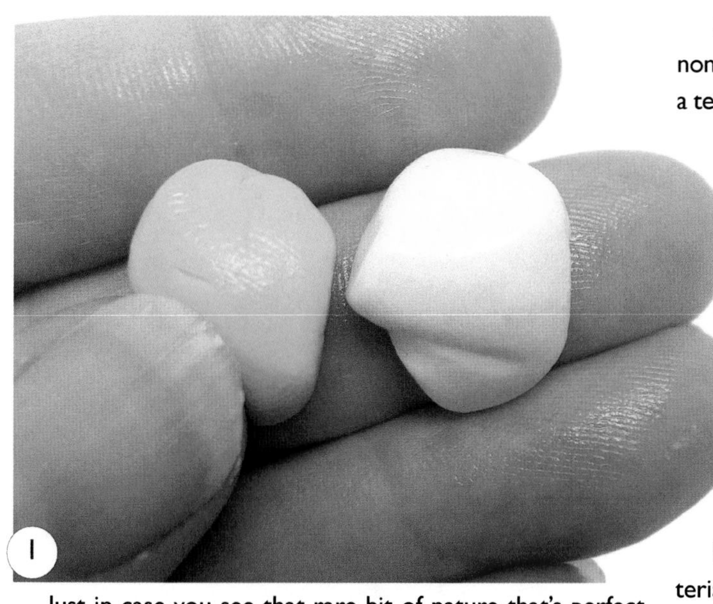
1

Just in case you see that rare bit of nature that's perfect for a miniature mould. Never be without your moulding paste pots!

In the last few years I have played more and more with the use of moulds to augment my limited sculpting abilities especially where the wonders of nature provide me with readily available forms to copy or as I call 'grab' for my miniature work. I call it 'grabbing' because of the Spanish word for to record is grabar and also because it feels a bit like pinching someone else's work. In this case the hard work of evolution and nature. Yes, I continue to be obsessed with nature and although I thought it was colour I was interested in I find that texture and form also excite me. Especially what I call the fractal nature of nature which solve many of my miniaturising problems for me.

The uses for these forms are not limited to miniatures, They can also be used in jewellery and other polymer clay arts you just need to keep your eyes and mind open to possibilities. Keep a notebook and 2 pots of moulding paste and whenever inspiration hits you you can 'capture' it for later use.

2 part mould making materials

There are several brands of silicone moulding paste. My favourite is my own brand, of course because I'm most used to it. 'My brand' Minitmold is a non toxic very fast setting material with a low odour. I will be using this material in this book of course, but there are many others available which may be as good or even better for specialist jobs if you want a slower setting time for example, or a firmer material. They include Silicone Plastique, Siligum, Alumilite mold putty, Prochima (Italy). They all share the similarity that they come in 2 parts and are technically known as "addition vulcanising". Basically that means that the hardening process begins only when the two parts are mixed together.

They all have a 'shelf life' which is usually about 18 months to 2 years from purchase.

Using fast setting mould materials which are easy to handle, non toxic and non staining means you can make a mould or take a texture from just about anything from delicate art objects to fibres, to natural forms. The limit is your imagination. And you can then use it for many craft materials and also with edible items, like cake decorating elements. Though it's recommended that you make separate moulds if using for moulding food items.

A few rules and recommendations for making moulds

Before you start, if at all possible, you should have clean hands and a clean work surface. If you're out 'in the field' this may not be possible.

Firstly, especially if you are using a super fast setting material, be ready with the exact item you want to mould from before you start mixing. Then, once you have started making a mould remember not to answer the door, the phone or the call of nature until you're ready to leave the mould to set, otherwise your material will go off before it's properly shaped and will be useless.

Check your mould or the first side of your mould before you continue. Look for over smooth shiny patches. Any shiny bits could mean air has got between the object and the mould. Throw away and start again.

If your mould is wrong or disappointing don't try and salvage it unless the original is broken and you have no alternative. Start again. A poor mould will never be a good mould.

You can use moulding to save stages in a work. For example you could be working on a model of a cat. You may want to work more on it but may be afraid that any more work might spoil it. This would be a good time to take a mould of the original and work on the new copies.

Right! Lets get started with a simple 2 part push leaf veiner for a small leaf.

Making a simple leaf veiner

Select a garden leaf with the shape of veins you want. Bear in mind the scale you're working to. If you're working in 12th scale you certainly want to be looking for very small leaves. Also bear in mind the shape and how the veins lie. A vine leaf does not have the same shape as a rose leaf for example ... but does have the same basic shape as a marrow or a maple leaf.

Copyright Issues

When taking mouldings from existing items of other peoples work, do not mass produce unchanged. This is immoral, un-artistic and in many cases illegal. You can however take elements and alter them so significantly by your own work, that their original is not recognisable in the new work.

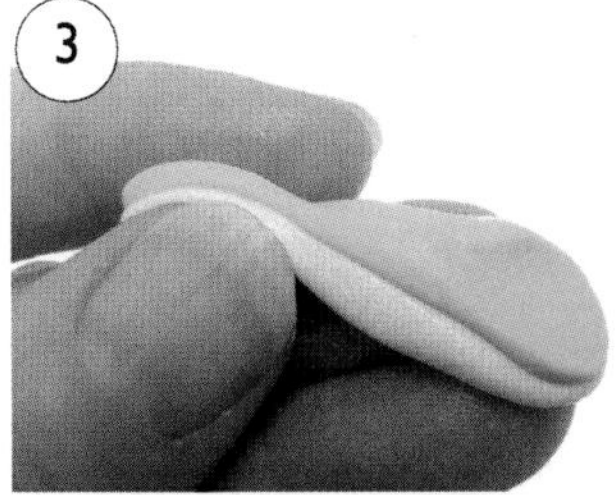

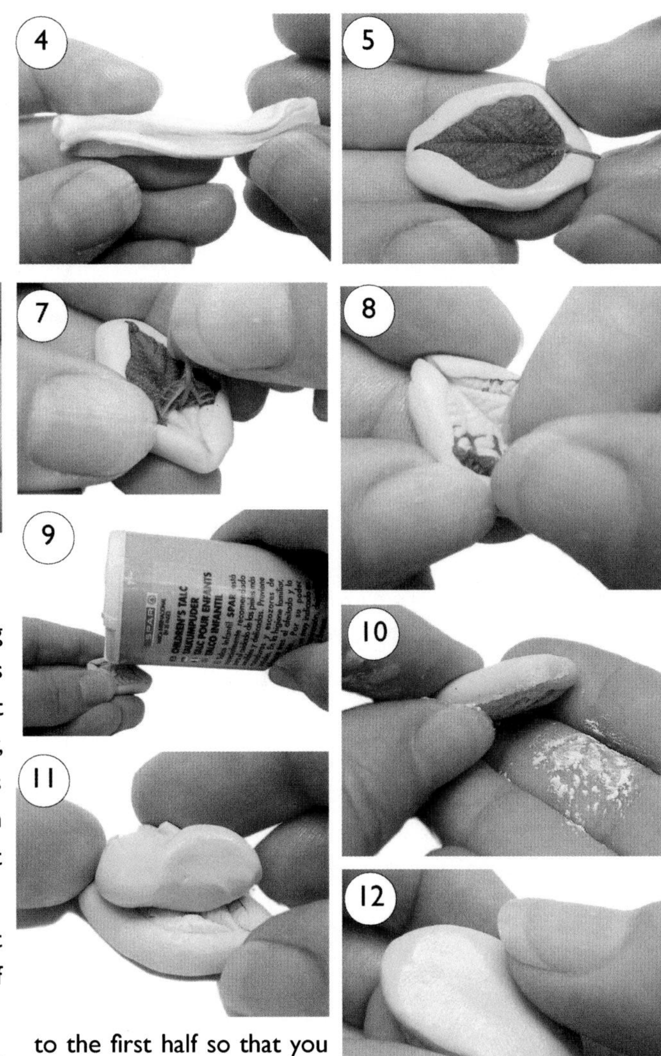

Then be sure that the veins on your leaf are clearly defined. Avoid any leaves that have very thin feeble or indistinct veins. You need to exaggerate a little. You can always press less firmly to get a lighter vein pattern when using your veiner. But you can only accentuate a light pattern a little.

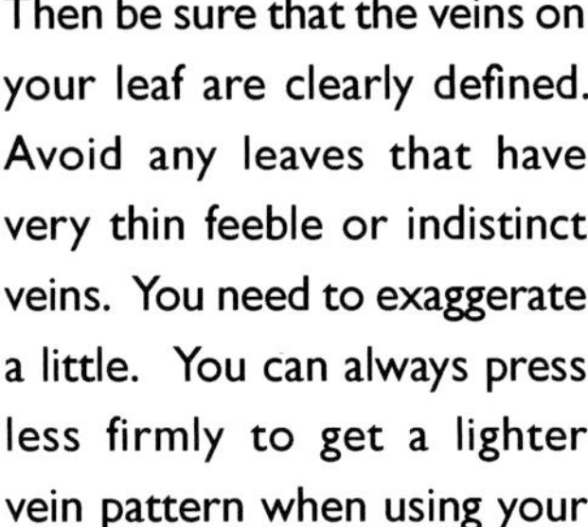

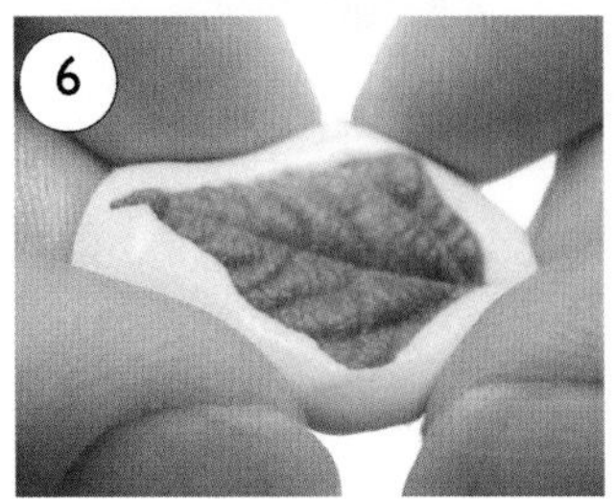

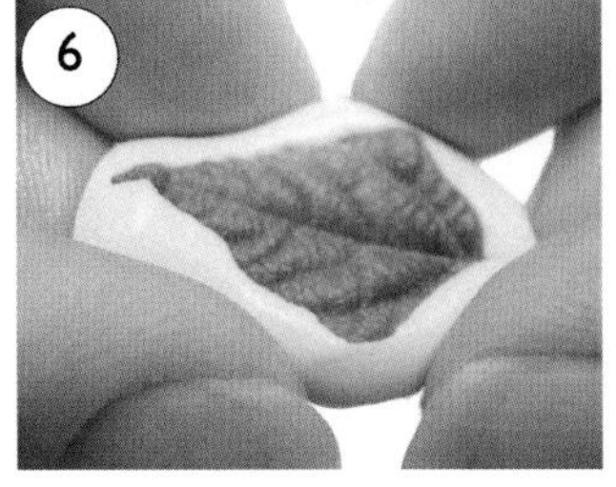

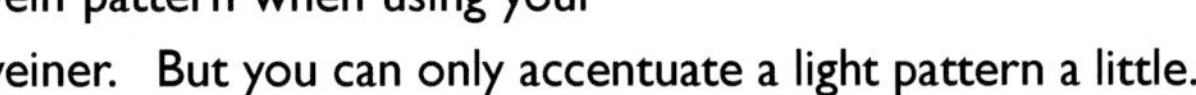

For this example I've chosen a bean leaf, (2) a climbing bean from my garden. The reason I chose it is because it has strong veining as it's a young leaf, the veins are regular, that is to say they're side by side like a mirror image. And finally, turning the leaf over, the back is really strong texture. If it's summer when you're doing this project you will have a wealth of leaves to choose from. If it's winter you might find it a bit more difficult.

So get ready to mould from your leaf. Remember not to be distracted. *(see previous page)* (3) (4) Mix equal parts of your mould material really well but quickly.

Form the silicone moulding paste into roughly the shape and a little bigger than the size of your leaf.

(5) Press the back of the leaf into the moulding material and gently smooth it round the edges so that the edges curve away gently from the mould. This edge gives you extra flexibility for using the mould in several ways.

Leave the mould to set. (6) If you are already an expert mould maker, here's a little tip. Just before the mould sets you can squeeze the edges a bit to make it set even more 'crinkly'.

(7) When this first half has set, remove the leaf. (8) If your leaf is really delicate it might leave a few shreds on the mould. If this happens you will need to remove the leaf bits with your fingernail or if it's really stubborn using a soft toothbrush and water. Don't pick these bits off using anything spiky as you can damage the mould.

(9) (10) To make the second half, talcum powder the first half lightly. Tap off the excess talc by tapping the mould against your palm or another mould. Use a face mask if making several moulds to avoid inhaling talcum powder.

(11) (12) Make up a similar amount of mould material and cover the first half with this pressing into the middle first and then flattening your mould outwards, taking up a similar shape to the first half so that you can tell which end is which.

Leave this to set then peel the two halves apart. Your mould is ready to use on leaf shapes. Here is an example of a leaf pressed with this leaf mould. There are several variations of leaf veiners and I will cover them in different tutorials as they appear. These mould materials are usually non toxic (check with the manufacturer) which means they can also be used for chocolate and sugarcraft work as well.

Types of moulds

These are the names I give to different types of moulds I make and teach in this book. Some are names already used in the industry and some are names I use to identify different ways of using the moulds.

Veiners usually 2 flat parts pressed together to leave an imprint of leaf veins. Often one part is made directly from the other part e.g. cabbage leaf, but sometimes the veins are 2 dimensional. That is to say, the veins have extra depth to allow for extra clay e.g chard veiner page 82. (1)

Two part moulds are 3d moulds which have an empty shape between the two pieces to form the item e.g. doll moulds and in this book pumpkin/squash moulds. You have

Variations on the basic leaf veiner

Leaf left in for depth page 76

Leaf stalk only left in for depth of stalk page 83

Push mould veiners page 60

Stem moulds e.g. aubergine tops page 75.

Veiners from home made masters, In this case you make a mould from a slice of cane describing the shapes in the home made leaf 'cane'. This results in veins that are more nearly matched to the placement of the veins.

to fill these moulds and push them together and trim off any excess see page 78. (2)

Push moulds are a type of two part mould where one part is usually less filled than the other but has the job of both pressing the clay firmly into the other half and also forming the back of the item. Push mould veiner is a veiner where there is a handle on one side to increase handleability. (3)

Stem moulds Moulds which form the stem of a flower or fruit so that the flower or fruit can be made without having to handle a stem directly e.g. aubergine tops, and calyx mould (I believe these are my design idea) page 75. (4) (5)

Imprinter moulds Usually just one part with a handle to press an impression into the clay e.g. Mediterranean tomato tops page 72. (6)

Texture sheets/plates usually just one part with a textured surface. Clay is pressed against, rolled on or rolled out onto these sheets e.g. potato texture, carrot lines page 30. (7)

The difference between a mould and an imprinter is that, usually, you press or pour something into the mould. An imprinter is merely pressed into the material to give it an impression or texture. You can use imprinters and texture plates either to add texture to small areas which you can duplicate randomly, or for more regular and predictable results.

Finding smaller versions in nature of the shapes you need

Where silicone moulds can really help is for archiving shapes from nature.

Where the real creativity comes in is seeing how economical nature is with form. It tends to repeat complex forms in different places, in different sizes.

If you look at a plant you wish to make in miniature and see if that plant itself might make the 12th scale version of it's own larger ones. (8) Other times you may have to find another plant with similar leaves in a much smaller scale for example the little weed leaf which to me looks like a tiny version of an artichoke leaf page 76.

In other small fruits and flowers. for example; the little fruits of the (carmine) poke plant which grows as a weed in Spain look like tiny satsumas. Be careful moulding from this plant as it is poisonous. (9) The tiny cups on some of the Australian gum trees which look just like tiny acorn cups. And the young flowers of the pine which look a lot like pine cones! Some flower shapes formed on alder trees in spring which look like tiny pineapples. You will see many more examples in this book but the most impressive of all is what I call the 'fractal' cauliflower.

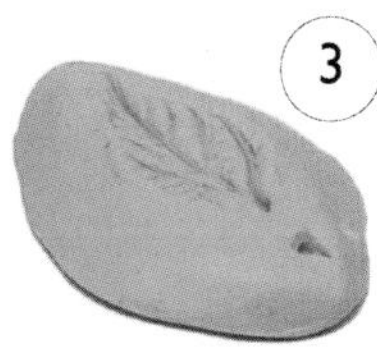

3

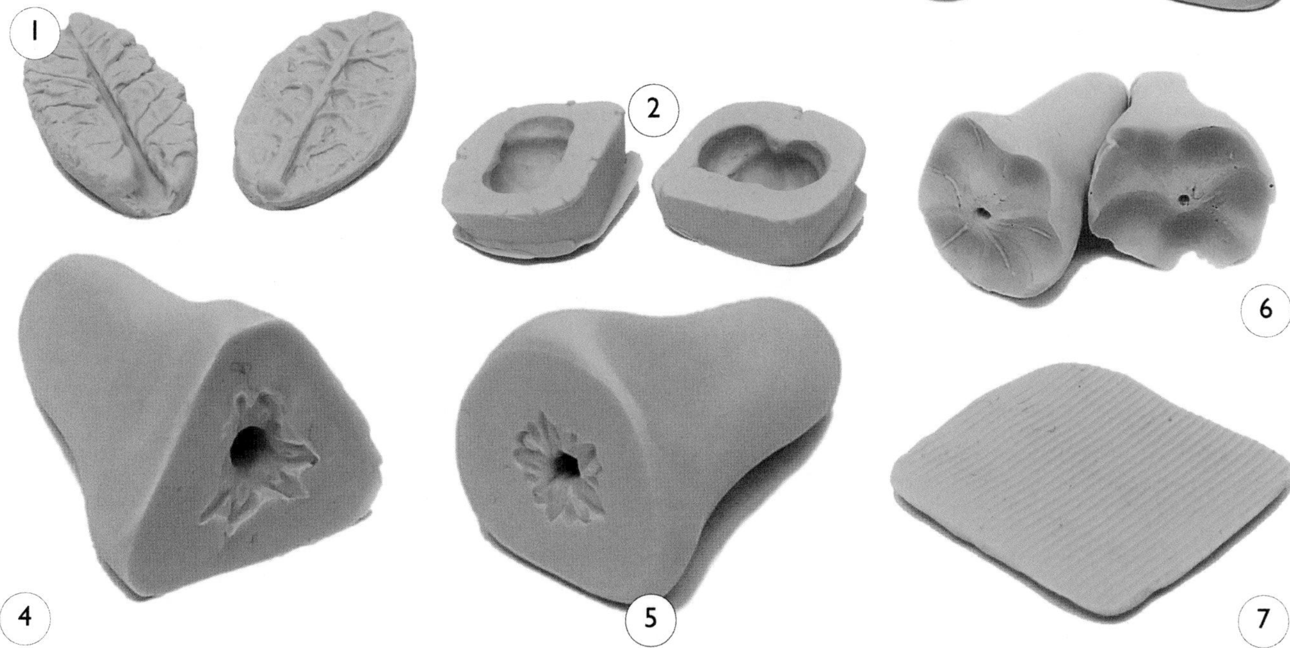

1 2 6 4 5 7

Also known as the Romanesco cauliflower in England, which is made up of tiny whorls each of which are a miniature version of itself. (10) (11) All this is why it's a great idea to carry the two little pots of silicone mould material wherever you go.

8

9

10

11

Professional Tips: Check for lost definition through air bubbles.

When making a mould or texture sheet from a master. Once the mould has set examine it carefully. If any part of your mould or texture plate comes out shiny you will have lost definition at least, or worse you may have introduced visible errors. You will not be able to repair this and your best option is to start again. Certainly don't waste material making a second half of a flawed first part of a mould. Better to make a new first part until you get it right. If a master produces air bubbles consistently in the same place you may need to drill into the master. An extreme example of this is on my octopus mould master where I had to drill holes all the way round. Sometimes a gently curving wall to the mould master can cure this on its own.

Another way to minimise air bubbles is to work from the centre of the mould outwards allowing air to slip out sideways or in the case of complicated moulds like this press a little material into each of the places where air might collect first. My husband is actually better at making this mould than I am and I always ask him to make my octopus moulds!

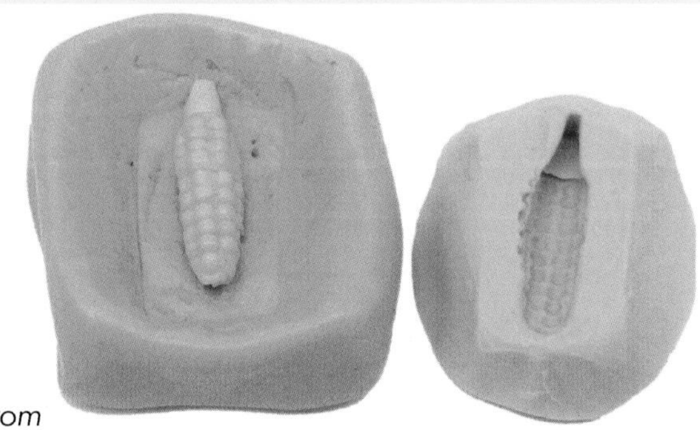

Here is a sweetcorn mould and the master it was produced from

Plants that make mini versions of themselves, or other things from nature.

SELF		OTHER	
Fig Leaf	*= self*	*Putka Pods*	*= pumpkins*
Bean Leaf	*= self*	*Pokeberry Seeds*	*= satsumas, a shape for garlic*
Grapevine	*= self*	*Young alder*	*= pineapple*
Chard Leaf	*= self*	*Bougainvillea*	*= tiny flowers*
Cauliflower	*= self*	*Asteraceae*	*= artichoke leaf*
Romanesco	*= self*	*Ivy flower*	*= artichoke head*
		Feathers	*= leaf veins*
		Mimosa Leaf	*= fern leaf*
		Rocket seeds	*= pea pods*

Simple texture plates.

Silicone texture mould from heavy sandpaper

You can use this texture sheet to add random texture or dust on random colour or dusts as in the case of making potatoes on page 55.

Get a sandpaper of the largest grit you possibly can. Often these are to be found in the professional and power tools sections of your DIY shop.

This plate can be used to texture potatoes for example

To make a texture sheet which is similar to the original texture but softer and in the case of sandpaper) less likely to shed particles you may need to do the ´double step´. That is to say you need to make an impression of the original texture ... and then a new texture plate from that. You can either make the first step from mould making material as well, in which case you need to remember to dust the first side with talcum powder to prevent sticking) or you can use scrap clay and bake for this step. Be aware of the lost definition check (as below) because this can be quite common with the second generation of this technique.

Texture sheet from the threads of bolts.

I use a lined texture sheet to make various vegetable textures including the stems of celery. And I use a distressed version for carrot lines The master for the mould is simply made by rolling the thread over the clay, I had bolt threads without a head to do this. If your bolt has a head you should roll it at the edge of a cutting board or bench so that the head doesn't stop the bolt touching the clay. Roll in one swift movement or you will get a bumpy texture.

Growbags

You will need

liquid polymer

glue

flower foam

scenic scatter/soil substitute

2 stationery clips

Photocopy the growbag page in colour on white paper.

Spread a thin layer of liquid polymer over the surface. Ensure that this layer is very thin and very even. Bake the paper in the oven at the normal temperature for your liquid polymer (make sure the paper is not too close to any elements in your oven).

Cut out one growbag and slit the squares across each of the crosses on just one side of the grobag (usually the one with the side nearest my web address however you can hide this if you wish) using a single sided blade on a craft surface. Or you can cut those squares right out. (Some gardeners prefer to leave the extra plastic to keep weeds down).

To make the filling

I use flower foam because it 'grabs' the plant stems. Cut a thin piece to fit in the bag: height 4mm, length 80mm, width 25mm. Coat one side with glue and sprinkle on soil substitute.

Wrap the growbag round the filler and glue the long edge down to close it.

Put a little glue inside the edges, and use a clip to hold closed until the glue dries. Please note. The growbag is very light in weight and putting plants in it can make it top heavy. To cure this you can either stick the bag to your garden/display using double sided tape. Or you can put weight inside the bag before gluing down such as sand, or magnets.

Mr Frank's **GROWBAG**

Mr Frank's **GROWBAG**

Mr Frank's **GROWBAG**

www.angiescarr.co.uk

Mr Frank's **GROWBAG**

Mr Frank's **GROWBAG**

Mr Frank's **GROWBAG**

www.angiescarr.co.uk

Mr Frank's **GROWBAG**

Mr Frank's **GROWBAG**

Mr Frank's **GROWBAG**

www.angiescarr.co.uk

Mr Frank's **GROWBAG**

Mr Frank's **GROWBAG**

Mr Frank's **GROWBAG**

www.angiescarr.co.uk

How to prepare garden bases

No two gardens should be the same! I'm not giving you exact instructions because this is not my area of expertise. But remember gardens can be messy. So as long as the original component parts don't show all shapes and qualities of work are acceptable!

First of all select a shape and size of of garden. Think about whether you will have time to complete a larger garden or whether you will be happiest to complete a small garden in a shorter time. Bear in mind if you want your garden to be 'stand alone' or to fit with a dolls house. The garden I made as a commission on the base I show on the next page took most of a month to make but nearer three weeks full time. Including a couple of days to make the base. The base is the smallest part of your work! Think about whether you want your garden to be L shaped and wrap around the side and back of your dolls house or square, or rectangular.

Simple Frame Project

For a nice, simple small frame try Ikea's Ribba Marco frames. Here I'm using the smallest one. It is made of solid fibre board so It can easily be cut and re-formed to make an L shaped garden. L shaped gardens are particularly nice for adding to an existing dolls house. This shape is pleasing as a stand alone or several can be put together to form a larger garden. Don't forget to take out the glass and base before you cut the shape! You can cut down and re-insert the hardboard as the base for your soil instead of using mesh if you like but don't forget to add some 'oasis' plant foam to the back to help hold your plants in place. I used 2 part epoxy resin glue to attach the broken pavers and brick pieces for a really firm permanent hold. See ① ② ③ ④ ⑤ ⑥

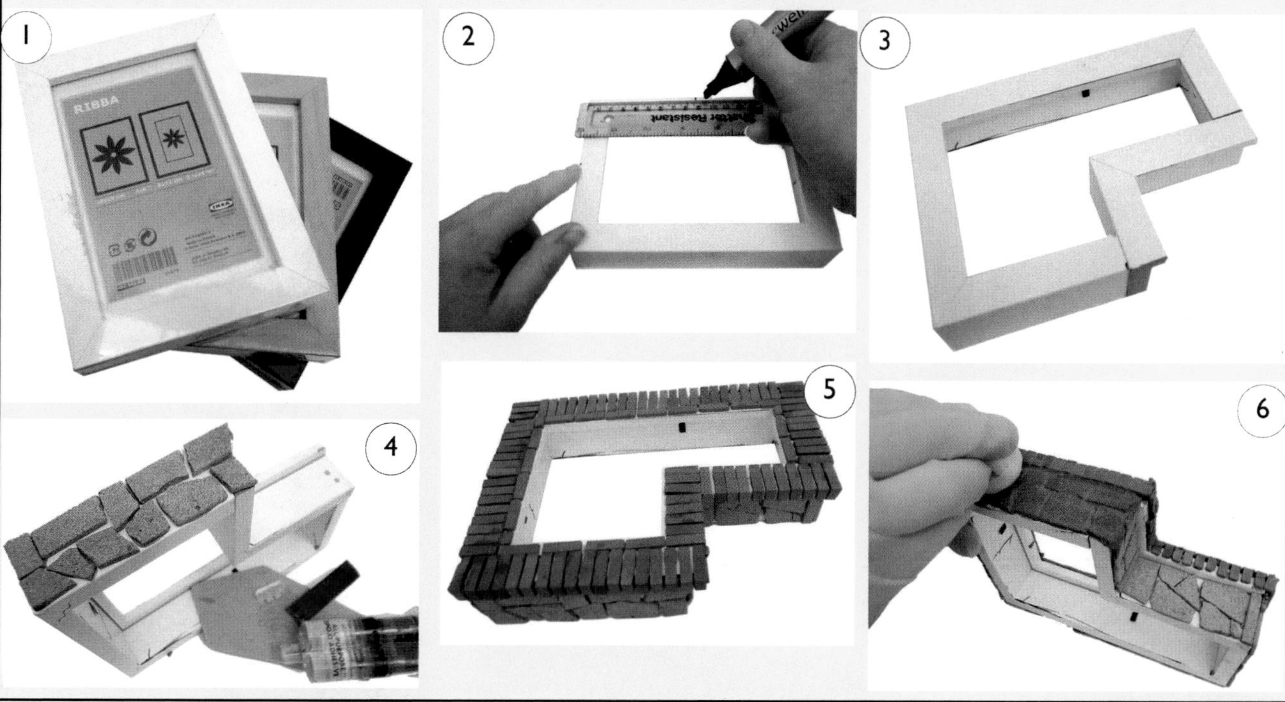

Larger Gardens

For a larger, more complex garden take your measurements along to one of the many 'cheap imports' shops around these days and select a photo or picture frame with a shape that you will be able to cover with bricks, tiles wood etc. Look at the layout of any subdivided photo frames. Will they make a pleasing garden shape. Will it look modern or old fashioned? Eastern or western?

Frames that are divided into smaller sections are best but you can also decide to sub divide your own simple frame with strip wood or even smaller frames if you wish. Any curved shapes will be more difficult, but can be attractive

Think about whether you could cut a shape down if it's too big or the wrong shape. Will it still be strong enough? Could you build up your own subdivisions with small picture frames fitted together on to a bigger piece of hardboard?

Here are a few ideas from photo and picture frames I've found, see the top of the next page.

Buy your paving slabs / bricks / gravel. Stacey's Miniature Masonry sells a great range of bricks pavers etc. at www.miniaturebricks.com You can of course trawl your own garden for bits and pieces for your garden walls etc. The great thing is even damaged materials are great for gardens!

Don't forget you can also use real sand for pebbles you

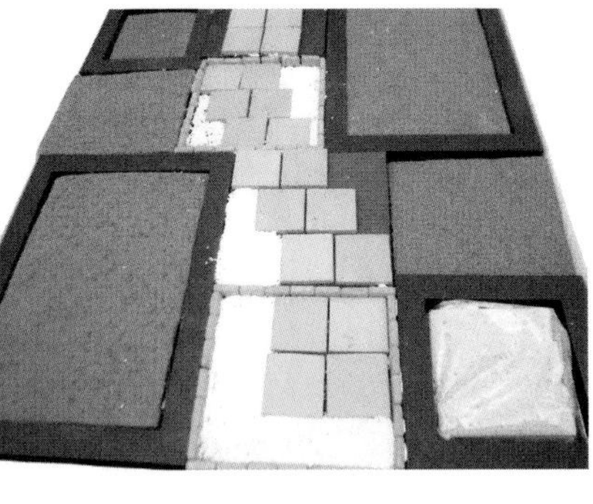

can sieve it to get the size of 'pebbles' you want. You can also use stones out of cheap aggregate to help you build a rustic looking garden. For a more modern looking garden you can build sections to look like raised beds from pieces of wood, dyed in dark oak colours. You can make them smooth for a sharp Japanese type look or distressed for a cottage garden look.

You might like to consider what walls or fences you would like. You can build them directly on to your frame or add them to the outside. Either way the simplest thing of course is to leave walls until you have filled your garden with plants. This gives easy access. I find cheap import shops also have trivets made of wood and place mats made of bamboo strips, both of which make attractive and realistic fences. They sell a range of picture frames and also various gravels in the plastic flowers section of the store.

To make soil inserts

Firstly tightly fill the holes with 'oasis' (flower foam) wrap this in plastic to stop it crumbling all over your work. (1)

Cut pieces of reinforcing mesh (available at garden centres and pet shops as pet cage mesh) to the size of the gaps in the picture frames. (2)

Mix up old polymer clay leftovers to make a brown sheet and wrap the mesh in this sheet. (3)

Press it together a bit so that the two halves stick together. (You can make this lumpy and bumpy if you want an uneven surface). Then paint the surface with liquid polymer (Liquid Fimo). You don't need to colour this but you can. (4)

Add a surface using soil substitute. You can often find ground coconut fibre etc. in garden centres or pet shops, or you can use dried tea bag residue or scenic materials from railway modelling suppliers. (5)

Bake these sections. They should fit tightly into the spaces in the frame.

The sections you want to use as pathways can be filled in with Foamcore and covered in pavers or gravel.

Add bricks, blocks, gravel and edgings using two part epoxy glue. Only mix a small amount at a time. Try to cover all the visible parts of the frame. You may find it easiest to spray the whole frame

3

4

5

1

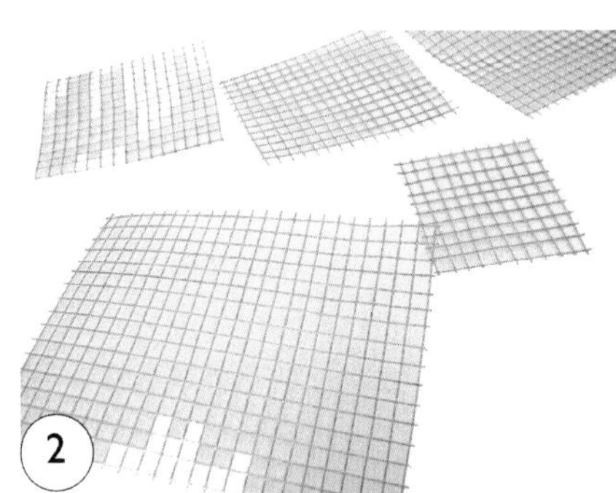
2

with brown spray paint in advance to make sure no 'plasticky bits' are visible. See the main picture.

You can make the individual sections later instead if you prefer, using fresh clay to attach the completed fruits and vegetables. These would then need to be baked again. See page 62 the weed garden.

Please note that the garden base pictured is very large and would take a LOT of filling. Do not over extend yourself and end up disappointed. However if you want to make a big garden long term, you can temporarily fill parts of a garden with gravel and path materials, seats and garden tools etc. until you have more time.

For the base of a tree

If you are making a garden with a tree you may wish to put the tree in one of your sections of garden. To leave yourself enough space it may be best to make a base with a 'hump' in it. To form a 'hump' use an egg cup or a large pebble and press the mesh over this. See (1) (2) (3) (4) (5)

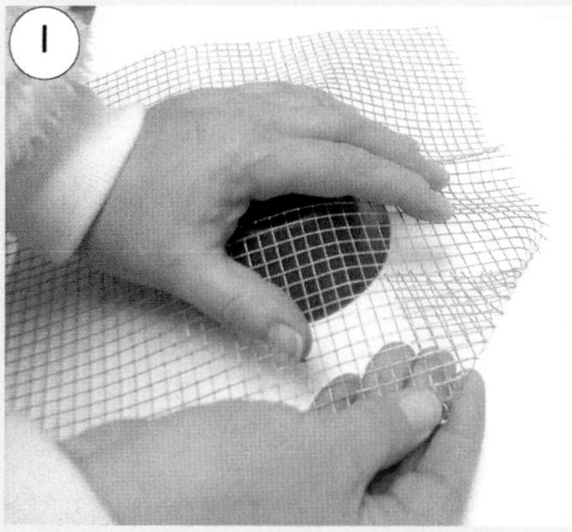

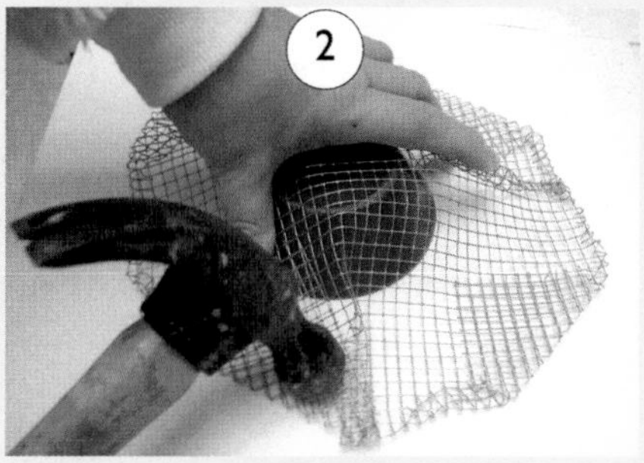

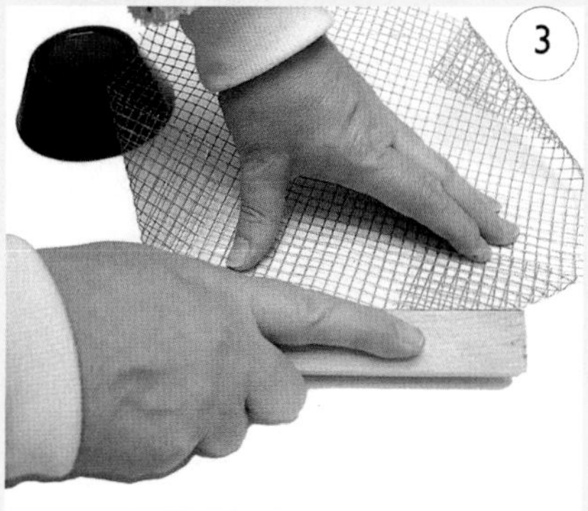

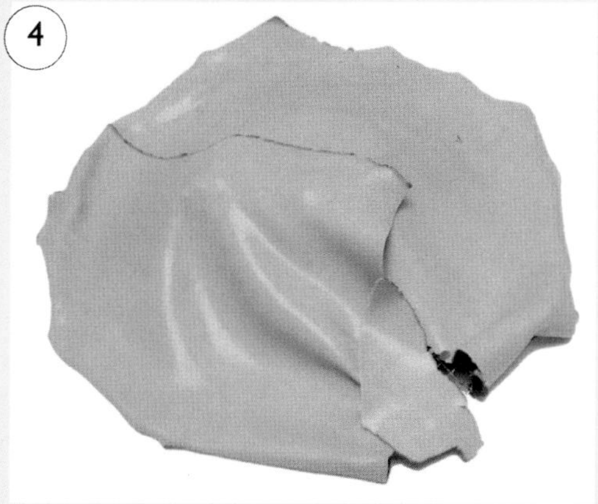

Furrows

Easy! To make a garden 'furrow' either as a part of a large garden (as in the Mediterranean garden) or as an insert in a planter or raised bed as in the allotment garden.

I used my metal safety ruler. If you can't find one, you can use bent garden mesh. The fine type used for small animal cages). Roll out leftover brown clay into a fairly thick sheet, I use a setting one or two down from the thickest.

Press the clay into your metal ruler or armature and trim the base so that the clay covers the support and is stuck firmly. Paint the surface with liquid polymer or Goo shown opposite (4) and cover in 'soil'. (5) This soil can be bought from railway and craft modelling shops. Or you can use organic soil substitute such as coconut peat replacement from garden centres.

Bake at clay temperatures and remove from the ruler support when half cooled. This can be used as an insert for your planter and can be cut to size filled around to fit into the space and drilled to receive the plants. You should put some oasis under it to hold the plant stalks if you're wanting to plant and remove the vegetables.

The Kitchen Garden

Lettuce Project

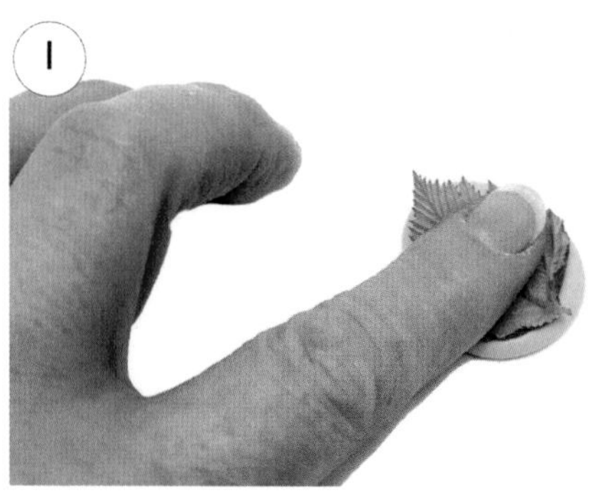

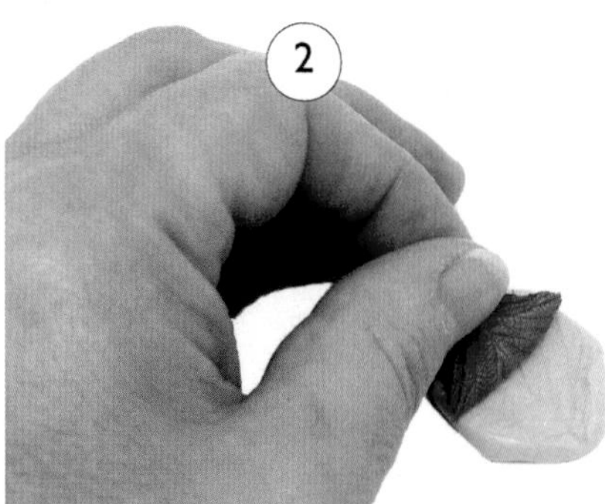

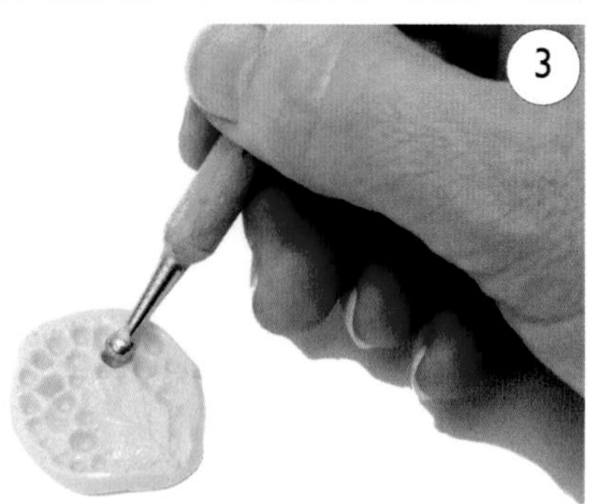

You will need

Silicone mould making material or lettuce mould
Lots of translucent clay
Spring and summer green clays
Ball tools
Pasta machine
Single sided blade

Making a lettuce mould

To make a special mould just for crinkling lettuces it's really difficult to find a leaf that has the correct 'crinkle' so I simply press a normal leaf right side down (1) into a piece of moulding paste and then when the mould is half set, (this takes a little experience to know) take the leaf off (2) and using a ball tool or two sizes of ball tool quickly press indentations into the shape around the edges, and another line further in to the mould. Make the second side from the first after powdering it with talc. (3)

Clay colours

Firstly you need to remember just how translucent lettuce is. And then you need to remember how bright the green colour is, to balance the effects of about 80% translucent with it's slightly whitening fillers. But avoid at all costs the horrible unrealistic green pigments which are difficult, if not impossible to mix into a natural colour and go for mixing from yellow and ultramarine. These produce much more realistic greens. In some cases the optical brighteners they put in polymer clays mean you have to 'quieten' these greens a bit with a touch of orange or muddy ochre but generally, for lettuce you can get away with a fairly bright green. *There is more information on mixing greens in my Colour Book (ISBN 978-8-46169-757-1)*

Making a shaded lettuce cane

You will need a pasta machine for this process.

Making a shaded cane might seem like going a bit over the top but especially when you are making garden veggies with longer stems, it really does make a difference to how the base of the plant appears.

This time you need to mix two greens. One based on a bright summer leaf green, and one based on a pale spring green to which I do add just a touch of white. Each needs to be about 20% colour and 80% translucent. You also need a translucent white (again 80% translucent) with just a touch of green.

The Skinner shade technique

Make up 4 triangles of the darker and lighter green colours by cutting 2 equal rectangles in half and placing the second piece on top of the first. Put two triangles together to form a new rectangle. Repeat this with the light green to white. If your pasta machine is wide enough for the quantity you want to make, put these pieces together into one. If not you'll need to do two separate shades and join them at the next stage. (4)

Pass this rectangle through the pasta machine once on a fairly thick setting, and then fold in half in the same direction as the direction it passed through the pasta machine and pass through again.

You need to continue doing this over and over making

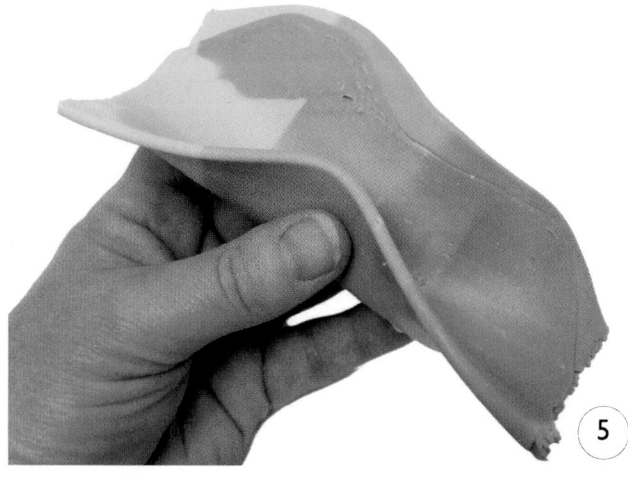

sure that you always fold and pass the clay through in the same direction. (5)

Sometimes the clay gets a little out of control and it's quite difficult to explain in black and white or even through photographs how to deal with this. Basically, when you have folded, pull outwards on the parts that have a lot of clay and push inwards on the parts where there isn't so much.

Makes no sense? OK! Go to my YouTube channel to see a full tutorial about how to control a wayward Skinner shade!

At first the clay looks streaky and you can't believe that it will ever look nice but it soon does have a nice gentle shade between the colours.

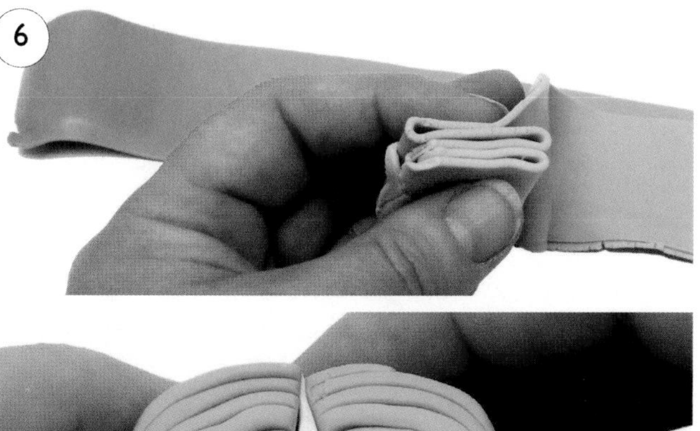

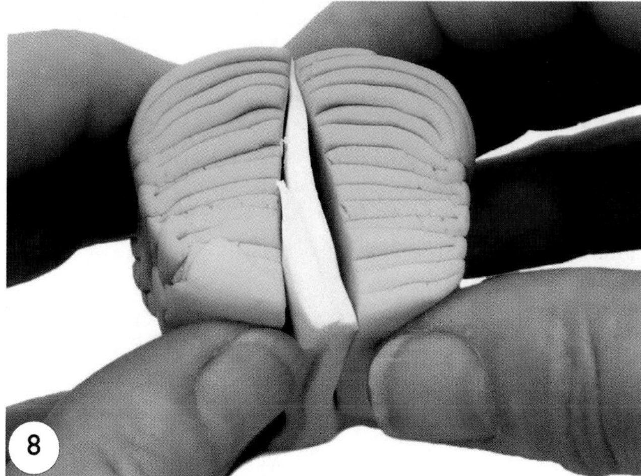

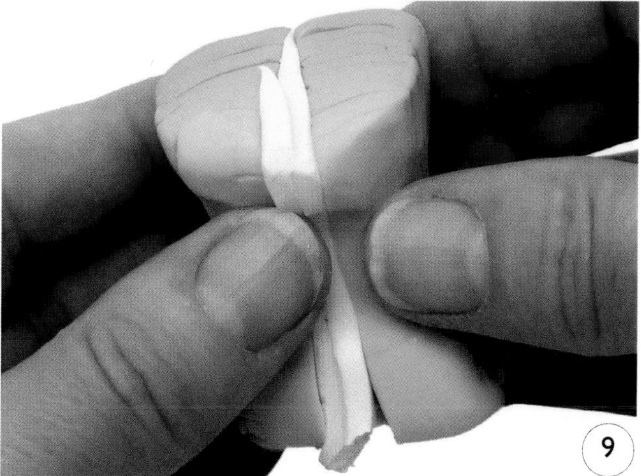

The 'fan fold'

Now we need to convert the shade into a block and then a cylinder, so the next step is to pass the shade through the pasta machine in the other direction once. Then set the machine a bit finer and pass it through again so that you get a long ribbon of clay.

Starting with the lightest colour in the ribbon start to fold over and over until you get a stack with the top slightly wider than the bottom. I do this slight widening to help me make the leaf cylinder graduate in a more realistic fashion. At each fold try to gently press and smooth the pieces together to avoid air becoming trapped between the layers. (6) (7)

Finally turn the stack upside down and trim off the folds. This also helps minimise air bubbles.

Now gently curve the outer edges around and slightly fold the bottom edge together to make a short, fat cylinder.

You then need some very translucent clay with just a little white. I'd say use no more than 10% white in this mix and a tiny scrap of green just to take the starkness off the white.

Form this clay into a triangleThe bottom of the triangle needs to be about 5 times as thick as the top. (8)

This triangle is inserted into the cane but in this case do not go right to the top. In later projects like the cabbage project you do take the lines to the edge.

Now it's time to lengthen your cane. Apologies to anyone who has done this a hundred times already for repeating this process. (9)

Take your cylinder firmly between your fingers and working round the circumference, squeeze your fingers into the edge of the 'cheese' to start to form it into a 'capstan' shape. In other words, give it a 'waistline'.

I now recommend you lengthen and take your cane down to, or nearly to, the final diameter that you will want to use, so approximately 2cm for 12th scale. Cut your cane into

pieces if necessary. Wrap in cling film and leave it to rest for a few hours or a day as it works best when it's cooler. You can keep and use this cane at room temperature for up to a couple of months depending on the quality and flexibility of your clay. (10)

Cutting fine slices

There are 2 methods of cutting very fine slices for vegetable leaves. Or three if you include machine cutting with a cane slicer. The safest is not necessarily the best. And the machine slicer isn't the quickest or even the safest! Here is the safe method. You draw your blade up the face of the cane and bring it just back from the face at the top by the smallest amount possible then cut down.

As you finish cutting pull the cane backwards away from the blade. Often the slice will remain standing as you also draw the blade away. But sometimes you need to angle the blade slightly away from the cane and scrape the blade backwards too. This can take a bit of practise. This method can squash a really fresh cane a little, but the slices can soon be re-shaped.

You can also cut leaves by holding the blade firmly in your writing hand and rolling the cane against the blade.

This is a tricky process and you have to be very careful to keep the blade anchored and not moving. It's so difficult to explain in writing and with still pictures I can only suggest you go to my youtube videos on the subject. It should certainly not be suggested for people with shaky hands, nervousness or for children. There is an expensive guillotine machine available from Lucy Clay which will cut slices of any thickness. I have one but I rarely use it, finding it easier to cut by hand. However if you have a disability which makes cutting these really fine slices difficult, it may be an investment.

Veining & making up

Put your leaf shape on the mould with the line down the middle and press. Then open and remove the leaf. The leaf can go anywhere in the mould top to bottom, as long as the line is in the middle. To remove the leaf from the veiner effectively simply squeeze it inwards. *Don't bend outwards as this can break both the leaf, and can lead to early cracking of the veiner.* You don't need any powder, oil or any kind of resist on silicone moulds. Any leaves that don't work, simply remove them and try again with another leaf. You'll soon get practised at veining and you'll be able to do it at speed. Depending on your variety of lettuce you can build the head up either enclosing the centre or with a fairly open centre rather like a crinkly rose. This is my preferred style but of course there are many types of lettuce including red ones which you can make in the same way just adding a red colouration to the edge by building it into a cane, or by powdering afterwards ... or both!

Don't forget if this lettuce is for your garden. It shouldn't look 'table trimmed'. It may have large outer leaves. It certainly should have a longer stem for pushing into your garden!

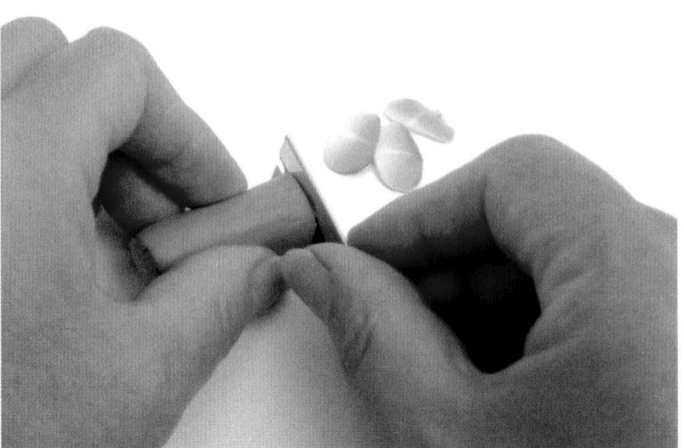

The safe method

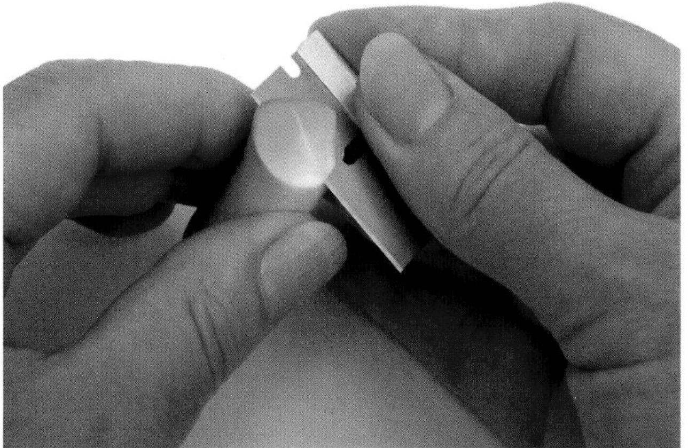

The unsafe method

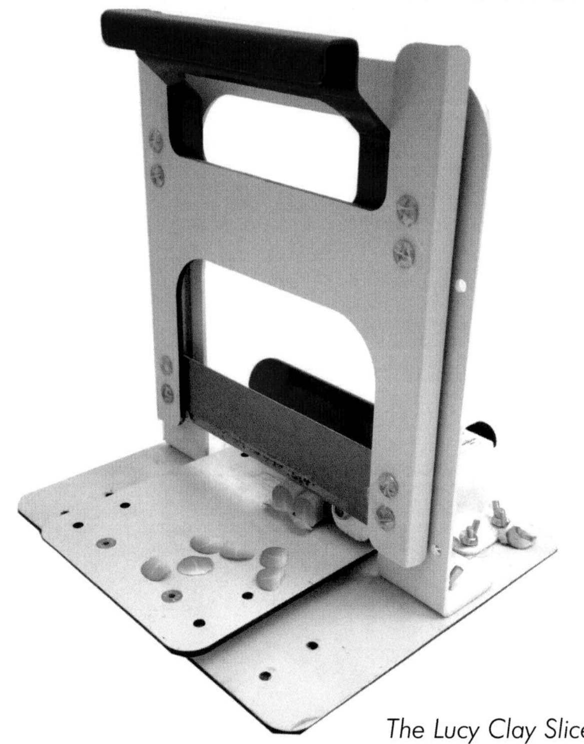

The Lucy Clay Slicer

The Herbs

Chives

You can use an extruder to make chives but you do want a variety of shades of colour. So make a stack of different greens and the extruder should push these through at different rates, effectively shading your colour for you. Extrude around 2.5cm (1") of clay through the narrowest holes and then grab the ends of the extruded clay and gently pull until the clay snaps. It may snap off at your end, at the end of the extruder or half way between. If it breaks at the extruder lay the pieces down on your baking surface and cut the bottom into a clean line. If it breaks off at your fingers, discard the pieces you're holding, turn the extruder round to line the base of the spikes along your tile in one line and cut the extrusions off at the extruder. You should be able to build a long line of chives ready to bake. The pompom flowers on the chives can be made using pale lavender colour flock, flower soft or snipped embroidery thread. Simply dip a baked stem or a flower wire of a similar colour into a pot of white Goo to stick the threads on. Then into the flock or threads. Bake again using a zigzag paper to keep the heads from pressing flat on the baking surface. After baking grab a big bunch of chives and slide a few of the flowers in to the bunch. Wrap them temporarily with flower wire, chop the bottom end to make a clean cut and cover liberally with PVA glue. Press the glue end onto some tissue paper to keep it from sticking to the surface and leave it to dry. Then you can remove the supporting wire. You can then plant in your herb garden or in a pot.

I made all the other herbs, including **parsley and rocket**, using stencils which I designed with my husband Frank as we went along.

Lavender and rosemary are particularly difficult to simulate in miniature because they are so tiny. Plus they have green tops and pale underneath to the spiky leaves so I choose not to make very big plants for these! Mine were made with a two part stencil and I played around with putting 2 layers of Goo in the stencil to achieve the 2 different colours Rosemary is usually a fairly dark green on top whereas lavender is much softer. The two parts were put together back to back (shiny sides together and twisted into fine flower wire

I made **mint** in the same way but with a larger stencil and just used a single bluey green. **Sage** has a very particular colour which is close to olive green in Premo. It also has a powdery look to the surface which you can get by dusting with talc. And a lighter underneath to the leaf. You can make individual leaves with double sided clay and join them in pairs on flower wire before twisting each pair into more flower wire, or use a herb leaf stencil.

For **basil** I made some pots of basil using a shaded polymer clay leaf cane cut very fine with my Lucy Clay Cutter

Carrots

You will need

Single sided blade
Clay: soft, light green, carrot orange and translucent
Hockey stick shaped tool
Craft drill
Teabag dust
Green Goo
Green pastel chalk
Texture sheet (optional)

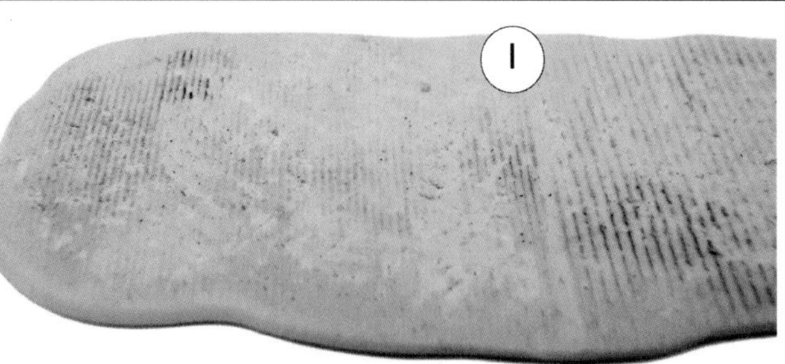

Make a roll of clay and add a point to the roll. Cut off a carrot shape and slightly round off the top edge. Note don't round the top off off you need it to be flat or even very slightly indented to make drilling easier.

Add texture to the carrot by rolling on a scratched off texture sheet. (1) You can add more lines and spots manually but if your carrot is in the garden re-member it won't be seen, so how much detail you put on depends if your carrot will be permanently fixed or not.

I use old tea bag dust to add some dirt to the carrot and I also like to dust the top slightly with green pastel chalks, as if the sun has got to the tops. Real garden carrots will often have this colouration.

Leaves

This is one of the new techniques which I've only been using for a few years. I used to use coloured lichen for the tops but I prefer this effect and it's fun to learn to do.

For carrot leaves you need a mix of spring and summer green as you have to get a balance between the lighter stalk as it leaves the root and the darker leaves. You can also choose to powder the edges for a change in the greens.

You need a slightly sticky mix. This time you extrude through a clay ex-truder on a very fine setting. Or you can simply roll short lengths of clay by hand. (2) Using a curved ended tool, press down the very edge of the clay at a diagonal, effectively dragging some of the clay out from the stem. (3) (4) Do this down both sides. (5) Sometimes, when you get your hand in, you can even subdivide those fronds again making very fine shrubbery, dill 'fronds' and carrot leaves for example. This is quite a dif-ficult technique to perfect but is very useful and once you 'get it' it's real fun! The trick is to have your clay soft enough and be comfortable with whichever tool you use. I use a hockey stick tool which is actually used for embossing paper in Pergamano (paper) craft.

When you have completed these 'fronds' remove them from the tile using your single sided blade (6) and place them on zigzag paper to bake. You can put the fronds into twos and threes to make the stems narrower for putting in the carrots. You can also twist them and shape them at this stage to ensure you don 't have a flat and shiny back, but a more natural movement. (7)

When both parts are once-baked I drill into the tops. (8) (9) Use a little green or brown Goo on the ends of your fronds and push two or three fronds into the hole in the carrot. Re-bake the whole carrot. Remember if you want a good spread on the leaves, take them out of the oven hot (they are flexible when hot) and as soon as you can stand them up to allow the leaves to cool in your desired position otherwise they will set wherever they are left. (10)

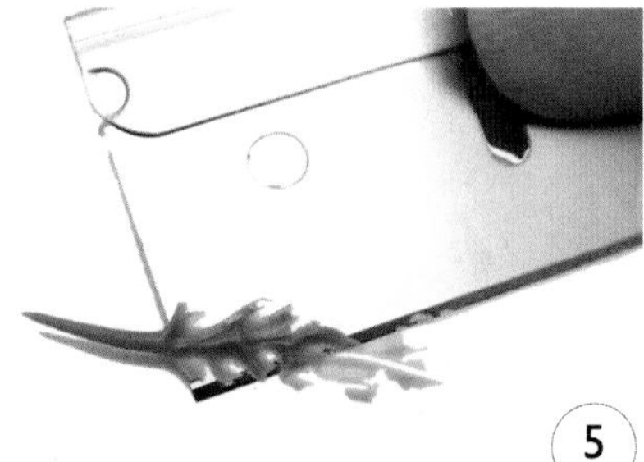

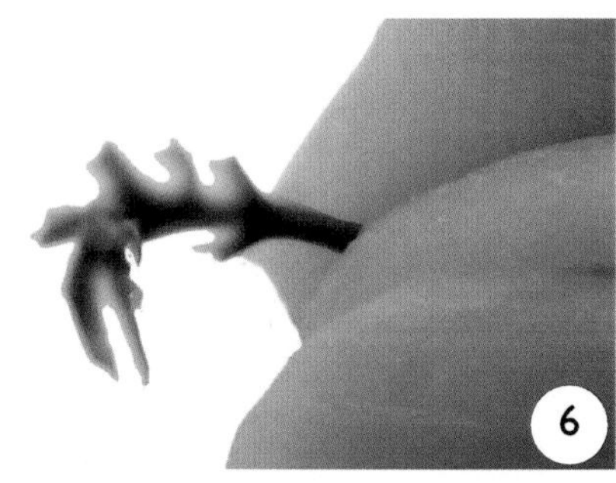

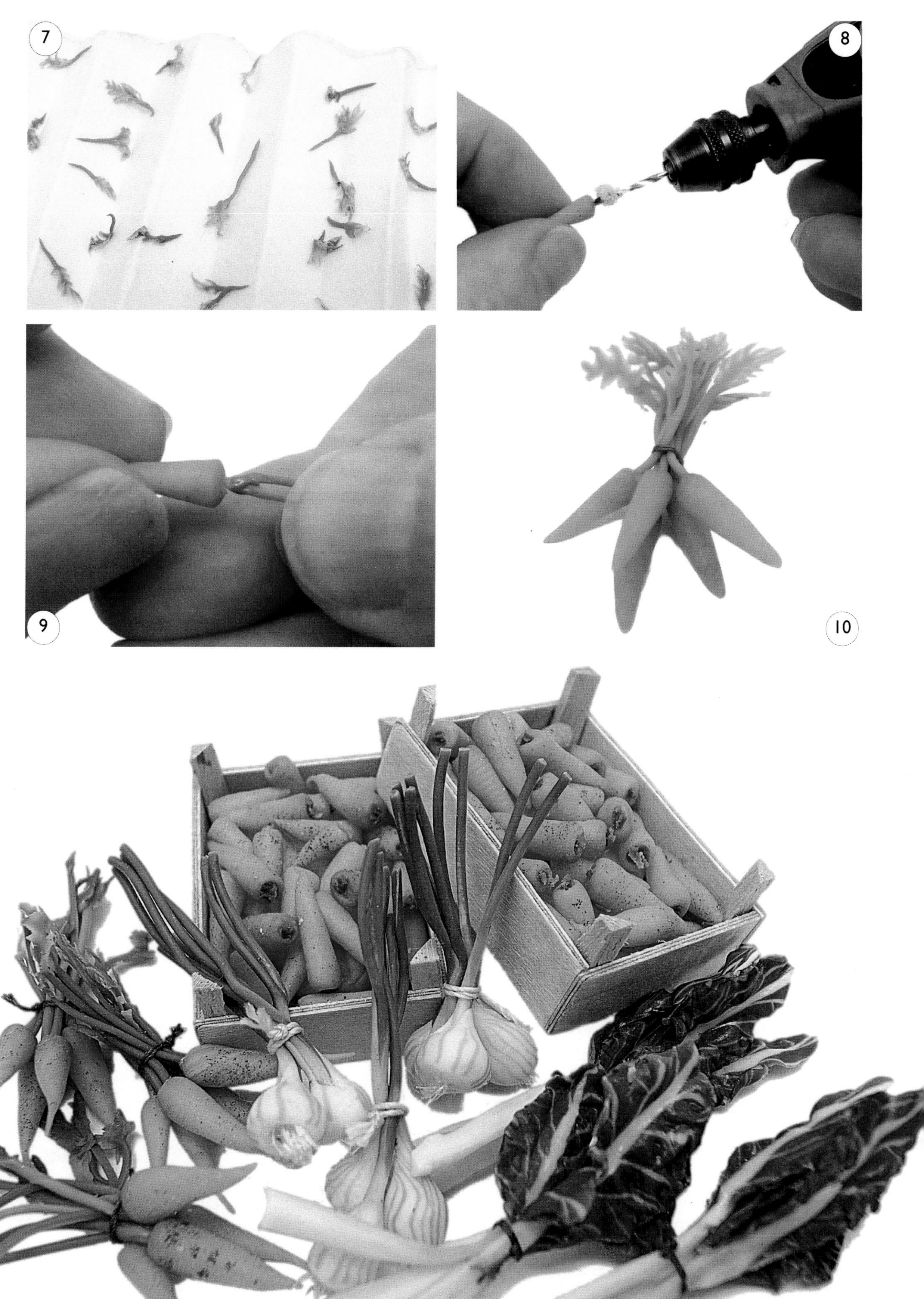
7
8
9
10

Beetroot

You will need

Clay: burgundy, marine blue, green clay: summer green, spring green, dark green and translucent

Single sided blade

Chard veiner or home made deep veiner

Small knitting needle

To make the leaf cane

Make a Skinner shade from dark summer to light green and fan fold it as in the lettuce project on page 26 into a cylinder ready to put the central and side veins in. You may also need to skip forward to the brassicas on page 50 to see how to put the side veins in if you are new to caning.

Caning is the word we use to describe putting patterns into polymer clay in a larger size (often, but not always a cylinder) and lengthening it to reduce the scale.

Once you have added the side veins you also need spots. (1) You put these in by piercing the entire cylinder in several places with a knitting needle (2) and inserting a thin roll of burgundy in each hole before squeezing back together and lengthening the cane. I make the cane slightly more leaf shaped as I'm lengthening it. The leaves are sliced and then veined using a chard leaf veiner (or a home made deep leaf veiner). I then add stems which are cut in slices from a flat piece of clay using the same method as shown in brassicas on page 50 (3) I usually pre-bake these, it can be useful to bake the stems first so that they have some rigidity, (4) and add them to the leaves with Goo (5) but you may prefer to add them before baking. Bake the leaves and stems together. Yes you can bake polymer clay more than once!

Beetroot

Make a pea sized ball with a stringy tail by nipping the end of the ball into a point and 'twizzling' it until it finally drops off. (6) You can mark the beet to make it less perfect, but in the garden you wouldn't see this so it isn't strictly necessary. Bake the beets. Drill the beets, and add the stems using some green Goo before baking again.

Radish And Turnip

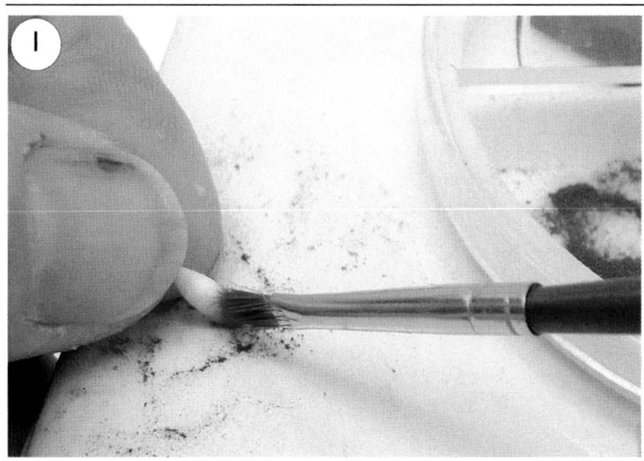

You will need

Conte crayon 39 or a carmine pastel
Porcelain, translucent and white clay
Spring and summer green clay
Cheap cutters to alter e.g. Makin's Nature
Pliers
Leaf veiner
Single Sided Blade

(1) Your clay should be a white and translucent mix. Approximately 2/3rds translucent to 1/3rd white. Make a small ball, not much bigger than a peppercorn and roll the end to form a point (see the beetroot project opposite). If you are making the 'French Breakfast' variety you need to make them longer than the little ball shaped radish. Paint the top half of the radish with red powder keeping the bottom as clean as possible. The round radish are more scarlet than the French breakfast which lean more towards the carmine colours. If possible choose your colours from looking at real life. Identify and copy the colours you use for future reference. My Colour Book (the physical version rather than the ebook) has useful reference strips down the bottom for colour identification purposes. If you want 'mud' on it I suggest you do that after baking as paints and powders can 'bleed' into the clay. Bake the 'roots' for a shorter than usual time as you are using a white clay and white clay can discolour when over baked. They won't be as strong so you will have to be careful when drilling.

Turnip and Radish tops

Make an oval cane for these tops either with the coloured veins for the beets in or just a plain colour for the radish, I recommend using a shaded cane if you want professional quality. See page 26 lettuce cane. Except you need a darker and less translucent colour. Using an oval cane allows you to cut a very thin slice of clay, much thinner than you can get from rolling it out. You can also add side veins as I do in the brassicas project but you certainly don't need to. You can then cut out and vein with a leaf mould. You'll need an altered cutter for the shape of your leaf as I haven't found a suitable cutter for the beet leaf shapes. (2) Then, choose a veiner with a reasonably close vein and deep texture. I often use a veiner made from a mint leaf. Or you can use the Swiss chard/beet mould. See the chard project on page 82. Radish tops (3) are a little smaller than beet tops so you can use the double cutting method if you want a smaller leaf, and you don't need to add extra stem if there is enough stem on your cutter. However if you want a longer stem you can add it at the veining stage as in the brassicas project.

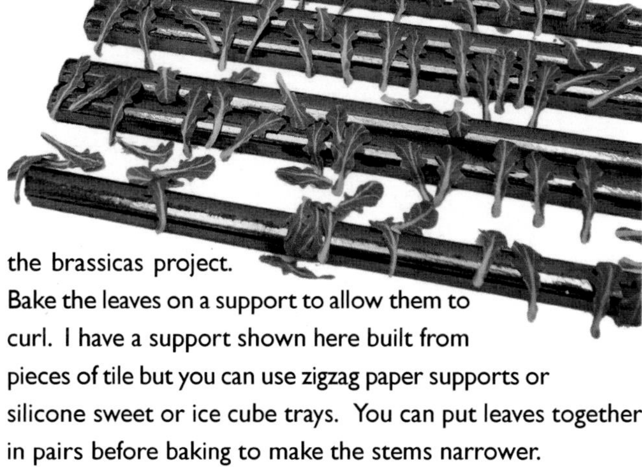

Bake the leaves on a support to allow them to curl. I have a support shown here built from pieces of tile but you can use zigzag paper supports or silicone sweet or ice cube trays. You can put leaves together in pairs before baking to make the stems narrower.

Just the same as with the carrot project drill the tops of the radish or turnip and add the leaves using Goo before re-baking. Don't use too much Goo as it can expand when it bakes leaving a crack. If this happens fill with 'dirt' so it looks deliberate! (4) (5)

Sweet Peas From Stencilled Parts

You will need

Flower wire, light green

Fine glass beads

Light summer green Goo (the green is more realistic if you add a little white and a tiny touch of navy blue)

A small quantity of pale pink/mauve etc. Goo

A sweet pea plant stencil

Cocktail sticks or pointed tool

Flower Foam pad from sugarcraft suppliers

Ball tool

Because pea leaves are really very tiny and don't have a great deal of texture, and because the flowers are so fine I've chosen to use them to demonstrate how stencilling can produce really tiny elements in polymer clay Goo. For instructions how to make Goo please see page 13.

You can cut your own stencils with a lot of patience and a swivel knife but it is admittedly very fiddly so my husband and I designed these among a range of plant stencils. You can buy these stencils from me or from several suppliers. See suppliers list at the back of the book page 119.

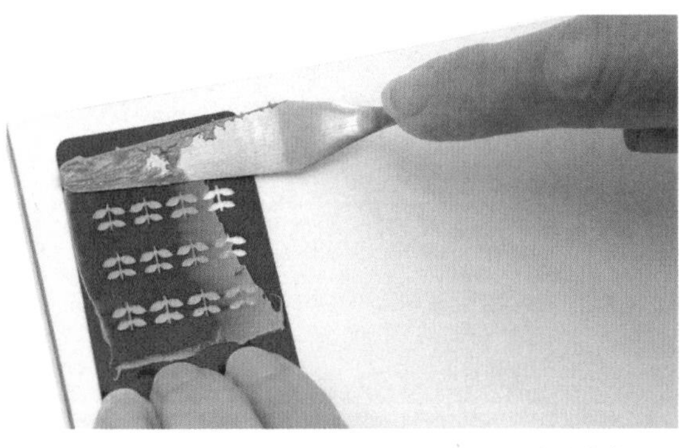

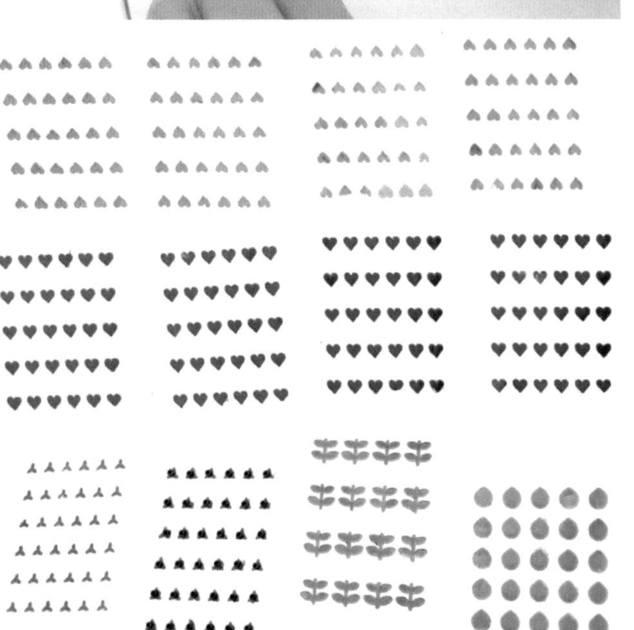

Preparing Your Stencil

We recommend that you wipe baby oil over both sides of the stencil and leave it to soak in. Wipe off any excess. This prolongs the life of the stencil and makes it easier to clean.

Cleaning Your Stencil

Remove as much Goo as you can, and then use kitchen roll and baby oil to clean the stencil on both sides. Store the stencil flat.

Baking

Remember, you can bake stencilled parts over and over again during several processes of constructing the plants so don't be afraid to divide this process up into stages.

Making plants

Add a bead to the back of the stencilled calyx part (using Goo) either before or after the first bake. I use a cocktail stick to pick up the bead and dip it in the Goo. You may need to use another or a fingernail to free the bead from the stick if it doesn't stick immediately to the calyx. Bake again.

Goo the calyx bead on to the top of a 6-8cm (approx 3") piece of light green flower wire (30-33 gauge) carefully pierce the bottom (fattest part) of the larger oval leaf with the flower wire and thread it up to around 2.5cm (approx 1") from the calyx. Add a second leaf immediately

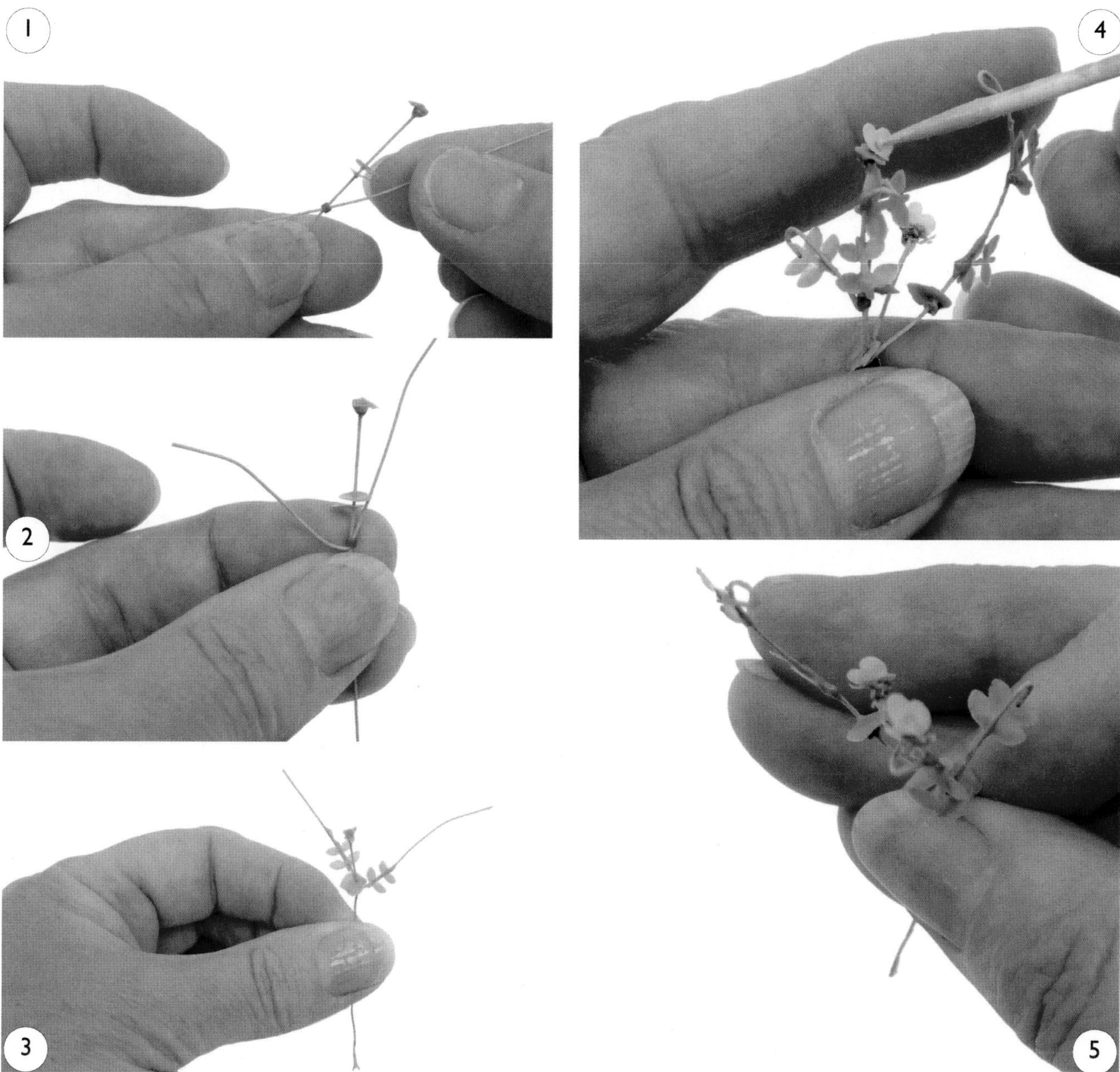

behind the first one and point them in different directions. Then thread another tiny bead (recommended Miyuki Delica 15/0) onto the wire and push up under the leaves. Then thread another wire through this bead. (1) It should fit snugly. Bend the wires diagonally upwards and then seal the whole 'joint' by covering the bead with Goo. (2) Then add the 4 leaf sets up these extra parts and below on the stem. (3) You can add more of these joints in varying formations. Curl the end of the wires round your pointed tool . You can snip off any excess later. Bake at this stage before adding the flowers.

Using one of your colours of flower Goo, or even better a slightly darker shade, Goo the tip of the heart on to the calyx. (4) Then you can either bake again or go straight on to the next stage of Goo-ing the smaller heart in the same direction. We want to try to make the bottom heart bend downwards so it can be easier to make them separate if you do this after baking the first part. (5) Either way the petals can be made to have a more natural form after baking and while still hot. You can also press a ball tool into the lobes of the hearts on a piece of Flower Foam, stiff flower making sponge available from sugarcraft suppliers, to encourage them to have more shape.

Strawberry plant project

You will need

Fine light green Japanese flower wire 33 gauge for example

Slightly thicker light green flower wire.

Fine, light leaf green sewing thread

Pastel chalks in ochre, orange, brown and reds

Small Petal cutter with 3 round petals OR a very small circle cutter (Kemper tiny push cutter)

Very tiny flower cutter with 5 or 6 petals. Kemper tiny blossom push cutter.

Green Goo and brown Goo see page 13

Foundation mix 2 polymer clay (appx ¾ translucent ¼ white)

Pale yellow clay

Strawberry colour clay

Clay in greens from light summer green green to darkest green

Plus some white and translucent for a lighter backing colour.

Craft drill (Dremmel etc.) & very fine drill bit.

Light green acrylic miniatures paint and a dressmaker's pin (to add seeds)

Bent pin tool

To remind/prompt you as to what a real strawberry plant looks like here are the range of leaves flowers and fruit. The leaves come in all colours. Various greens and various stages of decay. I took these examples late in the year. Earlier in the year there aren't so many partially decayed leaves and there are some brighter green leaves. If you're making a whole garden scene it's worth thinking about the month of the year and what plants will be at what stage of growth.

If you are making a mature tub or flower bed you will need mature green fresh green and also one or two of the dried out leaves scattered around the bed under the 'growing' plants for realism. If you are only making a small pot of strawberry plants you can certainly leave out the brown leaves.

real strawberries

Making the strawberry leaves push mould

(1) Take a very small 3 petal flower cutter and cut out a thin shape from a piece of clay. Choose a clay which is reasonably soft to work but durable and semi flexible when baked. For this job I've used Cernit. Use a different colour from your final leaves to distinguish that this is your mould master. You also need your clay thin but not extremely thin. Around 1.5 - 2mm is about right but this can depend on the size of your 3 petal cutter. If you can't find a 3 petal cutter you can use 3 single circles overlapped. Use the tiny Kemper circle cutter.

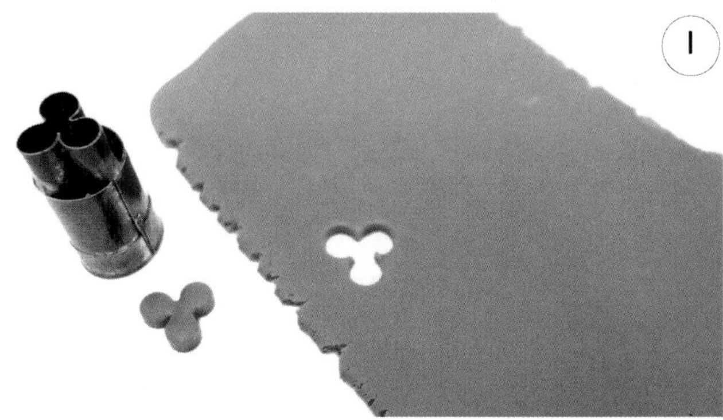

(2) Draw three veins on the centre of each leaf with a bent pin tool, cocktail stick or dental tool, then draw the veins from each centre vein to the edges. Draw fairly deeply and right to the edges for a good strong texture.

Finish the shape by pushing in at the edges at the end of each line to form deeply indented edge.

Bake this form at the recommended temperature for the clay you have used. This will be the master for your leaf veiner. You can try making more than one of different sizes and see which works best for you. If you have difficulty finding a small 3 lobed cutter try cutting 3 separate tiny circles from Icing nozzles and filling the centre where they join.

(3) Once the master is baked, press some 2 part silicone moulding paste over the original on to a ceramic tile. Leave

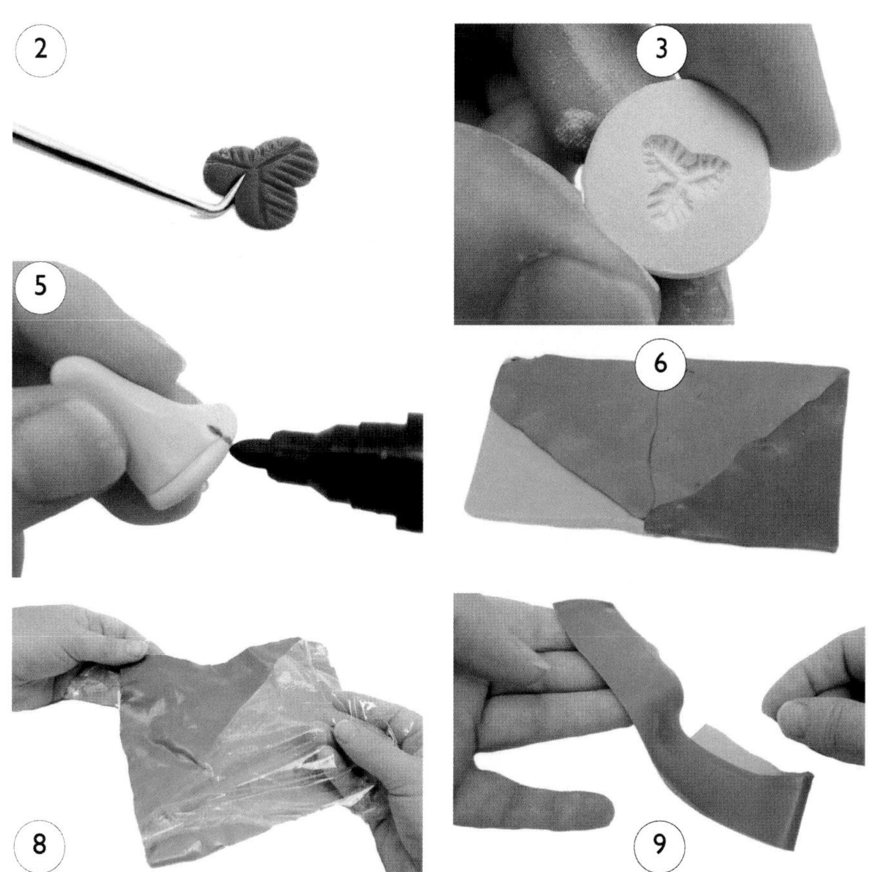

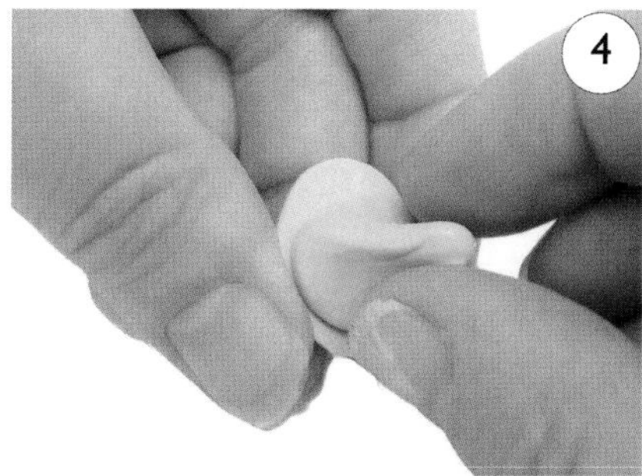

to set and peel the mould away from the master. If you see any 'shiny' patches on your mould it has got air between the mould and the original, you will have lost definition and you may have to do it again.

When this part is dry, remove the master, dust the mould with talcum powder and make the second side.

(4) As with all the push mould types, you need to put a handle on the second side. Make sure it's long enough to grasp with your fingers. A three sided handle is best to get hold of.

(5) Make sure you make some kind of locating mark.

Open and check your results.

Making The Leaves

Now make a a 'Skinner shade' from dark summer green clay to a fresher spring green. This is to give you a variety of greens in one sheet. (6)

Back this sheet with a paler green made from a mid green and white and translucent Sandwich these two sheets together and roll out on a thick setting.

Then roll again on thinner, and finally a very thin setting. (7)

(8) Wrap the sheet in cling film to keep it clean if you aren't using it immediately.

When I am ready to make the leaves, I cut a piece of this sheet and I then stroke and stretch the leaves even further to make them as fine as possible. (9)

Try to use this prepared clay over the next couple of days as very thin sheets don't remain flexible long. The clay can be re-mixed and re-made though.

Make a similar sheet of (autumn leaf colours) brown clay also with a lighter colour underneath.

(10) Cut a good number of the 3 sided petals and mould each one between the two parts, making sure the dark green side goes downwards into the flat side of the mould. (11)

Cut as many leaves out as you feel able to 'vein' in a session and leave any extra clay under a sheet of plastic film.

(12) With the darkest colour down into the flat half of the mould press the clay with the press mould and open.

The clay normally would stick slightly to the first mould. However, depending on the stickiness of each side it may stick on the other side instead. You may need to use a smooth cocktail stick to help you delicately remove it. As you're removing it curl some of thee leaves slightly sideways.

To take the clay out of the mould squeeze the edges of the mould to encourage the edges to come away from the mould.

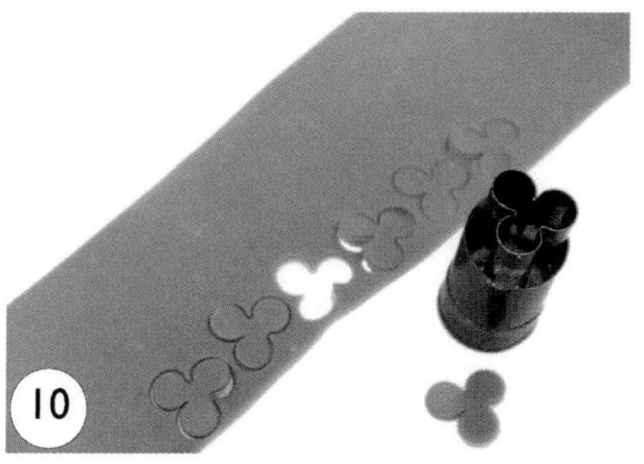

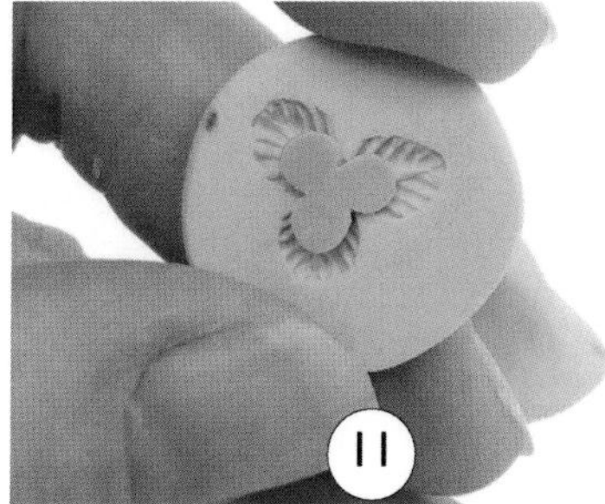

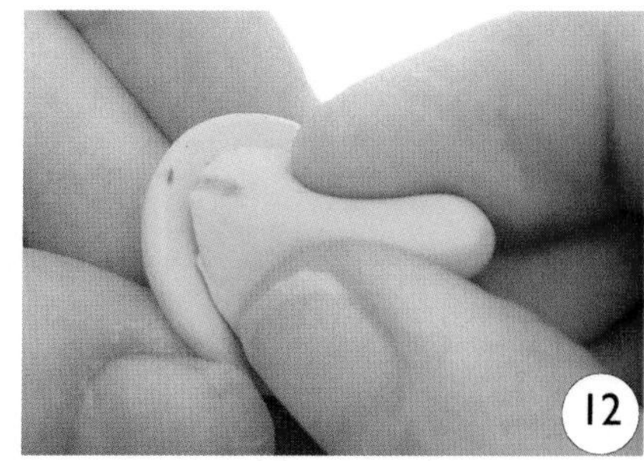

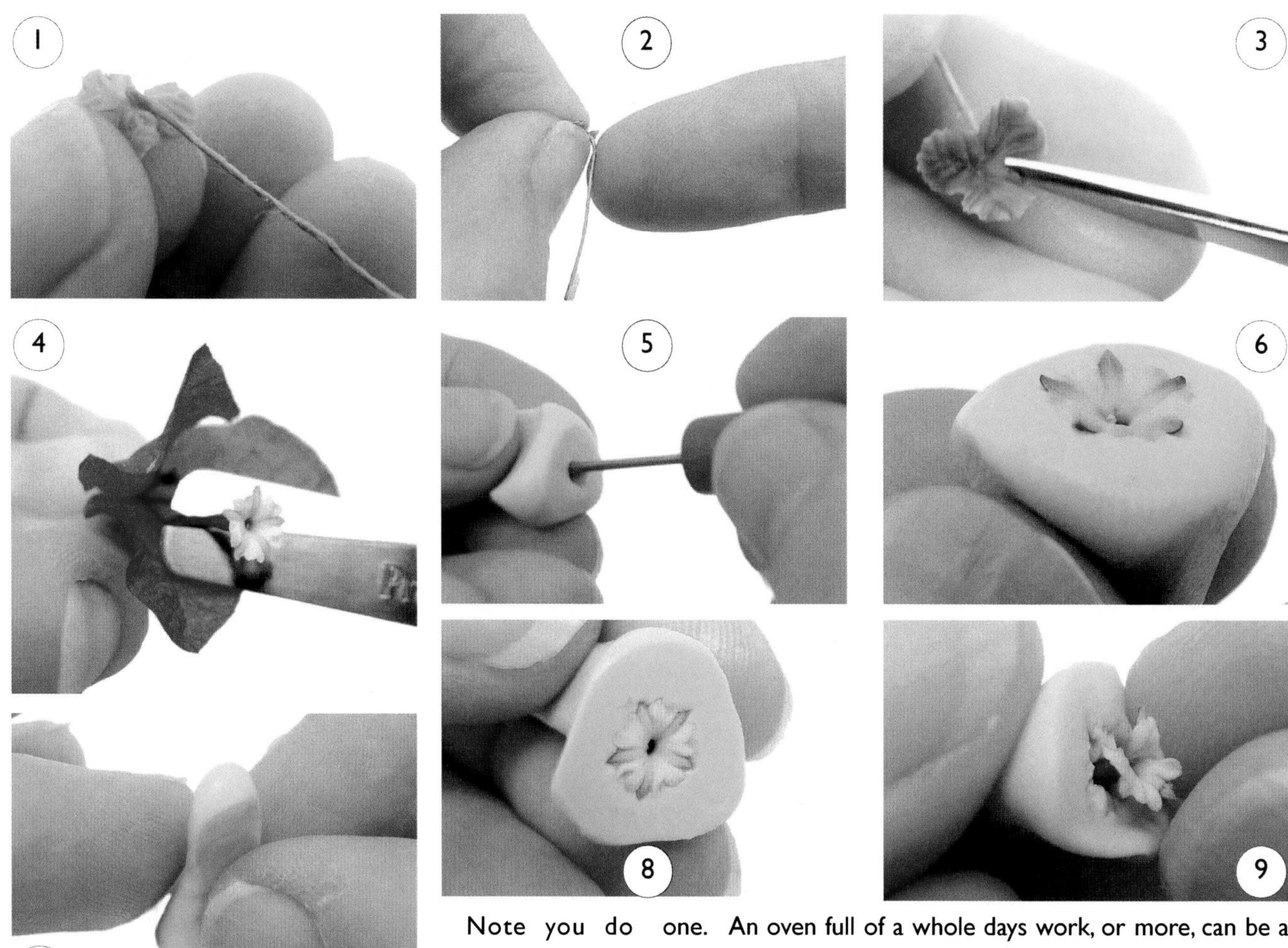

Note you do not need to put any 'resist' on the mould. However If your clay is very sticky indeed you may find brushing the very smallest amount of fine talc on your sheet of clay may help it not to stick to the mould.

Glue some of these leaves onto different lengths of stalk using Goo. (1)

the leaves should be upside down and the stems attached to the back. Bake. You don't need to add stems to all your leaves nor to any of the brown ones. The leaves with stalks will stick out a little higher than the rest so it stands to reason that you should add stalk to only the best of the best especially of the lighter (therefore apparently younger) leaves. You can bend the stalk after baking. (2) You can accentuate (3) the separation of the leaves after baking the stem on because the Goo serves to hold the parts together more firmly and flexibly.

When you are making a lot of individual elements for a big project. Try to bake as many of the elements as possible at the same time, as this saves on oven use. You may need to have a safe place to put parts waiting to be baked where the cat won't stand on them or shed on them! If you have an oven specifically for craft use I advise you to use several small ceramic tiles to work and bake on and just add tiles to the oven as you go along. Until the oven is full. But one note of caution: put a timer on your oven if it doesn't already have one. An oven full of a whole days work, or more, can be a disaster to lose by over baking.

To make the calyx mould

Making this mould was the single biggest step I took from food making to making gardens and I found it while looking for a way to make tops for Italian peppers and indeed this calyx mould works for making these tops too! (4)

If you have a bougainvillea plant, snip the tiny flower inside the pink 'leaves' leaving about 1cm of stem. (5)

First make a blob on a stalk shape like an inverted tear drop. Make sure you make a hole to pop the stem in because otherwise the flower stem may not be strong enough to push it's own hole and may bend. (6)

Push the little flower carefully in to it. This flower is very delicate and you must do it immediately while it's stem part is still firm. You will only be able to use it once.

When you have put the flower into the mould material, make the stem square or triangular shaped. Please note: it will not work if you make it cylindrical. This is because of the way you remove the clay later. Cylindrical shapes just slip through your fingers. (7)

Upturn the mould and put it on a flat surface to set. You may need to keep gentle hold on the mould 'stem' to stop it drooping. (8)

(9) When set you can release the flower by squeezing the mould until the tiny petals come away from the mould material.

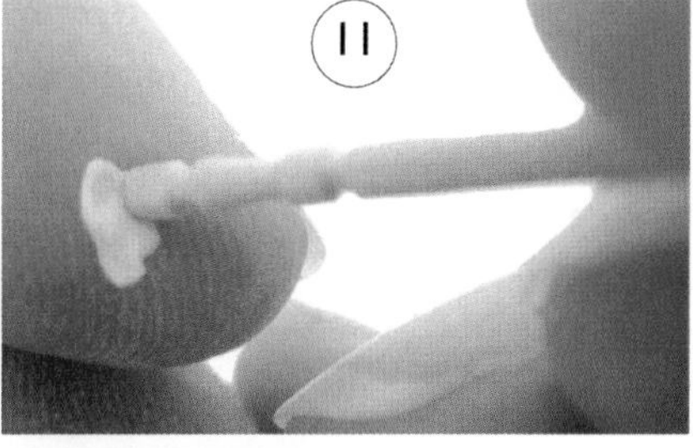

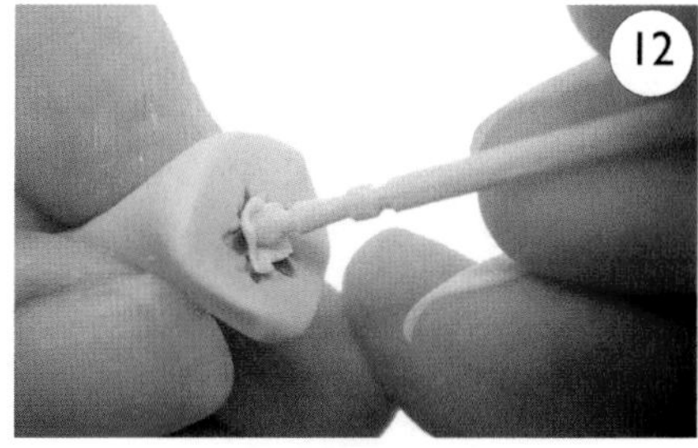

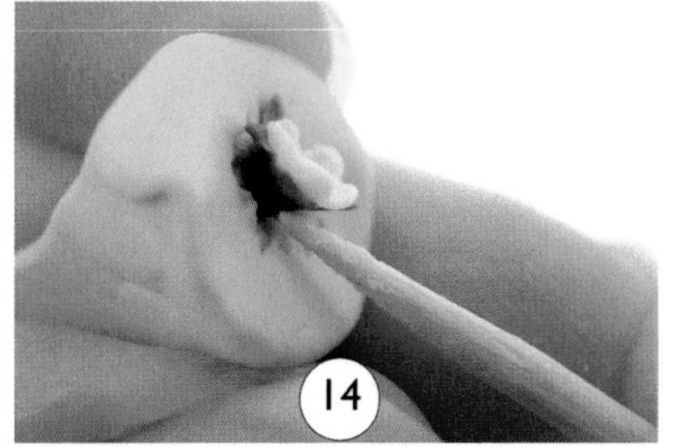

Then pull the flower out. You may find it breaks during this and you may have to gently 'dig' the stem out with a thin knitting needle or cocktail stick. Take care not to damage the mould.

To make the flowers

(10) Press some green clay into your stem/calyx mould and scrape back with your fingernail until you leave green clay only in the calyx part, (the star shape) not in the flower part.

(11) Make the thinnest possible sheet of pale translucent white (Foundation Mix 2).

Cut a lot of little white flowers with a tiny blossom tool and press with the back of a cocktail stick or with a ball tool into some flower foam to shape each petal then press in the centre on to the calyx to ensure that it sticks. (12)

(13) Then make the tiniest cone of yellow clay and add it to the centre. If you can't form a tidy cone just make a really tiny ball of clay. (14) To remove the flower from the flower mould roll and squeeze it until it loosens and lightly 'pick' it out using your bent pin tool or a cocktail stick.

Sometimes the whole stem will not come out. Don't worry just leave this flower on a short stem and start again pushing more green clay into the mould. I put many of my flowers together into pairs or threes before baking. (15)

Strawberries

You can choose to make your strawberries with solid colour or with shaded colour as in my book "Making Miniature Foods" instead. Or you can use a pale cream colour clay and simply dust with pastel chalks to produce several different shades of scarlet to red for increasingly ripe fruit, whichever method you use for making the fruit I make the shape into a cone and cut off the back rounding it off. Make the strawberry calyx using the 'cut and cross' method. (16)

(17) Simply make a thin snake of clay and press onto the surface of the tile. Then shave tiny slices from this 'flattened snake'. To release these slices from the blade hold the blade diagonally with the safety edge of the blade towards you and push the blade backwards along the surface. The clay should stick to the surface more firmly than to the blade and should be released by this motion. (18)

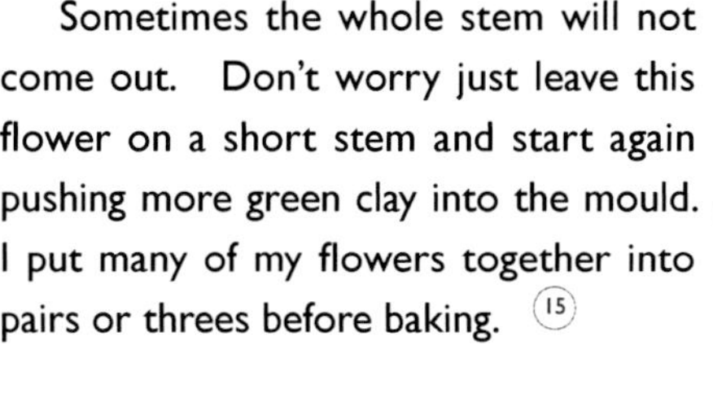

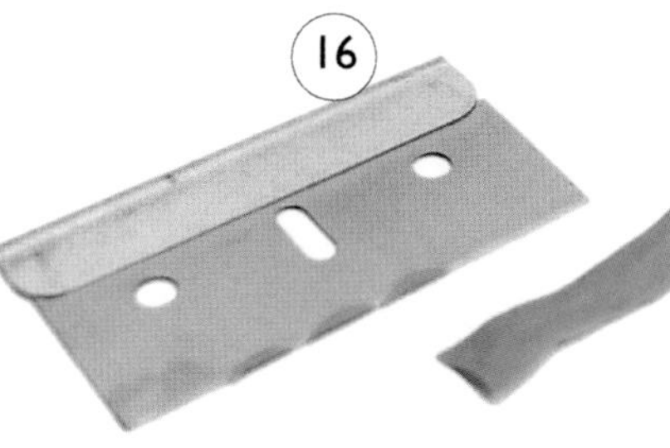

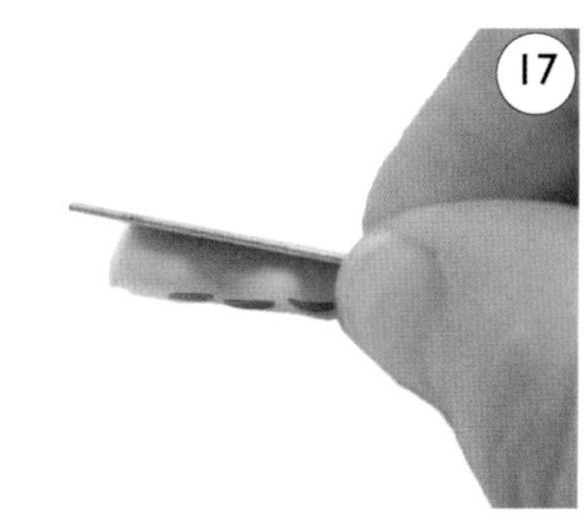

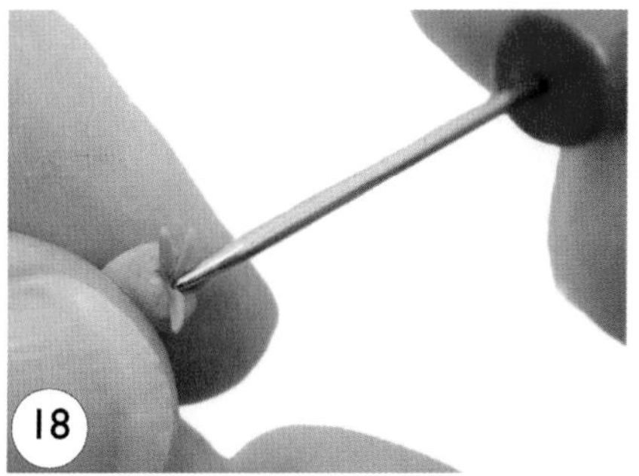

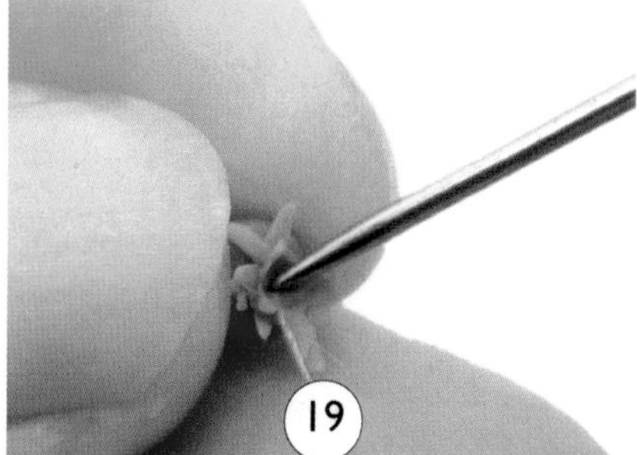

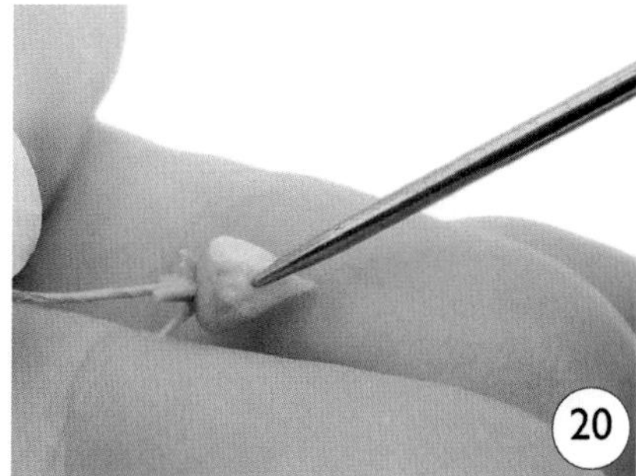

(19) Lay these pieces one over another to form a star shape and press onto the back of your strawberry shape. Then with a little Goo on a cocktail stick, add a small piece of green sewing thread for hanging down strawberries, pushing the thread a little way into the strawberry shape. You can also choose to make some strawberries with wire stems to stand up in the strawberry bed.

(20) Make little indentations for seeds with your bent pin tool.

Assembling the plant

You can either glue the pieces into a pre formed soil surface or you can assemble and re-bake using Goo but remember the white flowers can change colour if over baked.

1

2

Drill several very small holes in the 'soil' surface a centimetre or so apart (half an inch) and blow away the dust caused by the drilling.

Starting at the base layer glue a few of the brown 'dried leaves' to the soil. Build up layers lightly attaching the other leaves firstly any badly coloured misshapen or ill-defined leaves plus any 'bits' of leaves that fell off or just didn't look good. This is a beauty parade and the rejects get to be the support, making everything else look good!

Then start to glue in a few of the standing up leaves. (1)

You are aiming to get a nice 3 dimensional, loose feeling, joining of the leaves so that some will simply be suspended over others. Disguise the glued base with extra leaves (use the curly ones) add few flowers in clumps of 3 and a few fruits on stems.

Make sure that a few of the fruits hang over the side. At this stage sprinkle a little more soil substitute on any glue that is still visible. You need to fill in the levels up to the ones on stems which can stick up fairly rigidly. You can disguise the flower wire by breaking up the line by putting other leaves close up to it. (2)

Finally with a tiny pin, or shaved down cocktail stick, dot a little light green paint into the indentations on the tiny strawberries that you made earlier.

I don't do this earlier in the process because it's quite laborious and there's no point in putting the seeds in where they can't be seen. Most people won't see even the visible ones!

Colour Tips: easy mistakes to make

(when colour mixing for nature)

Professional Tip

This book isn't about colour mixing. I have a book which does that and which I recommend that you have on hand to help with your colour mixing, but here are a few key points to help you think about how you mix colour for your garden project.

My pet hate is using colours straight from the pack. It's so obvious when you do this and the colours are never right. Even with a good natural green like Fimo's leaf green or Premo's olive (more the colour of tinned olives than fresh). Not forgetting that Cernit do an 'olive' which is a lovely colour but not in any way related to the humble olive! They're not perfect. They are 'one size fits all' mixes. The colour is sometimes dull and opaque. If you want a garden that looks alive you must mix the colours yourself. Preferably from the base colours (yellow and blue etc.) and you should add variety. Not every leaf in the garden is the same green although many are closely related.

When I mention dark green, summer green and spring green they are the three colours which I suggest you pre-mix as they are the standard which you can intermix with extra translucent for 'lightness' (in perceived weight) and white for paleness.

I have made almost all of the following colour mixing mistakes so, although they might seem obvious. They aren't always!

Assuming that you have to add translucent to your colour when making very delicate items like grapes and lettuce etc. Actually you need to add a small amount of colour to a large amount of translucent.

Assuming that carrots are orange and tomatoes are red etc. The truth is the subtle differences in tone make all the difference in realism.

Ripening fruit (naturally ripened)

In a bract of fruit such as tomatoes, raspberries etc. generally the fruit closest to the stem swells and ripens first. The mistake is to reverse this order.

Red isn't just red

It is also tempting to think of red as just red whereas, when looking to mix colours or buy paints or pastels you should note that strawberries tend towards scarlet (a yellowy red) and raspberries towards carmine (to my mind a 'bluer' red). I'm not sure my interpretation of colour is the same as yours will be so look at nature and make your own colour interpretation.

real garden fruits showing a variety of reds

It's a fair cop! (cheating the seasons)

Some readers might by now have noticed that I'm cheating the seasons a bit. That is to say I'm including vegetables fruits and flowers that may not be in season together. I make no apologies for this. You may also say that one vegetable is in season in your part of the world when it isn't in mine. This is not a book to stick slavishly to. I tweak the quality of the plants or the seasons they appear and even, on occasions the scale I prefer to blur the line between fantasy and reality. If you're a purist you may wish to do the research into seasons and set a time of year on your project. These are my miniature gardens and I much prefer fantasy to purism. In my mini world I can have my leeks at the same time as my potatoes and my raspberries!

Raspberries & Blackberries

You will need

Moulding material
Accent beads & Glue
Cocktail sticks
Clay: carmine red, green, black & translucent
Small leaf cutter
Light green flower wire
Small leaf veiner (homemade or bought)
Single sided blade

The berry 'masters' are made by glueing tiny no-hole beads to a wire or cocktail stick. It is important that your beads are really tiny. The accent type beads are ideal but make sure that they are of even sizes. Some you can buy have very variable sizes in the same pack and this can spoil the result. (1)

Use a really good glue, but be prepared that your master will be destroyed in the making of the mould as de-moulding the master can pull individual beads off. If you try using more glue to keep the beads on the excess can 'blur' the nice sharp definition of the individual beads. So it's worth losing the master for a really good mould which will last through very many mouldings. Make as many masters as you want moulds since the masters are unlikely to stay together long enough to produce more than one mould.

Make the mould mix and upturn the cocktail stick or wire into the mould mix. Leaving the cocktail stick on and holding it or propping it upright will help you see if you're making a level mould.

Remove the master. Make several moulds as, sometimes, you leave the raspberries in the mould to bake and making them one by one would take way too much time and electricity. *(A version of this 'beads method' was first published in my book Miniature Foods Masterclass.)*

You can make the berries using coloured translucent clay. (2) (3) Be prepared that your mould material may affect the clay in the first few times you bake in it. It can help to wash the mould out first to remove any oils. But the first time you use it don't expect the results to be great. Don't forget to make berries of different sizes and colours and to bunch them together on the plant. Alternatively, use a Liquid Fimo mix as described in Miniature Food Masterclass. Or you can use a liquid / solid mix I call Goo. However making with polymer clay allows you to make a little indentation in the top if you want to make 'fresh picked raspberries'. You can add a calyx and stem to the back of your berries using the same methods as with the strawberry project, either using a calyx mould or by the cut and cross method or using a stencilled calyx. I prefer to make all the berries at the same time, bake them and then add them on to the stems later. I like using flower wire as it's really fine for the bunches of fruits and flowers. But for the canes (the long straight upright branches) I use a thicker wire or 3D pen work. See the patio projects chapter for 3D pen information. Remember raspberry canes are long and straight and very light coloured. (In real life they can reach 6ft or more) (4)

1

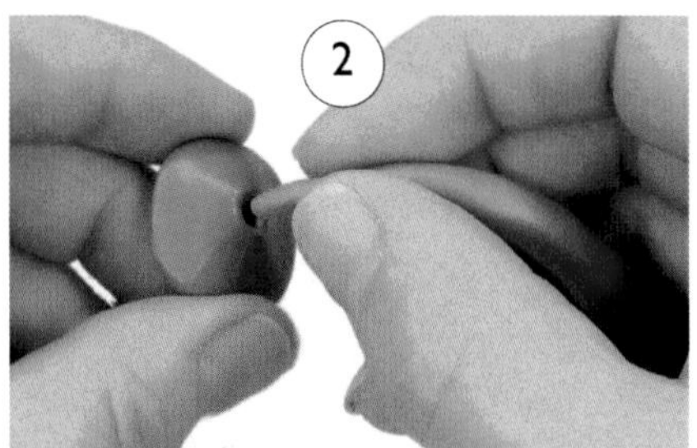

2

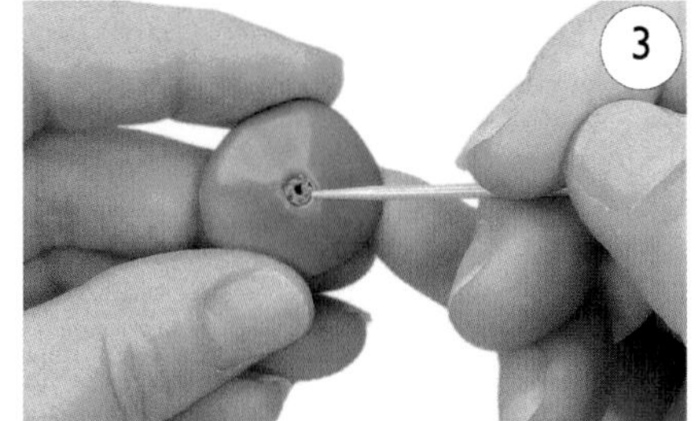

3

Blackberry canes are even longer but more straggly and will usually start to bend over at around 5ft. They are very fast growing as any gardener knows and shoot branches out in all directions! (5) The leaves of both plants can be made individually which of course is a work for the very patient! I do them this way for the raspberries because you can then have a paler back to the leaves. Note that raspberry leaves are grouped together in sets of 3 and blackberries more usually 5

4

5

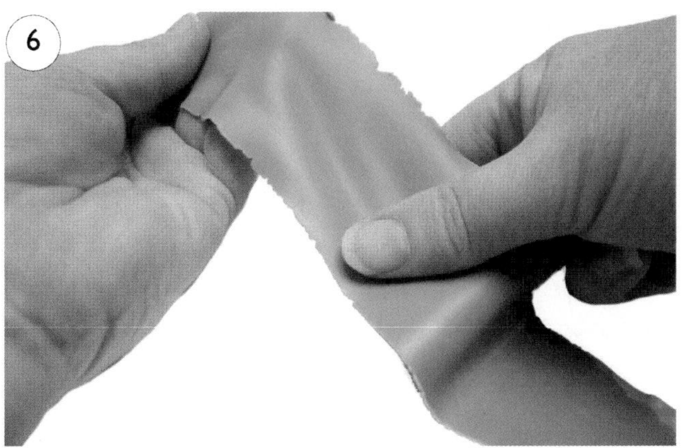

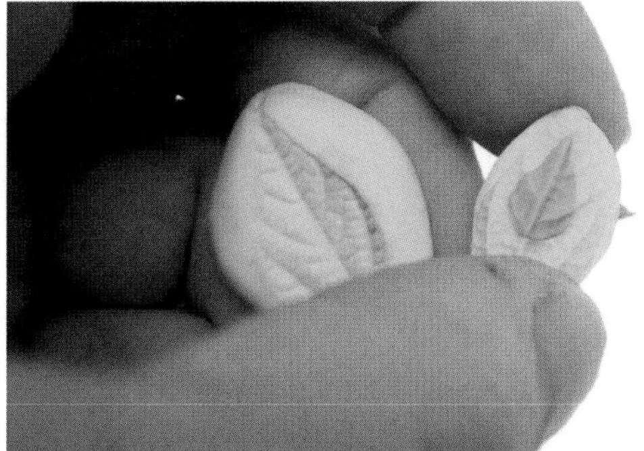

or 7 (or more)

When making with polymer clay, the leaves are cut out of a thin sheet of clay with a lighter colour on the back

To make a 2 layer leaf sheet with very much lighter under side you really need to add a sheet of a porcelain colour clay (foundation colour mix 2) with just the very smallest amount of the darker of the greens added to take the brightness off a touch. See steps 6 and 7 of the strawberry project on page 37. Then the clay needs to be stretched absolutely as thinly as possible without tearing it (6) and veined using a very deeply indented veiner. The best leaf to use for this veiner would be made from an actual tiny raspberry leaf, or you can use my veiner number #5. It doesn't matter if the veiner is a bit big as you can put the leaf in any part of the mould. (7)

Add the leaves to the ends of longish pieces of light green flower wire and then twist some of the wires together but not too closely because raspberries do grow on canes rather than bushes. Add the fruits and flowers if you have made any. (8) (9)

When making blackberries, before adding the leaves to the flower wire I 'dab' my wire in Goo so that the Goo clings and forms spiky peaks. (10) I then bake it and then add the leaves. In this case I used the plastic leaves from the length of flowers which I took apart (see page 107 "Cheap Tricks"). It wasn't possible to re-bake these afterwards so I had to use glue instead of Goo. PVA glue isn't a good enough bond for this job. Oh yes I tried it and they all fell off. I make all the

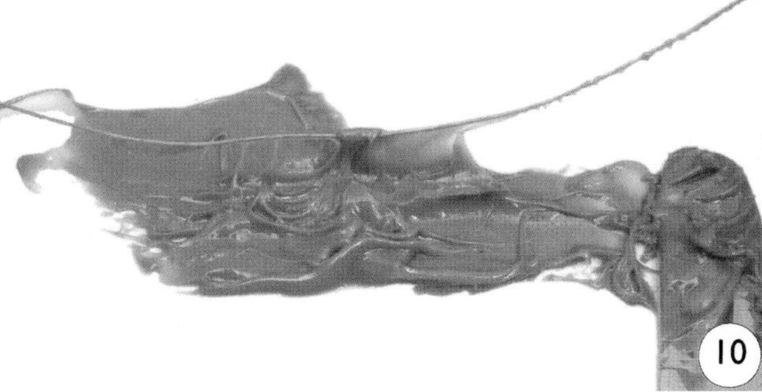

mistakes so you don't have to! I advise using a plastic based glue instead such as a jewellery or textile glue. I made both flowers and calyx for these brambles with a stencil.

Rhubarb

You will need

Single sided blade
Green chalks
Veiner (home made).
Translucent and white or porcelain coloured polymer clay
Red and dark burgundy clay
Dark green and lighter pale green colours
Flower wire
Large leaf cutter

You will need to make a leaf mould for this project. There are several leaves out in the wild which have a rhubarb leaf look and it's great to search out one which you think looks just right. Just be careful as these leaves may be poisonous if consumed as indeed are real rhubarb leaves. The internet has loads of images including botanical illustrations. It's worth taking a print out with you when searching for inspiration for leaf moulds. Remember the leaf doesn't have to be the exact size. It can be bigger. (1) You'll also need cutters the shape of a pointed shovel.

If you don't have a cutter these shapes and sizes (I didn't), you can alter long leaf cutters (available from cake decorating suppliers). I've chosen this set because it's fine and flexible metal. But I won't use the serrated side of the cutter. (2)

Roll out a very thin two layer sheet with dark green clay on top and lighter green clay underneath. (3) Roll it really thin and then stretch even further so its as thin as possible (4) Cut out and vein lots of leaves remembering to squeeze the veiner in to release the leaf and NOT bend it outwards. This helps the clay to come away from the veiner without cracking and also increases the texture in your leaf. Then bake your leaves ready for later. (5)

The colours used for the skin of the rhubarb cane are red and dark burgundy. Make sure your clay is nice and elastic. If necessary by adding a little mix quick or Sculpey Mould Maker. This material is great as a clay softener/elasticiser. Make a thick square of red The red you use depends on whether you want to make forced rhubarb or an open air rhubarb plant. You then need a much thinner sheet of dark burgundy. Not too fine though as the rhubarb will be so small you may not see the line at all if you make it too thin. (6)

Looking at a real rhubarb stick you won't see definite lines but this method creates a 'super real' effect which sometimes helps your miniatures to stand out. The sheets are stacked cut and stacked again. (7) (8) (9) Then a slice is taken and rolled out to form a thin skin on the cane. Make sure the skin does not overlap on the cane. (10) The centre of the cane is a very pale pink.

Wrap the skin around the circular cane and then using your thumb and forefinger of each hand to press the rhubarb into a square cane. When lengthening, make sure you keep this shape by smoothing and pulling the strip using the same thumb and forefinger opposition. (11) Lengthening a square cane without losing definition can be tricky and does take some practise.

Lengthen this strip until it is around 6mm wide and thread some flower wire through a small piece. (12) You can then stretch the cane even further to cover your wire. You want the final rhubarb cane to be around 3mm or even finer. The wire is to support the heavy leaves. You don't need to wire for the smaller leaves.

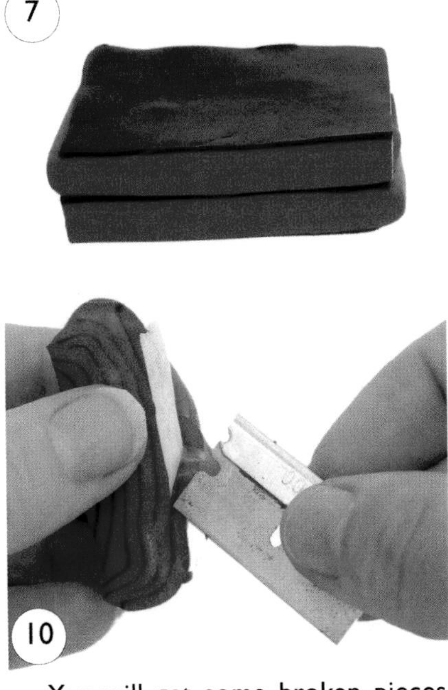

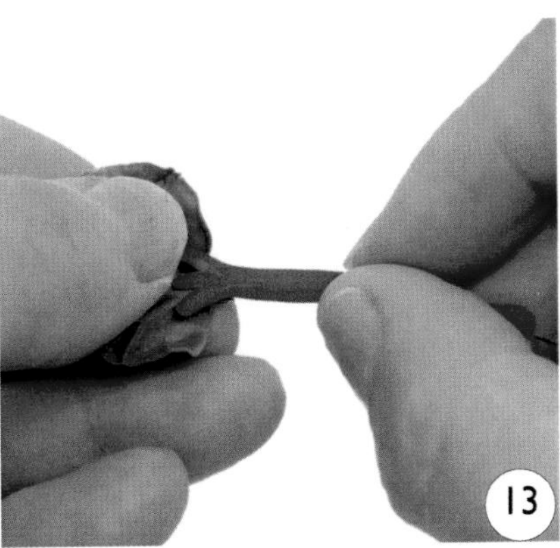

You will get some broken pieces. Bake them anyway and use them for making miniature rhubarb pie!

You are aiming for lengths of approximately 5cm (just over 2 inches) if possible with one end slightly narrower than the other. Using an old pair of scissors you can snip the wired cane into pieces. Then I use my blade to divide the top (narrower) ends into three.

Attach the stem to the pre-cooked leaf by simply 'smearing' this edge onto the back of the leaf , at the same time bending slightly so that the leaf lies at an angle to the stem. (13)

I then paint/dust with green pastel to disguise the join. And bake again. You may wish to make a zigzag sheet to support the bent over leaves.

For forced rhubarb (not shown) use tiny circles of the thinnest possible translucent yellowy green for the leaves. You can make this colour by adding only a tiny bit of green and yellow to a much larger quantity of translucent. The leaves are veined and then 'crumpled' over the top of a very thin pre cooked stem.. A forced rhubarb project appears in my Miniature Challenges Part 2 book.

I cut the base of each stem off at an angle to ensure I can cram a lot of stems into a small hole made in my base board.

I've made the stems very red but you may wish to make green stems and dust to make a little rosy at the ends instead.

Kitchen Garden Roundup

For the picket fencing I used some Chinese bamboo trivets. And cut them down and added spiked tops. Well, to be honest I passed them to my husband with a long list of sawing jobs.

Cut down to 4 inches remove the bottom bar from the smaller bits and re-attach. Cut the tops into a triangular shape. Attach 2 pieces together using the bottom bar glued with strong, fast setting wood glue. Add one of the smaller pieces that you previously cut off to each side of the main bottom piece. These fence pieces can be added to the base by drilling into wooden reinforcing blocks in the corners of the base (these need to be added and glued in first). To give the fencing a more 'lived in feel I covered with ivy. The stems were created using my 3D pen (more about this in the Patio Garden) and the leaves for the ivy are from my superfine range. The project for making this leaf cane if you want to have a go yourself is on page 97.

As a backdrop I decided to update a mini shed my mum made over 20 years ago by facing it in bricks. This shed is actually a garage which is a miniature version of my mums own woodworking shop complete with bandsaw, lathe etc. Since I don't collect dolls houses it was the only 'building' I had to hand and so I decided that if it looked like the side of a cottage it would do. The only problem was it didn't have brick walls. I didn't have time or money to go the 'brick slip' way so I rooted out an old brick stencil of Bromley crafts I had in 12th scale. Neither did I have the brick compound to go with the stencils, or if I did it's lost under a pile of craft materials, so I had very few options. I decided to have a go at using Goo!

I very lightly coated a ceramic tile with liquid polymer as a stencil adhesive and as a light bond between the bricks. Not too much, or I knew the top layer would run. I used a spatula to spread a terracotta coloured Goo on top. Then I simply shook grey sand (from Ikea) on top and pressed it in slightly. Removed the stencil and baked. The bricks were then just glued over a primer coat of mushroomy-grey paint using cheap wood glue applied very thinly over the paint. The edges were disguised using more ivy.

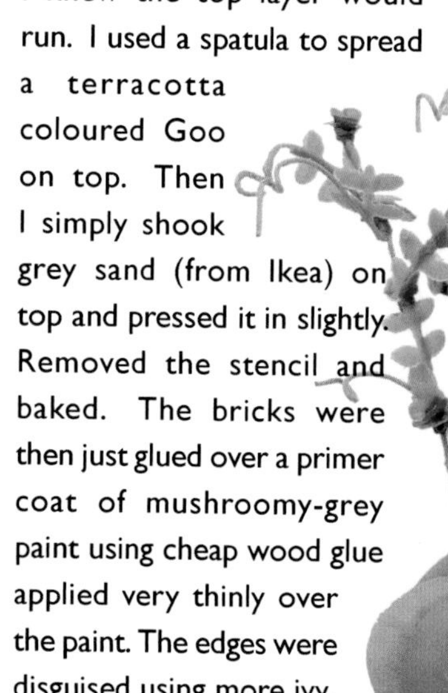

The base is simply one of the larger multiple

photograph frames mentioned in Making Garden Bases. The pathways I filled in with hardboard and covered with sandstone blocks from Stacey's, simply glued on with epoxy resin. The beds are filled with sections made in the way described on page 22. The edges of the raised beds are covered in a sheet made from a mushroomy-gray coloured Goo and sand. This was also baked separately and glued on later, using craft glue. Don't try to bake anything on these picture frames as they will melt!

The little bits of grass in the cracks and the infill are made from various scenic materials including a grass sheet which you can tear to tiny pieces, by a company called Imthurn. Underneath the flower beds I put flower foam to hold the plant stems in place.

To display the garden for photography I chose to add some 'trees' behind the scene which were simply made using plastic flower parts from a far eastern import shop. See Cheap Tricks page 107. The sunflowers and the rambling rose were made using my stencils.

The Allotment Garden

Brassicas, Garden style

This is where most miniature gardens come unstuck. People often assume that the vegetable plants in the garden look exactly as they do in the shop. Table trimmed to perfection and sorted for quality. All of an even size and standing in perfect rows with not a leaf out of place, close to the ground and with never a weed in sight. Nothing could be further from the reality of a real garden, especially an allotment. Nature is wild and unruly and to celebrate it I feel it's only right to appreciate it's wonderful imperfections.

There are several different varieties in the brassica family, and each has slightly different colours and shapes of leaf. Of course cauliflowers and broccoli have their florets, and brussels their tiny little sprouts. I'll give you a simple versions in each case and you can use the internet and seed catalogues to research the variety you want to make and 'tweak' the colours and shapes to suit you.

Look at and print out photos of entire brassica plants (untrimmed) if you aren't lucky enough to have the real thing in your garden! You will find that there is a surprising amount of greenery round your plant. They are also surprisingly tall and often quite scruffy looking. In short they aren't at all like the vegetables you buy in the shops are they? And look at the colour of the leaves. They are quite different from what you would imagine from your table trimmed varieties. Most brassicas have a 'bloom' over the outer leaves when mature which turns the outer dark green leaves to a powdery bluey green in aspect. This can be achieved in two ways, by mixing the clay colours. Premo does a Jungle green which is pretty close to this colour. With other clays you need to add navy blue and a little white to achieve the same effect. Or, as nature does, by using a dark leaf green and powdering with white pastel powder or talc afterwards.

1

2

Cabbages
(Savoy style shown)

You will need

Pasta machine
Single sided blade
Cabbage mould
Dark, medium & light green, white & translucent clay

For the leaves you need dark leaf green, summer green, and muted spring green mixes of clay and a relatively large quantity of creamy white which is approximately 3:1 translucent to white plus a touch of yellow to make it cream colour, and a tiny touch of summer green. You will be making all the veins for 3 canes of different colours and the additional stems to the leaves with this colour. Though, for the darker outer leaves I recommend adding a little more green to the mix. For more detailed colour mixing advice please see my book Angie Scarr's Colour Book.

3

4

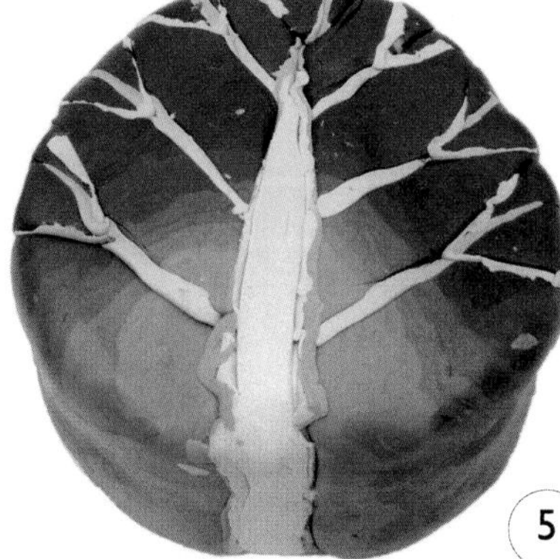

5

Using the Skinner shade technique make a fan fold shaded block, tapering at the bottom (see the lettuce project on page 26). (1) Form into a cylinder carefully trying to keep the blend of the colours. (2)

Cut the cylinder in half and cut each half diagonally into 3 or 4 depending if you want to add side veins. if not adding side veins cut into 4 on each side. (3) Please keep your pieces in place in order to avoid confusing which piece goes where! Add thin sheets of stem colour between each piece and the next. (4)

If you wish to add thinner side veins cut triangles from the cylinder. (5) Make sure you only do these one at a time to avoid having lots of confusing bits lying around.

Add the central triangle which is made in the same way as shown in the lettuce cane on page 26. Then lengthen the cane until it's diameter is around 2cm or just a little less. Then make the other two colour shades. (6)

Slice and vein leaves from each colour of cane. (7) Now form a central 'pea on a stalk' (8) shape with either the lightest of your greens or better still with leftovers from the vein mix. Wrap two light coloured leaves, one over the other. (9) The clay does stick to itself. Then you carry on with the medium colour leaf. I use 3 of these. These will stand up reasonably straight or curl back slightly.

Finally start adding the darkest leaves round the outside folding outwards for a trimmed savoy cabbage. Here is where the garden brassicas differ significantly from my other projects in other books and magazines. I like to put a fatter central stalk in each of the very outer leaves more nearly to replicate nature. Obviously these stems don't get seen in the inner leaves of a whole cabbage so you only need to put them on leaves where the base of the stalk is seen, so, in the case of cabbages that will be in approximately 5 outer leaves.

Make a long triangle cane either in the same way as you did for the central part of the leaf cane, or simply with your fingers as it needs to be long! Cut slices from this triangle at a slight angle so that the top is thinner in both directions. (10) (11) See the rest of the method for these outer leaves in the cauliflower section on page 54.

Note that cabbages from the field or allotment can be really big. Sometimes they grow nearly as much as a metre across including all the outer leaves which are removed when they are harvested! I need to keep within a limited miniature garden so I don't go that far! I finally add some smaller scraggy outer leaves further down the stem and leave the stem around 3cm long so it can be 'planted' later.

6

Bake your cabbages in the oven according to clay manufacturers instructions.

Of course there are many other types of cabbage. You may decide to use other colour ways, other veiners and a more open form when assembling. The internet and seed catalogues are full of inspiration!

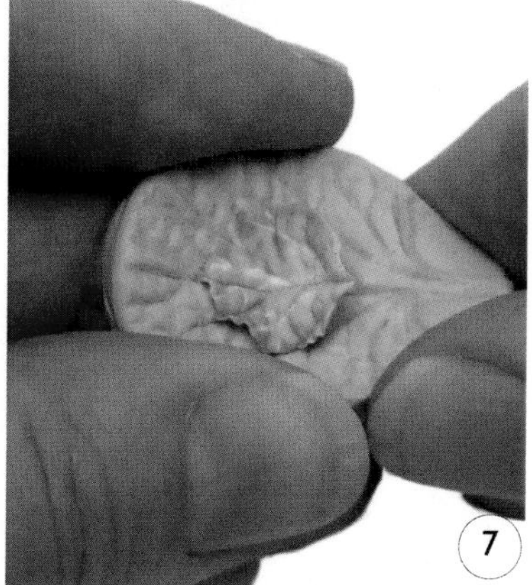
7

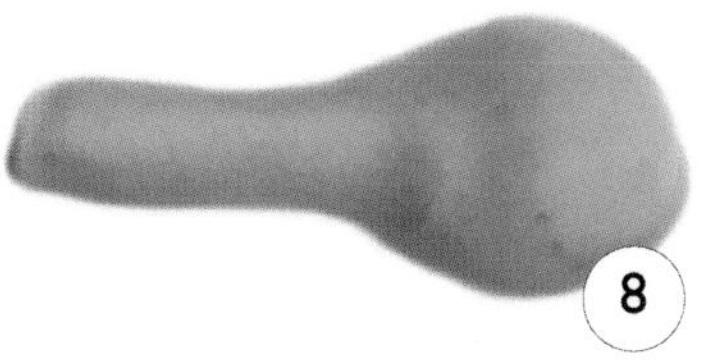
8

9

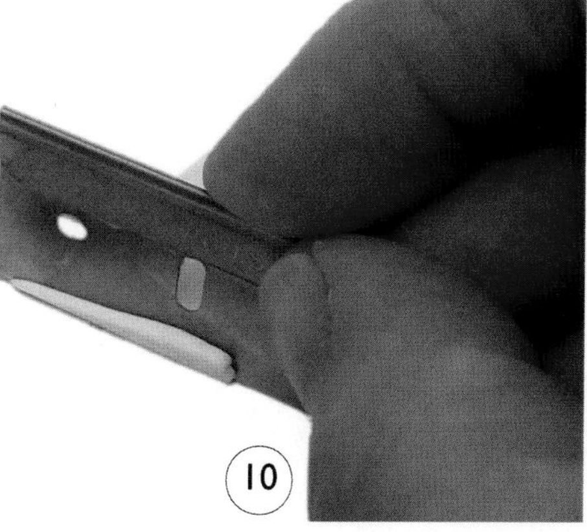
10

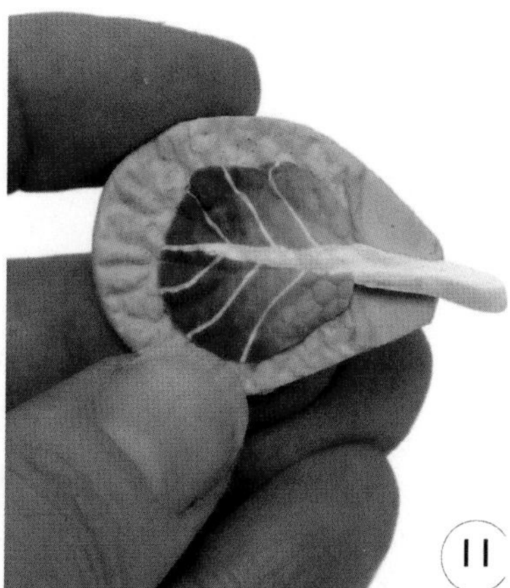
11

Brussels sprout plant

You will need

A dark brassica cane shaded from dark to mid green for the head and outer leaves of the plant. Just like other brassicas the Brussels sprout plant has a very powdery bluey- green leaf

A second much smaller Skinner shaded leaf from lightest stem green to medium powder green, put a very thin edge on this leaf by wrapping round the leaf with an ultra thin skin of the dark green

Goo in a muted (not yellowy) light green, you can make it from the stem colour below

Head and side leaves

Make up a sprout plant 'head' like an open head of cabbage, using small slices from your darker cane, lightly veined using a simple veiner. (You can make one from silicone moulding paste using a mint leaf). Make a lot of the leaves so that you also have plenty for the side leaves. (1) (2) (3) (4)

Now put stems on the extra leaves. Because these are very small I find it as easy to vein the leaves and add the stems just by pressing them on with the side of a pointed tool. (5)

Subtly brush talc or pastel powder colours on the leaves and top before baking both the head and the side leaves in advance. This makes assembling the whole plant easier later. You can drill into the back of the head after it's baked to help attaching it to the stem. N.B. use a mask when using powders to avoid inhalation.

Sprouts

(6) The cane for the tiny sprouts is made by cutting the outlined lighter leaf cane half and then cutting out the top of one cane in a curve to accept the second leaf. The space between these two canes are filled in with stalk colour to achieve a rectangular cane. (7) Note, making the infill (stalk colour) clay a bit softer aids the process of re-shaping into a ball and sticking to the stem.

Lengthen the cane until it's only about 6mm x 4mm (or even smaller). (8) Make the little sprouts by cutting a tiny slice from your sprout cane and folding the slice, (9) tucking the lighter edges in as much as possible and finally twirling the end between your fingers to make the pointed edge of the 'teardrop. (10) Practise making smaller and smaller sprouts as you can use sprouts of many sizes. Make a good number of these sprouts.

Looking at photos of real sprouts I noticed that they seem to grow in a little spiral. Some fatten up more than others and it seems fairly random whether they fatten up more at one end or the other or in the middle of the stem.

Stem

(11) The stem is clay extruded through a Core Extruder and needs to be wired. You need to make it about 6cm long with a pointed end. (12)

Bake the stems before adding the sprouts.

Make at least 3 stems, approx 5cm long, pointed at the top end. If you have time, make 5 remember, odd numbers are always more attractive than even!

(13) (14) Add the sprouts from the top

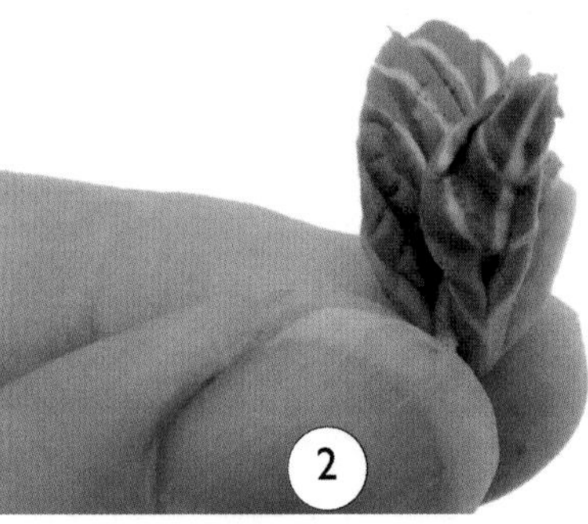

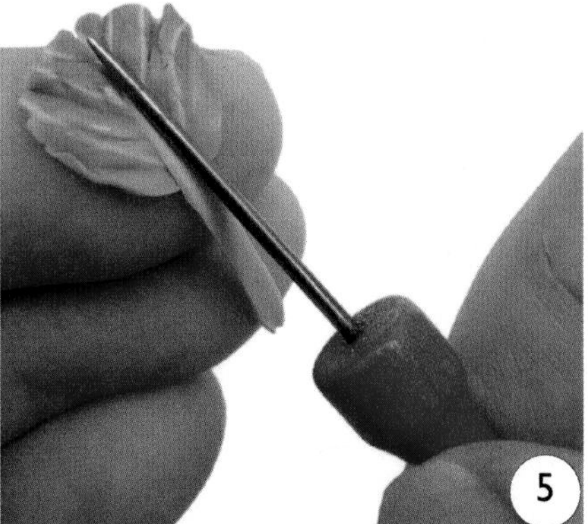

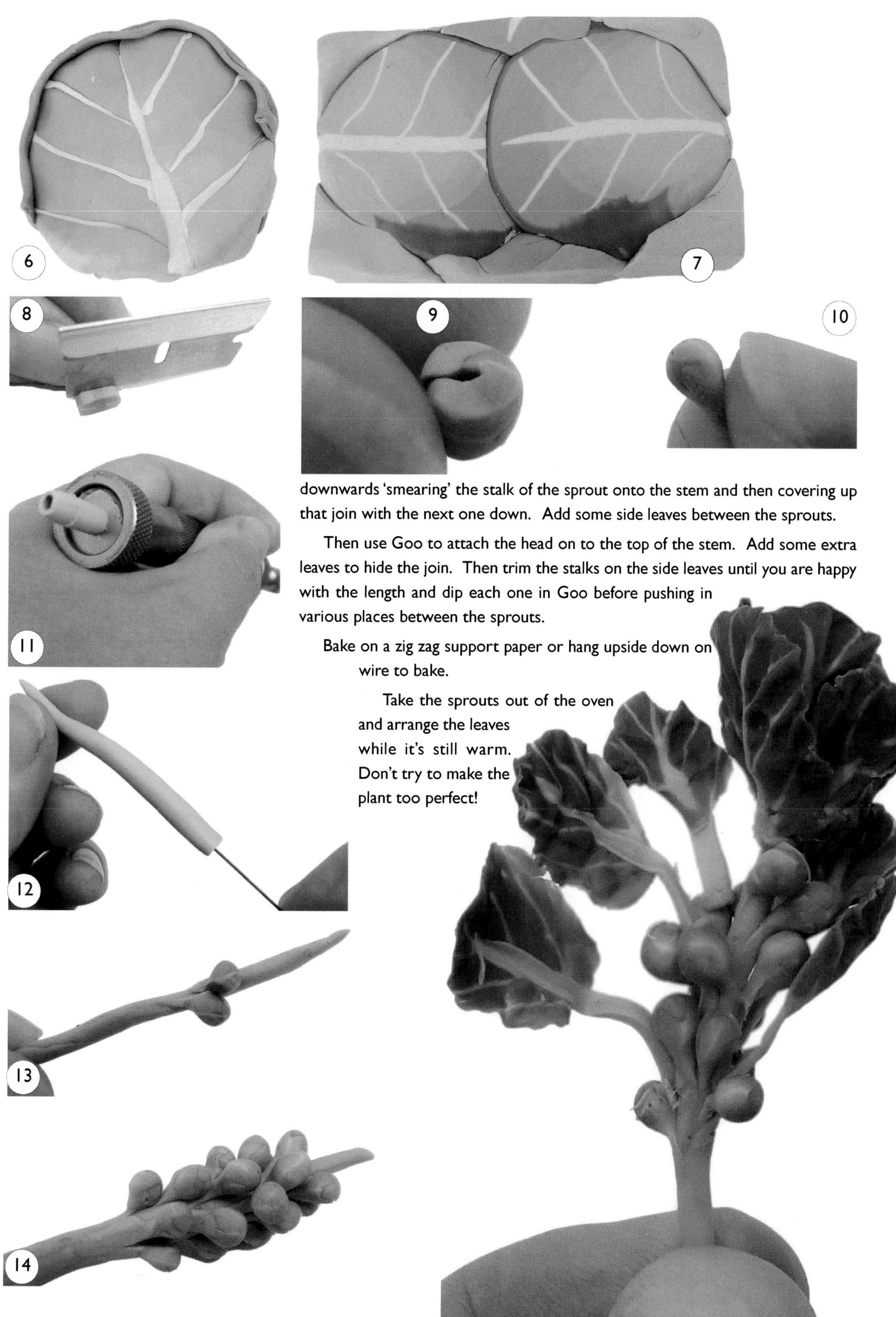

downwards 'smearing' the stalk of the sprout onto the stem and then covering up that join with the next one down. Add some side leaves between the sprouts.

Then use Goo to attach the head on to the top of the stem. Add some extra leaves to hide the join. Then trim the stalks on the side leaves until you are happy with the length and dip each one in Goo before pushing in various places between the sprouts.

Bake on a zig zag support paper or hang upside down on wire to bake.

Take the sprouts out of the oven and arrange the leaves while it's still warm. Don't try to make the plant too perfect!

Cauliflowers

You will need

A creamy white mix about 50% translucent for the 'curds'
The light and medium leaf canes from the cabbage project

Once you have the several differently coloured canes of the brassica family you can go on to make several different brassicas. I tend to choose just the lighter canes for cauliflowers in the shop and the light and mid colours for the garden variety although you can also use a darker cane if you powder it sufficiently.

Making a cauliflower mould

Select a really nice floret from your cauliflower or Romanesco cauliflower and, pull pieces off it until you achieve a really nice regular shape. Now here's the very important stage that makes all the difference to enhancing (exaggerating) the texture. Leave it to dry out a bit! This makes the gaps between the mini florets more defined. Simply press your floret into the mould making material and leave to set. One little caution, cauliflower juice on the hands can affect setting,.

Then simply press the creamy coloured mix into the mould and pull out. (1) Then shape the stem (2) and at this stage you can decide how big the 'curd' is going to be just by pressing more into the stem for a smaller curd. Pull away any excess clay leaving a stem of around 2-3 cm. (3)

The cauli leaves

(and outer leaves of some cabbages and sprouts)

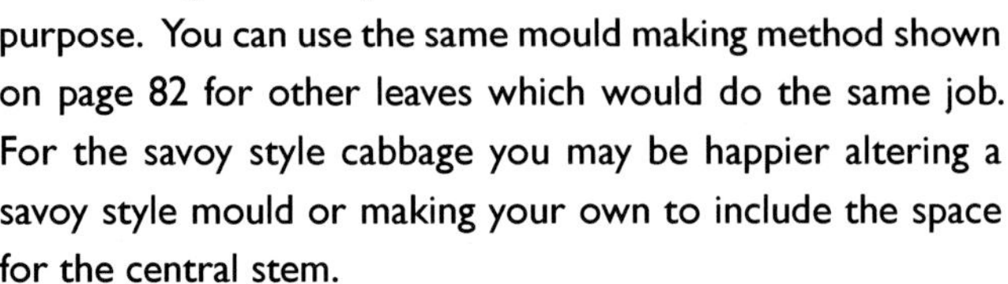

I use a mould with a central stalk to make many of the outer leaves of my brassicas now, so that I can add the stem separately. Because I show the chard mould in this book I will use this mould which is as good as any for this purpose. You can use the same mould making method shown on page 82 for other leaves which would do the same job. For the savoy style cabbage you may be happier altering a savoy style mould or making your own to include the space for the central stem.

Firstly for a garden cauliflower you will need a light coloured cane and a darker colour and you need your cane to be shaded from dark to light in both cases. See the previous project. Make a long triangle cane either in the same way as you did for the central part of the leaf cane, or simply with your fingers as it needs to be long! Cut slices from this triangle at a slight angle so that the top is thinner in both directions. Place a triangle into the stem part of the mould and lay a leaf slice over it. (4) Place a thin slice of leaf

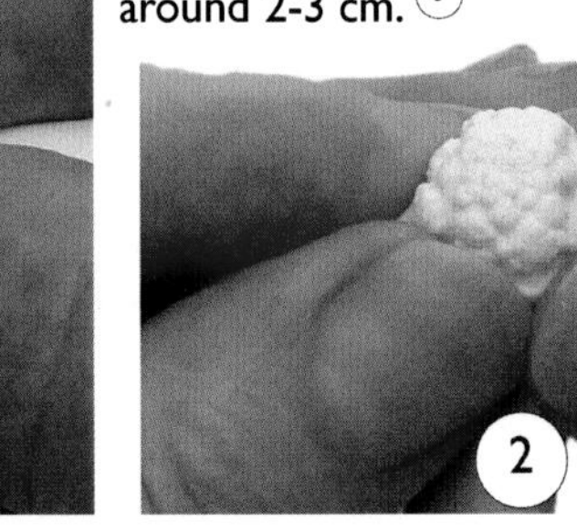

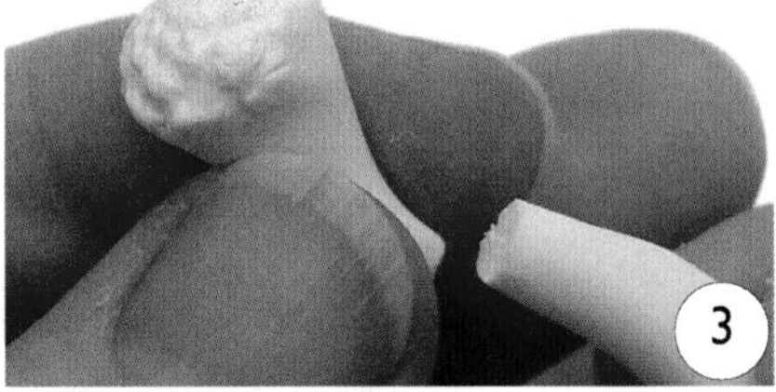

over the mould, lining up the central stem (5) and press to vein. Squeeze inwards fairly firmly to help the leaf curl in and to exaggerate the texture. (6)

Add three leaves of this light colour to the stem around the cauliflower 'curd' (7) (8) then add three darker leaves between. Then 3 more and just below. And then a few small raggedy leaves down the stem.

Potato plants

You will need

Single sided blade

Dust from tea bag packet

Translucent, white, yellow and ochre polymer clay (of the last two just a tiny touch)

Texture plate or old tooth brush etc.

Green and ochre dusting chalks

Green Goo

I made the potato leaves using a stencil but if you don't have a stencil you can make them using the same method as the raspberry leaves on page 43.

Roots

I haven't found a better way of simulating full size roots than to use real ones. I used grass roots for this project as they are nice and fine and very easy to find.

What better reason to remind you to weed your full size garden (if you have one) than to harvest the roots! If you don't have your own garden then you'll have a good excuse to go for a walk and can be the strange person who pulls weeds out of chinks in the pavement! Attach the stem on one plant to the roots using plenty of Goo. Then rub a little brown paint around the join to make it look more natural.

Realistic new potatoes

I used to make muddy potatoes very simply just rolling simple elongated ball shapes and 'dunking' them in soil substitute and brown paint but here is a more realistic new potato which will serve both as straight from the ground in your garden or semi clean in a harvest, kitchen or shop scene.

Look at the colour of your favourite local grown potatoes. They are fairly translucent and often a lot more yellow than you'd imagine. Of course potato varieties can vary quite widely.

Make a cylinder of the colour you choose. This means being fairly subtle about adding yellows and ochres to translucent and a little white. (If you have my colour book you can start with my foundation colour mix 2).

Outside of this cylinder wrap the thinnest possible sheet of ochre white mix. (1) This colour is stronger and more opaque than the centre but should still be in the same spectrum.

There are 2 reasons for making a skin on your potatoes. One is that it really does look more realistic with a skin on,

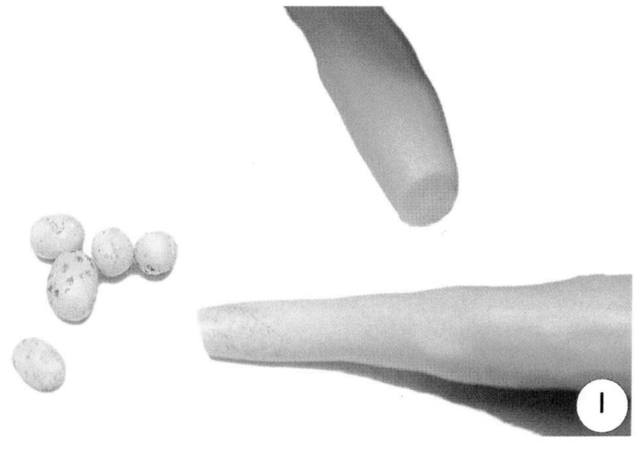

the second is in case you might want to 'peel' some of your potatoes in an interior scene, or slice right through with the spade or damage with the garden fork in your scene. Also the more true to life the colour inside is, the more realistic it will look on the outside as long as the skin is thin enough to give the effect of the colour showing through. Making a skin this thin on a very small cane can take practise but don't be put off doing it more than once if the colour or skin thickness is not right first time round. These experiments don't cost much and the ability to look critically at your own work and reject it on occasions, will improve you as an artist.

When you have lengthened your cane close the end and cut off a piece as if you were making a half potato. Then close the other end. This can take practise to bring the outer colour over the inside colour without leaving any streaks.

Roll into an irregular oval shape.

Using a texture plate very lightly dusted with tea bag dust, roll a little dusty texture into the potato shape. (2)

Finally, dipping the side of the top edge of your single sided blade into the dusting powder, make two or three small impressions of the edge. You will find that this forms very realistic 'eyes' in your potatoes. (3)

After this you may wish to add just a very subtle dusting of green chalk and/or ochre chalk. The green to make it look like it might have been close to the surface and got some light damage. The ochre to make the skin tone better and less uniform. (4)

Make a hole in your garden base and stick some potatoes within the plant roots at the base of a plant.

Allotment Onions

This is an update of my onions class which was shown in my first book Making Miniature food and Market Stalls. I've added the green for an extra 'punch' to the line. Onions are one of the most difficult canes to get the thickness of the skin right so err on the side of thinner rather than thicker as drying onions aren't as dark in skin colour as fully dried ones.

You will need

Caramel colour mix,

Dark brown mix,

Orange and the very pale green mix if you wish. You can leave this out but it does make the lines more obvious.

For the stems of the living onions you'll need a summer green colour.

For the very dry stems natural coloured Raffia or paper string. White flower wire painted fawn colour (or use Raffia) for the hanging onions.

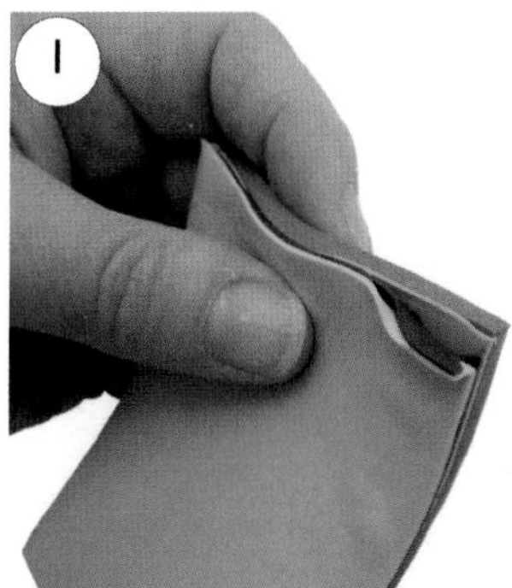

Fawn thread and a needle for threading the hanging onions.

I used some pale sandy coloured silk knitting yarn for the roots . You'll also need just a little liquid polymer to stick the roots on..

If you want to 'muddy' your onions you'll need a matte earth coloured acrylic paint.

Look at onions on the internet. Notice, onions which are still growing will have lighter coloured skins. The ones which have gone to seed will have thickened green stems and the ones which are ready to harvest will have fallen over.

To make onion skin for ordinary dry onions *(as in a shop or dollshouse kitchen)*

Roll out a thick rectangle of caramel coloured clay. About double the thickest setting on your pasta machine if you have one.

Overlay another rectangle, this time of orange clay, the same size but this time very thin and on top of that a slightly thicker strip of brown then add the green if you're using it. (1) You can roll this rectangle out with a bottle or rolling pin or use your pasta machine. Then trim the edges to form a fairly tidy rectangle where all the colours are visible. (2)

Cut the rectangle in half, down the middle and put one piece on top of the other (see the rhubarb project on page 44 for this technique). Cut and stack those two pieces together again. Make sure there is no air between the pieces.

Cut several (4 or 5) thin slices (around 2 mm thick)from this stack and lay them side by side to form a sheet of 'stripy' Fimo. (3)

Press these slices together so they stick together well. (4) Roll this sheet out very thinly. I use a pasta machine and pass it through one way and then thinner in the other direction. (The thickness depends on how big your cane is

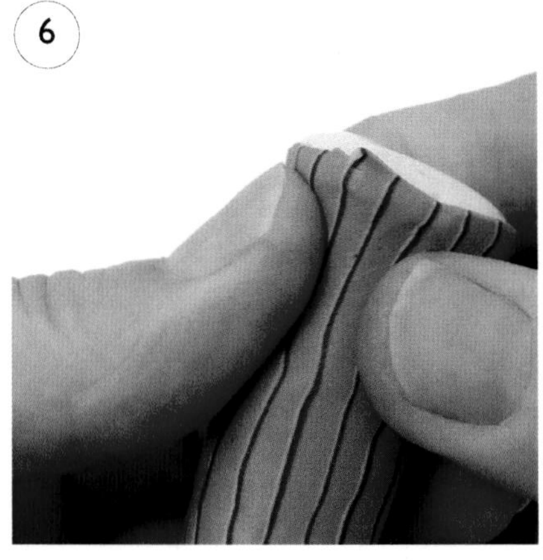

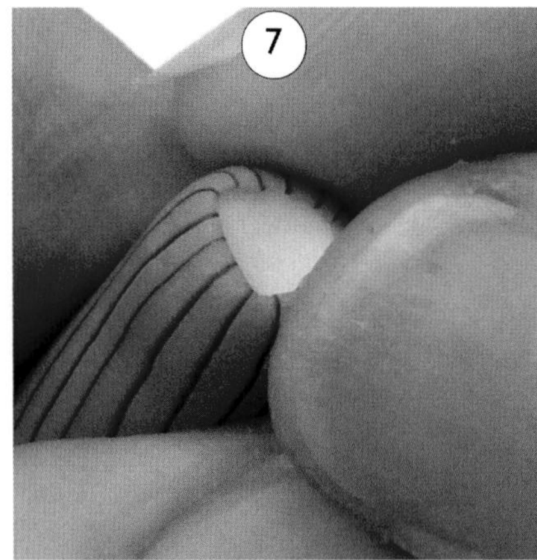

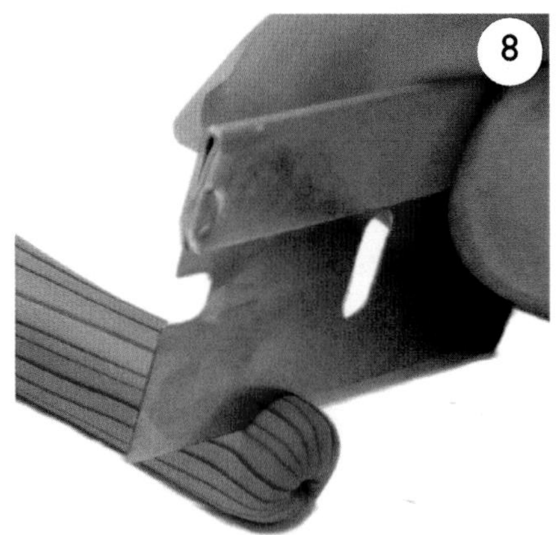

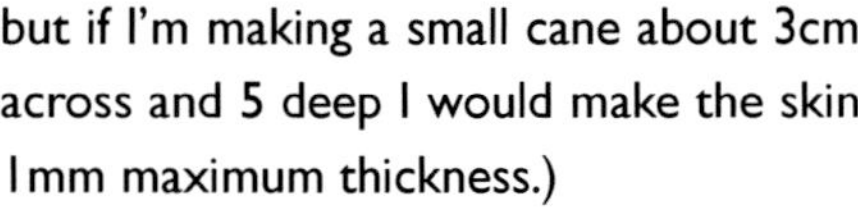

but if I'm making a small cane about 3cm across and 5 deep I would make the skin 1mm maximum thickness.)

Wrap the sheet around a cylinder of pale translucent yellowy green and join together making very sure that the edges meet but don't overlap. (5)

Look for air bubbles under the skin. If you find any, cut right through the clay diagonally to release the air, and press to stick it all together again.

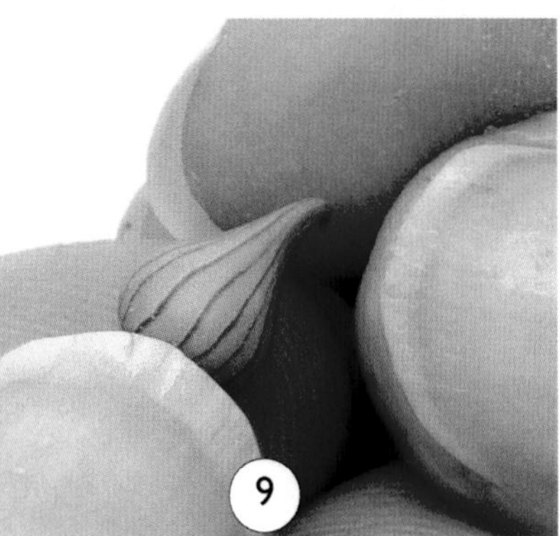

Lengthen the cylinder by squeezing in the middle and work outwards, in the same way as in the lettuce project on page 26, squeezing and rolling as you go. (6) Leave the cylinder to cool before making up your onions.

Starting with a cleanly cut end, close off the end by pinching the skin over the centre colour gently. (7)

Cut off and close the second end (8) this time carefully form a pointed end by rolling it between your fingers. (9) It is VERY important that you are careful not to twist the cane and to keep the lines straight and not twisted into a spiral.

For drying onions

After looking again at the real thing I wanted to re-do the cane to make the living and early drying onions a lighter colour with more split skins. I put a thin layer of yellow between the outer skin and the inner cylinder to make the colour inside appear a little "yellowy" I also then cut away some of the skin to reveal the inside. I then added some inner stalks made from a Skinner shade of summer green and the pale green from the inside of the cane, and the dried outer stalks from a shade between the leftovers from the onion cane mixed up to make a pale fawn mix. And more of the pale green. These were cut rolled and inserted into the onions. Some were standing up and growing and some were bent over as they do at the end of their growing season.

The final stage is the harvest. These onions had raffia stems. Shred some raffia cut into the onion and insert a piece of raffia. Insert the ends of the raffia into this slit (10) and press together gently. (11) If they don't stick well use a smear of liquid polymer. This is usually unnecessary. You can add natural coloured thread to the base to make the roots gluing them on using liquid polymer I used silk knitting yarn. Decide how you want to set your onions before baking. Some people stand then up with the stems bent over. Some lay them sideways and my brother dries his on wire racks with the stems cut off and the stubs pointing through the mesh. It's your allotment! Bake before shredding the raffia into smaller bits. Snip the ends so that they are narrower.

Perhaps you will want to have some still growing in the garden.. Some could be falling over and ready to pick. Maybe one or two which have gone to seed! I've made a skinner shade with both the green and the fawn colour to add these partly dried stems. (12)

The onion flowers on the ones I've left "gone to seed" in the garden were made by dipping the green stems (after baking) into white Goo and then into a mix of embossing powder and pale green flock. They were then baked again before glueing on to the garden. I made a slight indentation into the surface of the garden with some scissors. A reamer would be better for this purpose but I didn't have one.

For the onion string

Thread a needle with some fawn coloured sewing thread. Knot the end by winding it round your fingers, drag the thread towards the end of your fingers to form a knot. If you have never made a knot in this way before it may take some practice.

Thread the needle up the onion from the base to the

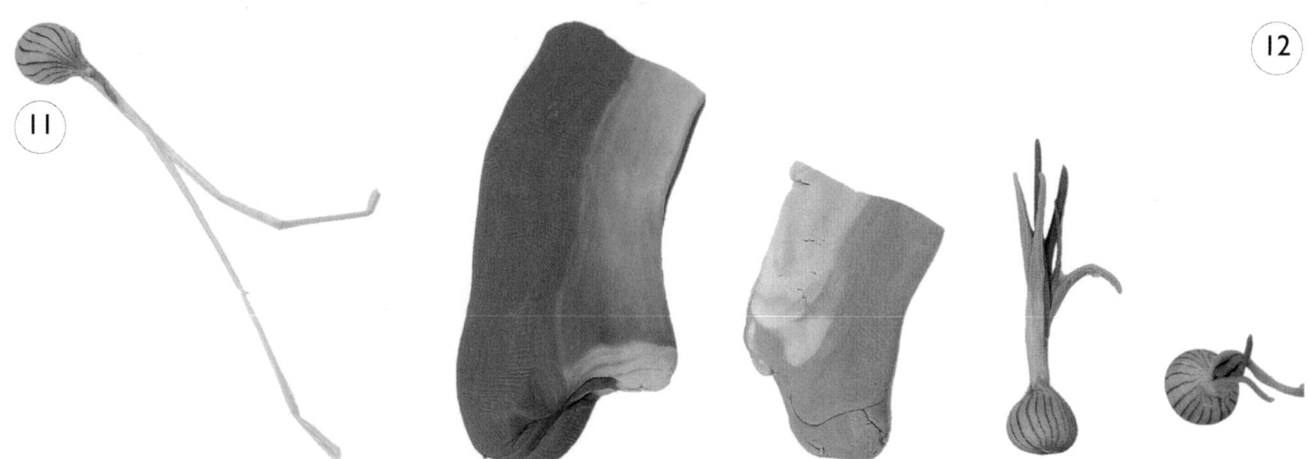

tip. (13) Pull the knot gently into the base. Cut off the thread leaving a good length of thread at the top. Repeat this process for as many onions as you need to make your string. You can make small bundles or longer strings. Bake the onions (with the thread).

When baked tie them together in pairs. (14) Cut off the thread as close as possible to the knot. You can add extra thread as roots using liquid polymer and natural coloured thread.

If you are using flower wire to join the pairs up into a string, paint it first using light brown paint. When dry fold it in half, put a pair of onions over the fold in the wire and twist the wire over them.

Add the pairs of onions one pair at a time twisting the wire twice after each addition. (15)

When your string is finished twist the wire a few times more to make enough to form a loop then twist the wire back on itself and round the whole string to the bottom. Trim off the extra wire and any over long threads from the bottom of the onions.

Extra onion skin can be made by using your leftovers from the onion stack. Stack them a few more times and pinch one end together. Then shave off bits to make very fine peeling skins.

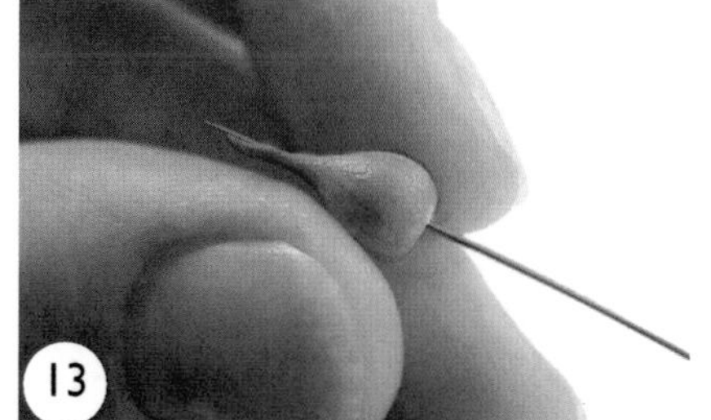

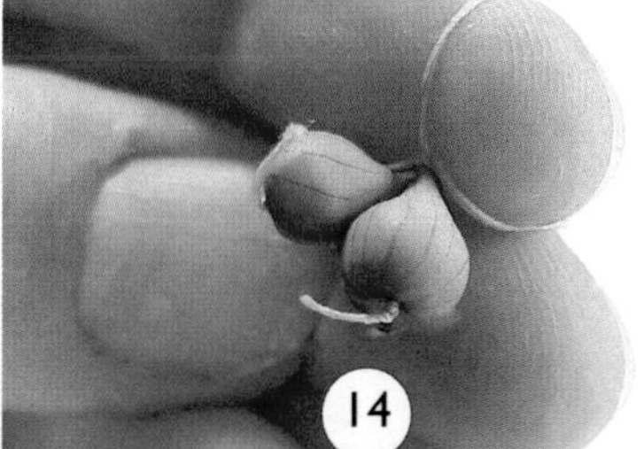

Runner Bean Project.

(A climbing bean project was first published in my Colour Book but has been re-done slightly differently for these runner beans) This project takes a fairly long time and lots of patience, so you should set aside a weekend just for the bean plants!

You will need

A pasta machine to do the Skinner-shade and to get the leaves thin enough. You can do it without but it's much more difficult.

Tiny teardrop shape cutters

Tiny printer-veiner or bought tiny leaf veiner #5.

Polymer clay extruder with very small holes

Small ball tool

Needle ended tool and/or cocktail sticks.

Softened and flexible light green clay a mixture of spring green and leftovers will do fine! @ 60% translucent. I recommend Cernit or, even better a mixture of Cernit coloured clay and Fimo translucent. This seems to make the most flexible mix.

Dark leaf green clay (Cernit olive) plus 50% translucent

Light (lime) green clay

Pale green clay (mixed with white and translucent)

A very small quantity of tomato colour clay (red and orange mix) mixed with translucent 50/50 approx.

Green Goo.

Making the leaves

Note, after each stage cover your parts with cling film, label the parts and leave to cool.

The leaf mix. Make a Skinner shade of dark to light green and one of light to pale green. Lay one over the other. (1) Roll to absolutely the finest setting you can get on your machine, and then smooth out between your fingers to stretch the clay even further until it's as thin as you can get without tearing. (2)

Lay on a ceramic tile, cover in cling film and leave to cool. Do not flatten on to the tile as it will stick and may be difficult to work with later.

The reason for making this 2 sided leaf sheet is so that the underside of each leaf can be lighter than the top and in order to make sure that all your leaves are not the same colour but a nice variety of related greens.

Using a tiny teardrop cutter, (Kemper teardrop cutters are good) and a slightly larger teardrop cutter, cut out a few dozen leaf shapes. You can change the sizes of some by pressing them on your tile and then picking up again with a single sided blade. Gently press veins into as many leaves as you can manage before you lose patience then go on to making the beans. Leaving the leaves to cool a little after handling makes them easier to assemble without 'squishing'.

Bean cane

You don't need much clay! Using leftovers from the lighter end of the leaf shade, Make a small but thick rectangle of leaf coloured clay just mixed down with 10% white to lighten it a bit. Roll this to your thickest setting if using a pasta machine. Cut this rectangle in half and add summer leaf mixed with 10% dark leaf clay rolled to a thinner setting to the middle to make a sandwich. (3)

The reason for putting this darker green layer in the middle is to form a slightly darker green edge to the bean as you will see later.

Roll the sandwich again on one of the thicker settings of your pasta machine and cut into strips of a centimetre or so wide. Slice really tiny slices of your strip of bean cane (4) and press and shape them on your finger so the edges are a bit thinner, you should notice that the very slightly darker edge is very realistic. I press this edge a little with the back of my blade to indent it slightly. The imprint your fingerprint leaves is surprisingly string-bean like! Then nip the ends into the shapes of the bottom and top of a long bean. Runner beans in 1/12th

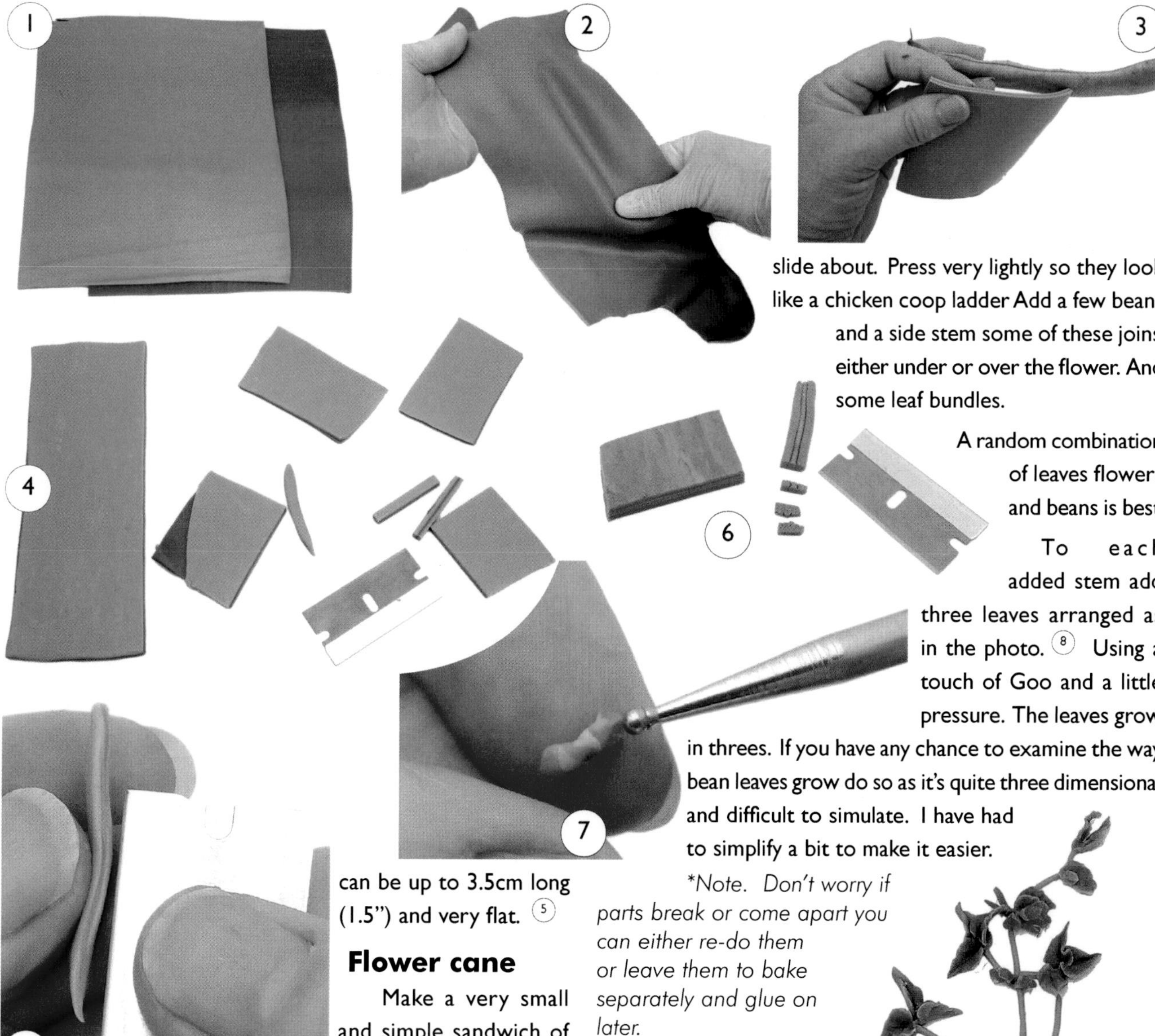

can be up to 3.5cm long (1.5") and very flat. (5)

Flower cane

Make a very small and simple sandwich of mid green in the middle with basic tomato red and translucent mix on both sides. This should be rolled out on the thickest of your pasta machine settings. Put to one side to cool so they can be handled without being sticky, Cut the flower cane in a similar way to the way you cut the bean cane then cut again to make tiny box shape. (6) Roll this gently into a rounded off cylinder and thin the middle with your needle ended tool, the back of your blade or a cocktail stick. Cut into each end of this flower. Then push a small ball ended tool into the top half of this cut, twice side by side to form almost a heart shape. This doesn't need to be perfect. (7)

Stalks

Soften a spring green clay really well, adding a touch of softener if necessary. Using an extruder with a fine holed disc, extrude a quantity of stalk material and cover and leave to cool a little.

Assembling the plant

Add these flowers to the stems around one inch apart using the tip of a pin's worth of Goo. No more or they will slide about. Press very lightly so they look like a chicken coop ladder Add a few beans and a side stem some of these joins, either under or over the flower. And some leaf bundles.

A random combination of leaves flowers and beans is best.

To each added stem add three leaves arranged as in the photo. (8) Using a touch of Goo and a little pressure. The leaves grow in threes. If you have any chance to examine the way bean leaves grow do so as it's quite three dimensional and difficult to simulate. I have had to simplify a bit to make it easier.

**Note. Don't worry if parts break or come apart you can either re-do them or leave them to bake separately and glue on later.*

When your stem gets to 6 or 8" high you need to top it off with some smaller leaves. I simply sub divide the tiny leaves to nearly the base and then 'twizzle' them together to form tiny bundles of leaves. I would use the very thinnest and lightest parts of the clay sheet for these leaves. Put one or two if these bundles on the top end of your stem. Bake your stems. Ensure the oven is hot enough to make a good firm but flexible bake but not so hot as to burn.

You can mount your beans one or two to a stake. You can also put three stakes together to form a bean pyramid or make a run of supports as I have.

Making A Weed Patch

You will need

Tiny cutters used for making various weeds OR stencils OR moulds

Clay in green, yellow, white & purple

Flower wire

Scissors

Single sided blade

Cocktail sticks

Glue or Goo

Make a base for your weeds to sit in

I chose to make a rough corner patch to fit in with the "Simple Frame Project" on page 21. (1)

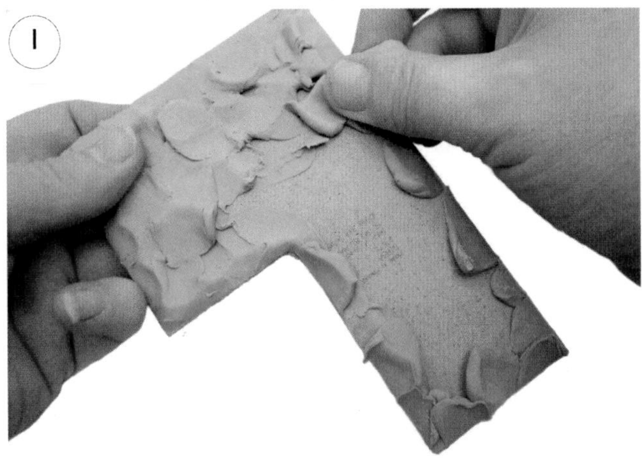

Using left over green mix clay (or you could use brown) I covered the I shaped frame insert with nice soft clay and then sprinkled it with various scenic materials (2) then started planting the weeds directly into the soft clay. (3)

Making weedy grass

for the weed garden and borders of other gardens

Make a very soft mix of fairly translucent light summer green and Sculpey mould maker.

Using a palette knife, very firmly 'smear' a very thin layer of clay onto a matte surfaced wall tile. You can use a shiny tile but it's more difficult to get it to stick well. You only need a thin strip about 2cm wide but don't worry if your 'strip' comes out wider or narrower. (4) I got the 'smearing' idea to make very thin clay sheets from Amanda Speakman who uses it to make lettuces.

Dab the edge of your knife lightly into this line all the way along at narrow intervals (as narrow as possible), causing fine line marks. Try not to cut right through, if possible. (5)

Make several of these lines varying the shade of green slightly.

Bake these. When baked you can use your single sided blade to cut out thin triangles leaving a zigzag of clay on the tile. Don't throw out the cut out pieces as they can also be used individually. (6)

When you have a run of around 5 'blades' of grass, cut this piece from the main line and roll using a blob of Goo in the middle to hold it together. (7) Immediately stick this into

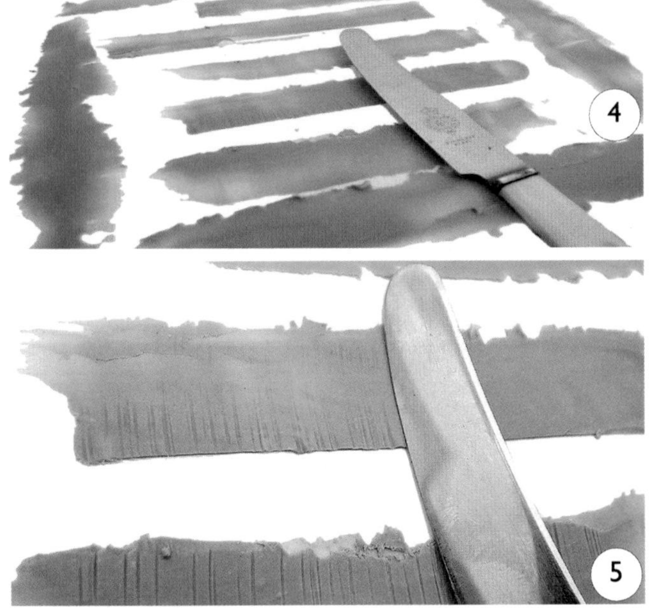

a hole poked into your garden surface. The hole should have a little Goo in it too. To hold the roll in place. (8)

Dandelions

I made these dandelion flowers using what I call the cut and cross method with my calyx mould. What using this mould does is enable me not to have to handle the flower at all. Thus I can make delicate elements even in the softest of clay without fear of 'squishing' them. The process is exactly the same as making the calyx for the strawberries on page 38 except in this case you keep adding petals until the top looks like a deep flower. (9) Then you squeeze the edges of the calyx mould to encourage the flower to drop out finally 'twizzling' the stem to make it longer and thinner. (10)

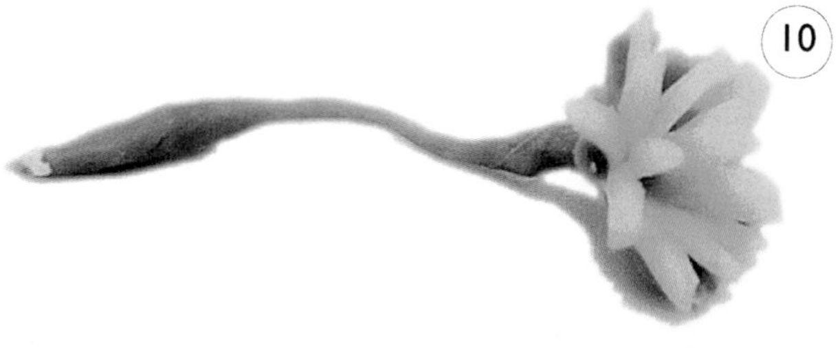

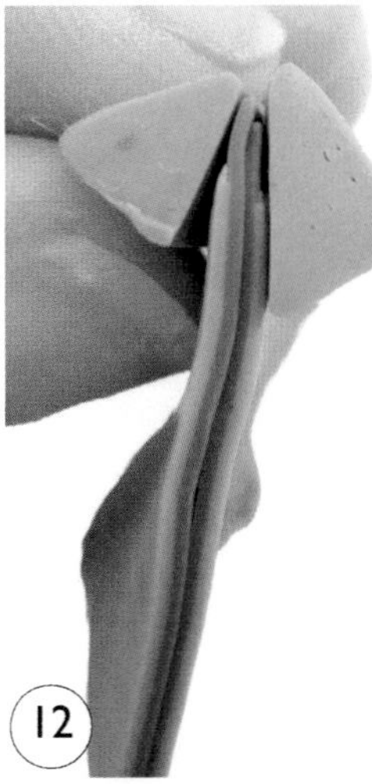

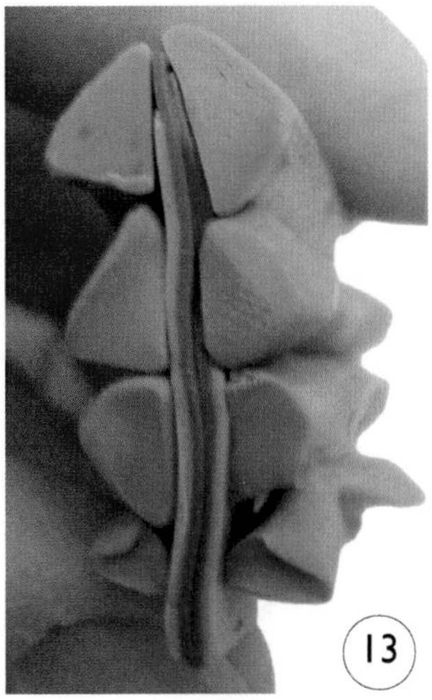

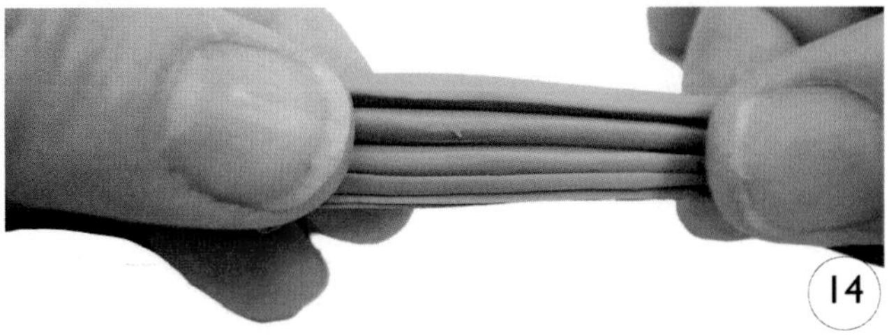

To make dandelion leaves I decided to make a complex shaped cane. This is where you don't pad out the gaps between the pieces of cane with translucent but simply make the clay soft enough that you can stretch the shape as-is. (11) (12) (13) (14) Then I baked the cane and sliced it very finely to make the leaves. After making the original weed garden shown below I made a stencil for dandelion leaves and flowers.

Dandelion seed heads are easily made by tying a thread very tightly round some polyester wadding (raid an old pillow or cushion) then trimming it back to a very small pom-pom. You can glue, or Goo, this on to the top of an extruded piece of green clay. You can do this at the same time as making the chives from the kitchen garden.

Daisies

You can make daisies by the same method as dandelion flowers simply adding a blob of yellow clay in the middle. You can also make tiny flower moulds using a drill burr pressed into silicone mould material. See this idea in the jasmine project for the patio. I have also made a stencil for daisies.

Violet

Violet leaves are really rather easy. You simply need a very small heart shaped cutter or preferably 2 or 3 different very small sizes.

Make a very thin 2 sided leaf either using the pasta machine and stretching or by using the palette knife smearing technique See grass, above.

Vein the leaf using a home made fan shape leaf veiner. That

is to say one with all the veins radiating out from the end of the stem. Or use a small vine leaf veiner (my veiner number 8). or the top of a tiny leaf veiner making sure the vein part does radiate from the bottom of the little leaf.

Add a stem to the back of the leaf using Goo in the same way as in the strawberry leaves project and bake before attempting to bend the stem.

Violet flowers

Mix the left over green clay from your leaves with some burgundy colour clay to make a dark reddish brown mix. This is the colour of your violet stem.

Fill the central stem only of a calyx mould leaving just enough clay at the top to attach the flowers to.

real and miniature violets

Using the cut and cross method cut 3 very delicate strips of purple and arrange two over the calyx mould as a tall narrow cross. Then add one more across the middle making a 6 pointed flower. With a cocktail stick, scrape a scrap of white from a block of white clay and add this to the centre of the flower. Then add an even smaller amount of golden yellow.

Remove the flower from the mould by turning it upside down and pressing and twirling the stem mould until it drops out. Sometimes it comes out without much stem. You can roll and add extra stem if you are practised in making flowers by now. If not. Don't worry, these little flowers can still be used and hidden in the 'undergrowth'.

Make the stem as fine as possible by turning the flower upside down and 'twizzling' it. Then fold (curve) the stem back on itself. If you can look at how violets grow from botanical illustrations on the internet it will help you understand this.

Yellow Wood Sorrel

This is an extremely delicate plant and can grow rather tall The tiny leaves look a little bit like clover. I used a 3 lobe cutter which I admit are hard to come by to cut out some extremely delicate leaf shapes. To make the clay as thin as possible I smeared the clay on to the tile as I did with the grass, but then lifted it again. (1) (2) (3) So it could be cut without staying stuck to the tile. You may need to have a little talc to hand to stop it being too sticky.

I then used a ball tool directly on the clay on my fingers to shape the leaf and thin it out even more. (4)

Wood sorrel flowers again need to be very delicate. Here's another way of making your clay really thin. Cut thin a very thin slice of bright yellow directly from a block of pre-conditioned but then cooled clay.

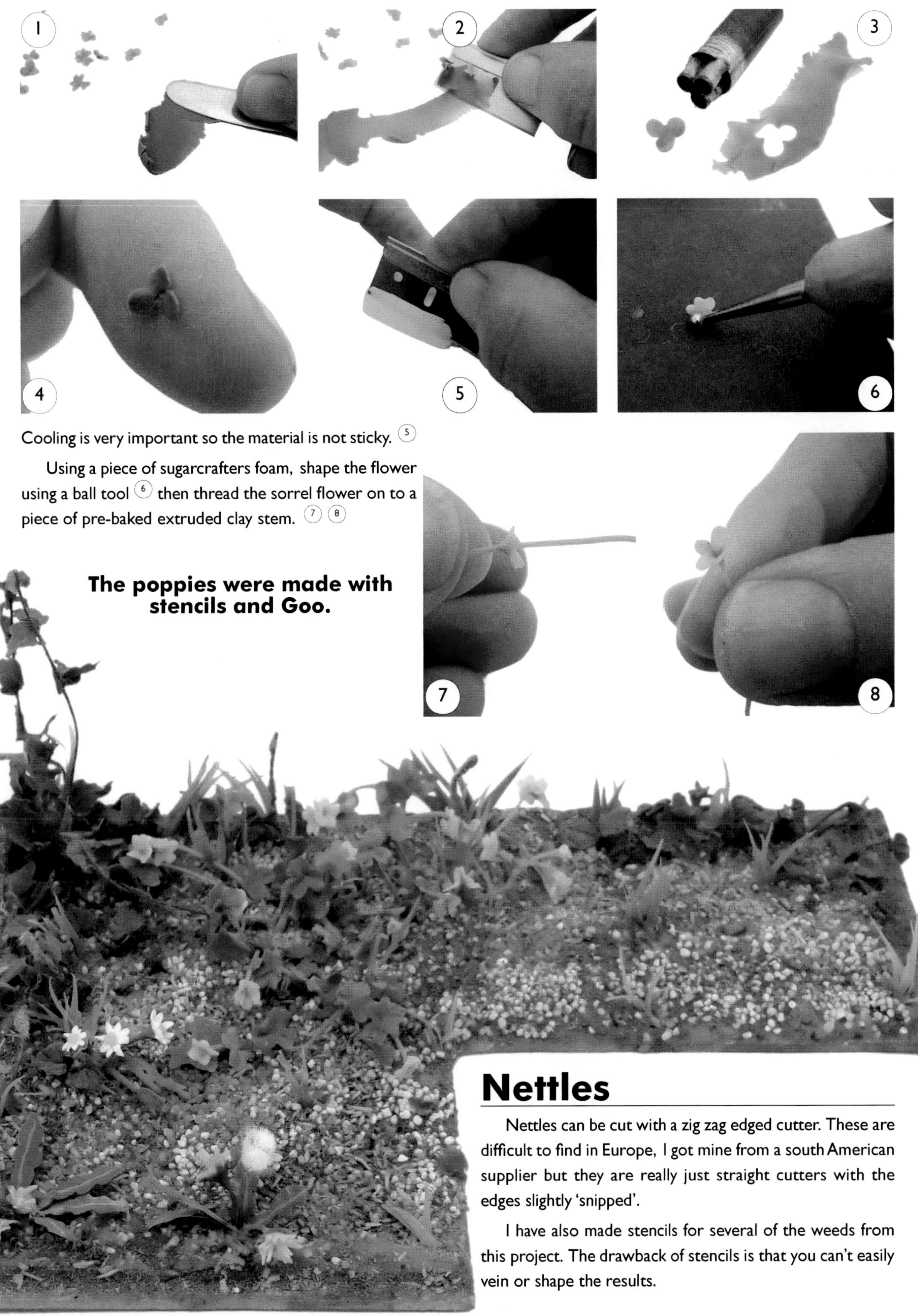

Cooling is very important so the material is not sticky. (5)

Using a piece of sugarcrafters foam, shape the flower using a ball tool (6) then thread the sorrel flower on to a piece of pre-baked extruded clay stem. (7) (8)

The poppies were made with stencils and Goo.

Nettles

Nettles can be cut with a zig zag edged cutter. These are difficult to find in Europe, I got mine from a south American supplier but they are really just straight cutters with the edges slightly 'snipped'.

I have also made stencils for several of the weeds from this project. The drawback of stencils is that you can't easily vein or shape the results.

Old Shed

based on the shed project in the appendix

You will need

Single sided blade
Brown & green paint
Grey & brown pastel chalks
Green Goo & sand (for roof felt)
A paintbrush

You can make up the shed according to the patterns in the appendix. These patterns were produced by Treacle Lane miniatures where you can buy the kit if you, like me, aren't a natural woodworker.

A note on copyright seems necessary here as many people are confused about this subject. You can make this shed up for your own use but if you are selling or showing as your own work you must ask permission from the original source. In this case Treacle Lane.

So, a shiny new shed arrived in the post to my house and I was very excited. I immediately put the roof felt on it but then left it on my shelf while I took a year off to be ill. I stared at it this way and that and just wasn't happy it was what I wanted. How was I going to convert this into a battered old allotment shed? I knew that there were books and articles out there on distressing. But, being an avoider of copying techniques especially for publication I decided not to read them and have a go myself! I'm sure there are better ways and advise anyone to go and look for them! What I do know is that this way is easy and worked for me and I'm happy with the result. So here is my inexpert method.

Firstly make the lines look like shiplap (overlapping wooden laths). The kit comes with lines already lasered in. But if you're making your own you'll have to draw the laths in using a pencil and ruler and then score with a single sided blade or craft blade.

Cut away the edges by deeply scoring the lines, if need be, and chamfering off a bit of the MDF on an angle (1). For an even better effect continue along the lines to take out some of the material under each line (2). Then score and scratch the whole surface with a blade and or scratching tool.

Start to paint by first putting a small amount of green at the base and then do a first brown wash over the rest of the shed concentrating on putting the colour more thickly into the grooves under each 'lap'. (3)

Rub a charcoal coloured pastel over each 'lap' again concentrating on the bits underneath each. (4)

Do a second wash over this. Keep applying browns and dark greys until you are happy with the colour. Trickle a little

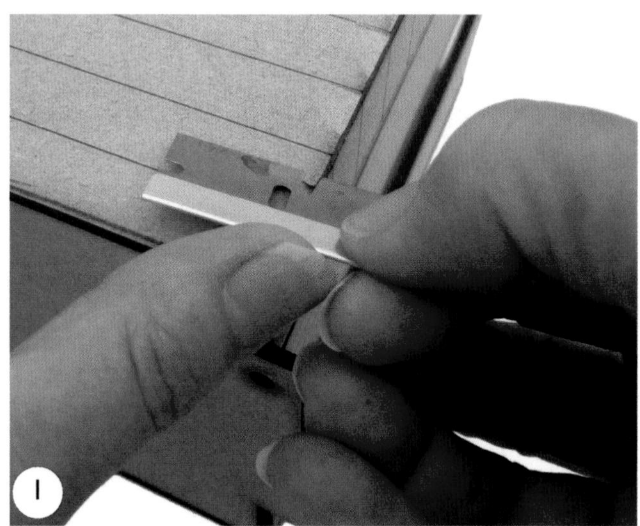

1

2

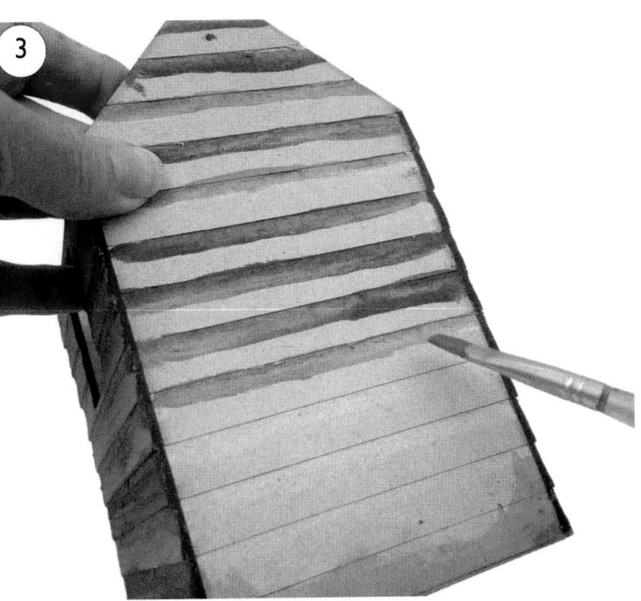

green under the edge of each window edge. Then pop the windows out to distress them too. You may need to prime the window frames with a plastic primer before painting.

You can make a simpler job of the inside of the shed.

Paint the edges of the roof.

Roof felt for shed

Using a green mix of polymer clay Goo spread thinly onto a ceramic tile and pour on grit. You can buy this from a Swedish homewares store in the plants department or you can get it from a beach! (5) Bake.

Strip the sheet from the tile and glue to the shed roof ensuring you tuck a little under the edges and hold on with small stationary clips until it dries.

I added some hinges and a door lock, laser cut for me by my husband out of card, as was the axe head

Allotment Roundup

I used a ready made veg crate style 'tub' for the raised allotment base. I sawed it into pieces and my husband tidied it up and made the hardboard platform tops. I decided I wanted to build raised beds as these are very popular now in allotments to help keep the soil in prime condition and to make weeding easier. I used the wood from wooden trivets from a far east import shop, which I took apart. They were dark brown stained already and so, matched the fencing which is also dark stained. These items are not well made and so wiggled apart easily. The thin individual staples have to be removed after you've pulled it apart. Each piece is approximately 13.5 cm (7") long so I cut 5cm (2") off each.

The beds were then assembled using the small pieces as the end pieces for the raised beds. These were glued on to the base using wood glue. They looked exactly like the raised beds in my brother's allotment, some of which were made with old grooved decking board. The fencing is made from Chinese bamboo place mats, shown on page 12.

The fencing was made by cutting the bamboo place mats mats in half down the centre. The same kind of wood (from trivets) as I used for the raised bed from the trivets was glued on as the supports. The bottom of the fence is held in place using 3M Dual Lock - Clear 250 which is a strong velcro-like fixing. This means I can remove each piece of garden and the fence for packing. Don't forget to stain the top of the bamboo if any of it is light coloured. The same with the wooden raised beds.

The 'bark chippings on the paths were made from the larger pieces from a bag of organic soil substitute (cocoa husk) These are glued on with wood glue.

The raised beds are then filled with the furrow pieces described on page 68. Each has a small piece of oasis flower foam glued underneath. The gaps were filled with a mix of the soil substitute and wood glue.

The roofing felt for the shed was made using green or grey polymer clay Goo spread on a 15cm (6") tile with decorative grey sand (available from Ikea's floral dept.) sprinkled over it and baked. When taken off the tile it not only looks like the real thing but responds like it too! This is cut to size down the edges and glued on with the bottom edges tucked under and glued in place. You may need clips to hold it down.

Shed & contents

The shed needs to be aged a little and the more cluttered the better! I distressed a little cheap table I'd found at the Arnhem fair which always has lots of inexpensive craft materials. I chose not to make a water butt and guttering due to lack of space, but you might like to add these too.

Jugs, buckets garden tools including axe and watering can and from our Secret garden Range of kits. Cheap table from a miniatures fair. Distressed with mud and mould (acrylic paint). The plant pots were from Mibako, distressed with white and green acrylic paint. The asparagus spears project is in my Miniature Foods Masterclass book.

The hangers for the shed walls were made from tiny jewellery hooks opened out and screwed into stained coffee stirrers. Stained with what? Coffee of course!

The Mediterranean Garden

Mediterranean Tomatoes

real tomatoes

You will need

4 pointed cutter
Single sided blade
Dental tool or bent pin tool
Clay: green, yellow, red, translucent
Pasta machine (optional)
Putka pod (optional)
Moulding material (optional)

1

The big Mediterranean tomatoes are pretty ugly and often have green patches, cracks and blemishes especially the home grown ones which would be rejected by any supermarket as there is no conformity.

I made an imprinter for the tops of my tomatoes using the tops of dried putka seed pods 'mini pumpkins' available on the internet from craft suppliers. I chose the smallest of these pods and I only mould from the top where the lines joined together and made one mould from a 'fruit' with with 5 sections and one with six. (1) The imprinter is simply some silicone mould material pressed onto the top of the pods just far enough to take an impression of the first part of the lines dividing the pod. Make a 'stem' to this impression so that you will have

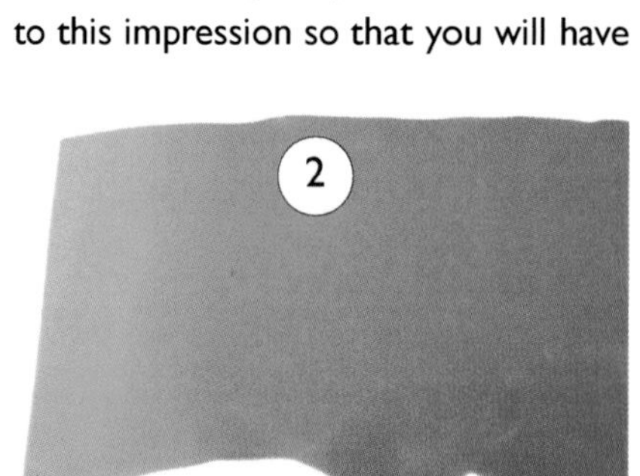

3

something to get hold of. As with all of these push type moulds and impression moulds you should make sure the stem is not smooth and round. An irregular or square-ish shape is much easier to get hold of.

Making a tomato cane

Your cane needs to have patches of different colours and I find the best way to achieve this is to make the top layers really very thin.

Firstly make fairly translucent colour

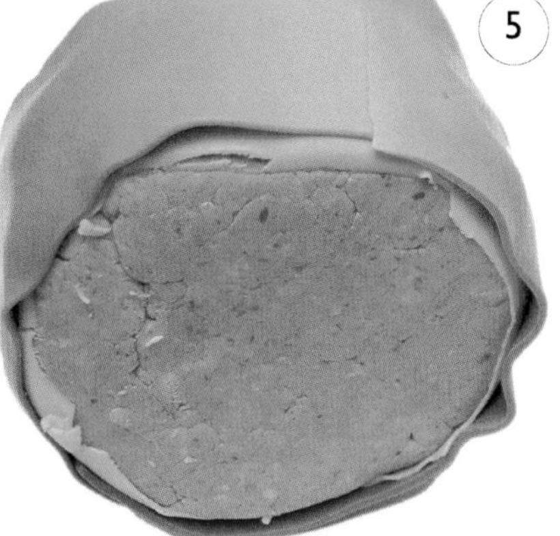

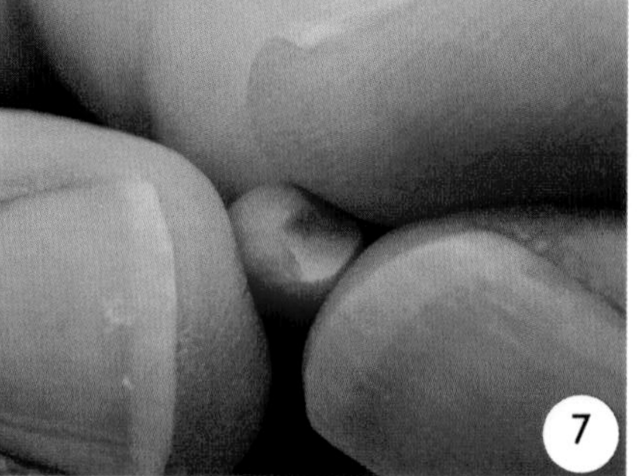

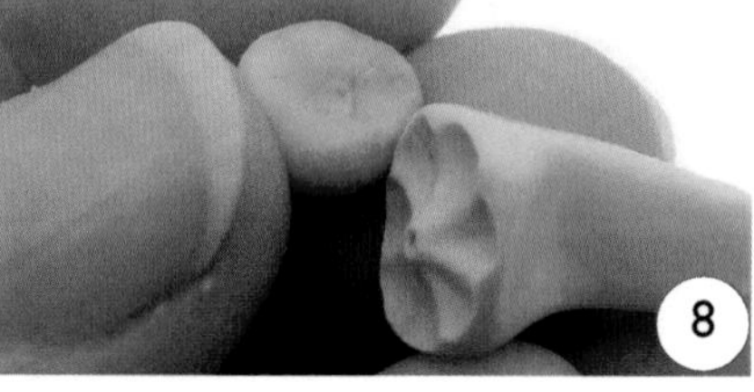

just as the centre. I use leftovers from orange and old tomato canes I use a thin skin of semi translucent yellow. On top of that I lay a very thin orange to green shaded skin. (2) (3) (4) (5) Make the tomatoes up by enclosing the centre with the outer colour on the end of your cane then cut it off as if you were making half of an even bigger tomato. If you're making tiny tomatoes of course you can just add the calyx at this point. (6) (7) (8)

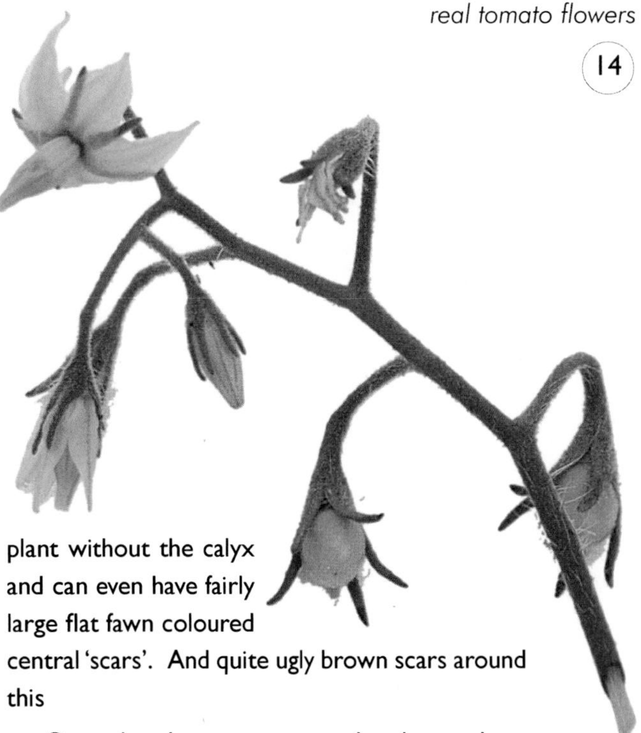

real tomato flowers

For the big Mediterranean tomatoes, remember, any that are harvested are unlikely to have a calyx, so you can then use the press mould to add a shaped indentation to the top before adding some fawn clay to the centre. Add a calyx and stem if you're making fruits to go on a plant. You can add the calyx directly to the top by using the cut and cross method (9) (10) Unlike store bought Supermarket tomatoes these are pulled from the plant without the calyx and can even have fairly large flat fawn coloured central 'scars'. And quite ugly brown scars around this

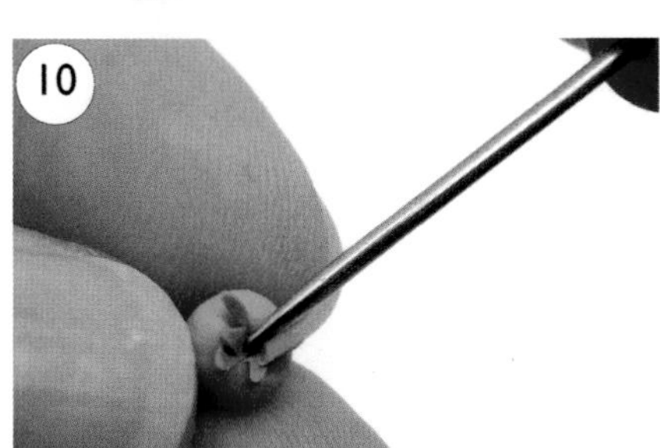

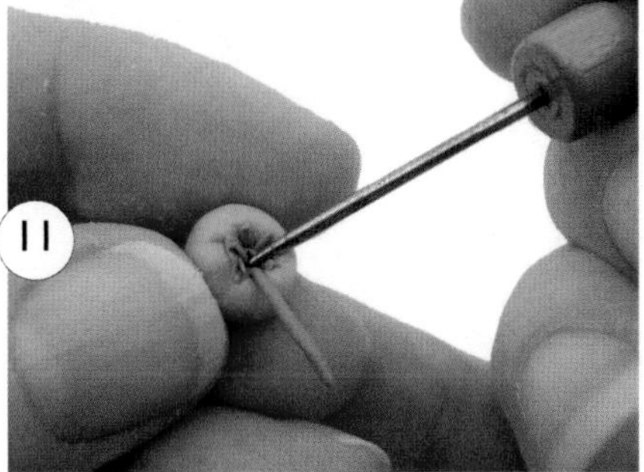

On a plant however you can barely see these scars. Add the calyx and a stem and put together in clumps of 2 or three fruits curving the end over so it can easily be added to the plant later. (11) (12) For extra realism some of the tomatoes on the top part of the plant can be greenish. Or even green. They are also likely to be smaller. Remember the order of ripening on a plant. Firstly the bottom tomatoes ripen but end tomato of a bunch first. Then as you go up towards the plant tip you will get younger and younger tomatoes and then flowers. Tomato flowers can be made by making a tiny cut and cross flower with a central pistil. (13) (14)

Tomato plant and leaves

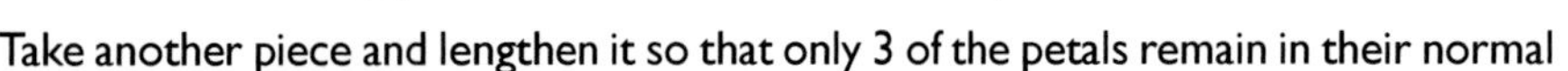

The tomato plant is made up of complicated bracts of leaves of different sizes. Otherwise the plant is made in a very similar way to the raspberry plant and the potato plant, except that the stems are a bit darker. Make a very thin sheet with a fairly dark green surface and lighter green underneath. (15)

The leaves are made by using a small petal cutter with 4 long petals, for example the micro fuschia cutter. (16)

Stretch the resulting piece to make it lie more like 2 pairs of leaves. (17)

Take another piece and lengthen it so that only 3 of the petals remain in their normal

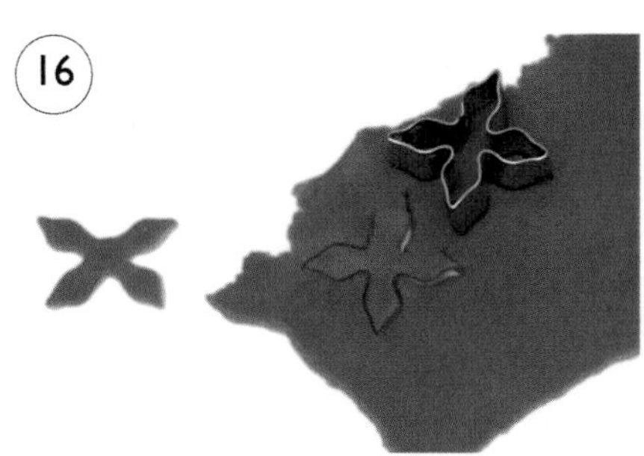

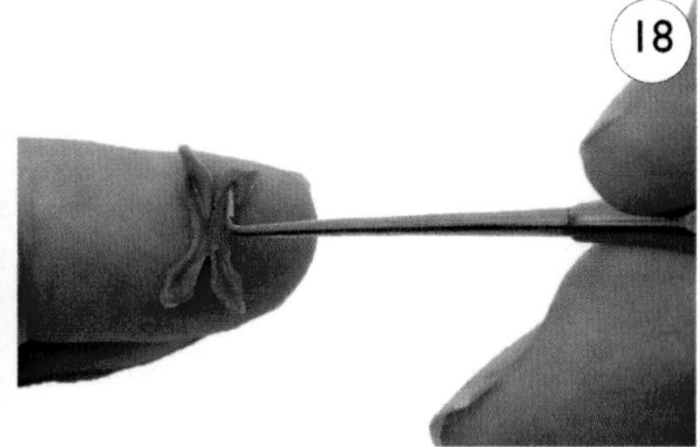

place and the extra one is rolled to form a stem. (18) (19)

Then press a line into each leaf as veining is very time consuming (20)

The first piece is then laid over the second to form a 7 leaf bract. You can add bits of even smaller leaf between those, but don't have to. And if you wish you can make the edges of the leaves more irregular by pushing your pointed tool against the edges of the leaves. This bract of leaves are then stuck to the wire using Goo. Pressed each against the wire stem using a pointed tool to make sure they bond and to make them look more realistic.

(21) If you can bake the leaves on a curved surface. You can buy various shapes of silicone baking formers in kitchen shops. These can help you bake in different shapes where a paper former might stick to the Goo. Here I show a silicone former I found in my local German supermarket. It's actually made for making breadsticks, but turned over helps to ensure a nice variety of shapes giving the plant more movement. Finally make up the plant by lining up in an uneven pattern and twisting the wires together to form a stem. As in the raspberry project on page 42. If you wish to make a taller plant you can keep adding extra lengths with leaves on as you twist. Add any extra leaves you wish to using Goo. It's also time to add some flowers which can be made using a home made flower / calyx mould as described in the Strawberry plant project page 36, and the 'bunches of fruit. The smallest and greenest at the top. Hang the tomatoes from joints in the bough of the plant and permanently attach, using thick Goo in the correct shade of green to hide the joints and attachments and baked again in a fairly flat position The plant can then be manipulated to a more natural shape before glueing into your garden. (22)

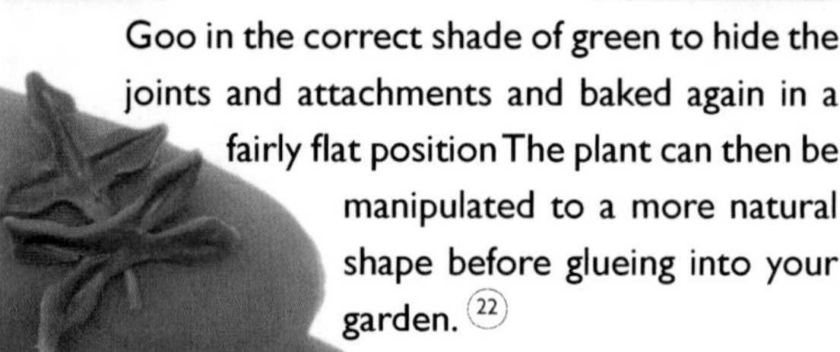

Since making this project I have designed 2 other methods of making realistic tomato leaves. One is baking Goo in moulds and the other is a set of stencils.

Aubergine Plant

You will need

Clay: white, translucent, burgundy, navy, black & purple
Flower wire
A veiner for the leaves
Silicone moulding material or bought aubergine top mould
Single sided blade

This plant has a slightly 'furry' look and as with all plants that have furry surface this turns the look of the leaf to a slightly 'bluish aspect. This fur cannot be reproduced well in miniature but you can go a long way to making your miniatures look a little more authentic. Here are some suggestions. Do not shine the leaf by adding any varnish. You can use talc or fine chalk/pastel powders but be aware that the granule size counts and some powders just look 'bitty' at 12th scale. The best way to get the look is by colour mixing appropriately. Usually this means adding a little white to the mix

Notice also that the centre vein like many plants, has a slightly red brown appearance. When making your cane make sure you add this for absolute authenticity.

Practise cutting fine leaves from the cane straight on to the surface rather than in mid air. You can thin the edges of this one out with your fingers adding the slight 'ruffle to the edge at the same time as the required thinness while leaving the centre vein a little thicker and therefore stronger. I use the top of my chard/beet veiner for the texture on this leaf. (1) The leaves need to be attached to wire with Goo before baking.

The flowers.

The flowers for an aubergine are very pretty purple and hang down on the plant. You can use a calyx mould and simply fill the whole mould with green and then add the purple petals by the cut and cross method. As you take the flower out of the calyx mould Pinch the green round the pale purple flowers and then just give the petals a little 'kick' outwards. I made a cane for my flowers in this photograph with a darker purple line in it. It's not too important how you make the flowers as they are small and less important than the fruits. (2)

I made a mould master (3) for the top of my aubergine fruits by cutting out a fairly thick piece of clay using a 3 sided flower cutter. I then squeezed in the top of this slice to form a stem, pressing little indents into the flower petals and then cutting each one into a double point rather than a single one.

Finally I cut off the point on my stem to make it flat. I left it sticking straight up to make a good mould. The copies from the mould can be manipulated and curved. (4)

For the fruit, simply make a pear shape of a very dark red blue/black mix. Then you simply fill the mould with a fairly soft green m ix and press it on to the top of this shape. As you pull the mould away. The top should be left on the fruit with the edges sticking out a little. You just press these down against the fruit and I then make a little hooked end to the stem which is how the aubergines do grow and also makes it easier to attach to the plant. (5)

Artichokes

real artichoke plants

You will need

Moulding material
A found leaf of similar shape
Leaf cutter
Burgundy powder
Clay: summer green, translucent & white
Single sided blade
Flower wire
Core extruder
A paintbrush

Sometimes a leaf shape is so complex that there is no way to get a cutter the right shape. In these cases there is another option. What I call 'hard pressing and cutting'.

The artichoke project is a very goods example of this technique. Nature has generously given us many different roadside weeds which produce this spiky shape. I chose one of the scrub land weeds near my home. And made a two part mould with the leaf still inside of the mould (rather than making the second part of the leaf from the first as in many of my other projects). This is particularly important because I then press the mould really hard on the material and the edges of the plant shape are almost cut through while leaving some 'substance' to the leaf itself. Put the back of the leaf in first and when that has set, dust with talc, and add the second half of the moulding material. Try and keep it to a shape that will help you locate it when you come to making the leaf pressings. I've cut my mould down so that the line-up is really obvious. Even a locating mark or two wouldn't necessarily help line up two halves of a mould with really indefinite edges. (1)

The Artichoke leaf is quite a bluey green in some lights and 'dusty' in others. I use a pale lavender green on the top and a pale almond green on the underside of this very thin sandwich. Just as in most of the other leaves the sandwich is thinned out almost as far as it will go without tearing, but in this case not quite so far as for the finer individual leaves of other plants. The artichoke leaf is a bit thicker and the stalk certainly needs enough substance to stand up. There is no substitute for practice when getting this the correct thickness. Too thick, and the cut edges will just look blunt and clunky. Too fine and the stems won't hold up or the whole leaf will fail and fall apart when being cut.

Also important is the mix of clays. I wanted a really flexible, tough leaf rather than anything crumbly. I didn't want a sticky clay for the moulding either, I used Premo with some Pardo (around 40%) translucent added. I could have used a mix of other clays I just happened to find this worked.

I dust the sheet gently with talc on both sides. This is fine for artichoke leaves as they have a 'bloom' effect on the surface anyway.

I cut my clay sheets roughly to the shape of the mould and putting the light side in to the back of the leaf veiner first, I replaced the top and press really hard. I then carefully removed the pressing and baked each leaf curled gently on a zig-zag paper former (2) to give it some form.

When the simple pressed sheets have been baked you can use fine tipped scissors to cut the leaf form out. (3)

How to make artichokes.

Mix the leftover clay from the leaves and roll out again to the finest possible sheet and thin out again as fine as you can. Cut into manageable strips about 2.5 cm wide.

Using a small tear drop shaped cutter, cut a line of shapes side by side and touching down the centre of this strip.

Remove the zig-zag strips from each side of this line and put them elsewhere on your tile/work surface. These will also be used. Press the spikey edges of both the tear drop shapes and of the zig zag edge bits down onto the tile with your finger to make them even finer at the edges.

Using the tip of the same teardrop cutter cut into the very tops of the teardrops and the zig zag waste bits just 'nibbling' a little from the centre of each. (4)

Using a reddish purple powder brush the tips of the tear-drop shapes with powder. Keep this subtle!

To assemble the artichoke take about 3cm of the bottom piece of the 'waste'. That's the bit that looks like a crown ... and wrap it round itself to form a 'core' for the artichoke. Then take an equal amount of the zig zag bit and wrap the 'core' keeping just slightly back from the tip and pinching a little to form a 'tail end' to keep hold of.

The extra little 'petal' shapes are then added around the central core in an alternate pattern . That is to say the tips cross over the joins of the line above. You will need between 5 and 10 of these little 'petals' to complete your artichoke. Each one gently leans inward rather than outward like a flower's petals. You don't want your artichoke to look like a weird green rose! These can also be baked in advance of assembly of the whole plant.

In order to assemble the complete plant you're also going to need some stalks. The stalks are made in the same way as the sprout stem on page 52.

To assemble, glue the leaves round the central stem using Goo between them. Use craft wire to hold the plant together. Your Goo could be specially made from the left overs from the rest of this project so that the colours match, although the sprout colour is a pretty good match. But don't try to use a fresh spring or summer green as they will stand out like a sore thumb! Finally add artichokes to the tips of the stalks by drilling into the back of each artichoke and attaching with Goo before baking.

Professional tip.

The form of the leaf can be further enhanced by folding the leaf gently and curving it and even snipping between the parts of the leaf and twisting them. All this shape must be put in before baking as it is very difficult to add any substantial change in shape afterwards.

The Squash Plant

You will need

Mould making material

A putka pod (optional)

Clay: green, yellow, white & translucent

Cutters in a large vine type leaf shape or Makins frog shape cutter set

5 pointed flower cutter 1cm to 2cm (1/2" to 3/4") across

Medium flower wire any colour

Green Goo

(This project is also described in my Colours Book)

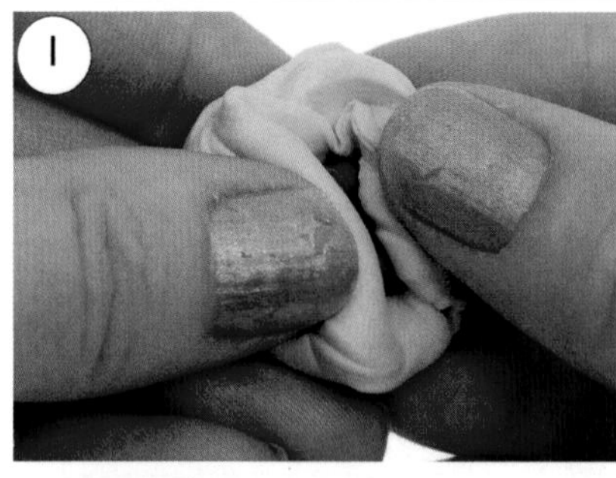

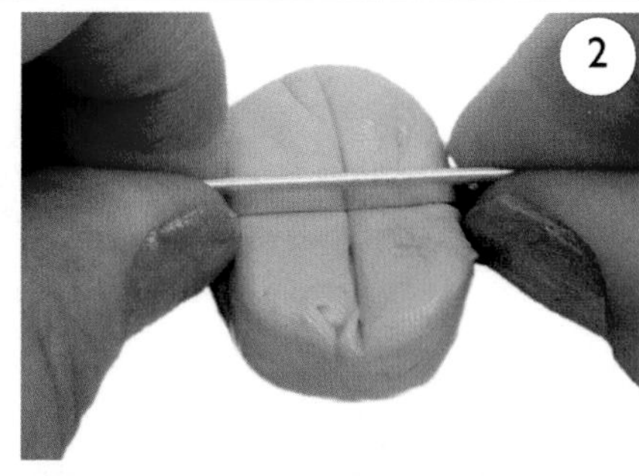

Making a solid squash or pumpkin

You can make a mould using a small putka pod. These are available on eBay and are the seed pods of a real plant which looks just like a miniature pumpkin. You could of course just paint these to the correct colour but I think it's fun to make them with clay. To make a mould for a whole squash, mix your mould material and wrap it round the whole squash (1) leaving an obvious long mark (2) where the mould material comes together in the middle at the top.

When the mould has solidified cut right through from top to bottom at 90 degrees to the line you left. (3) Hopefully you will be fairly near the centre of the pod. The line will help you to line up the two halves when filling with clay and pressing back together. (4)

The squash I'm making here has a fairly light coloured skin until it matures (after picking) to mid green. (5) When cut open its flesh is orange but of course for the garden it isn't open so you don't need to make the inside. You do need to put a stem on it and when still growing that stem should be anywhere from the green of the main stem to a slightly more fawn colour as it matures and dries out.

Flower cane

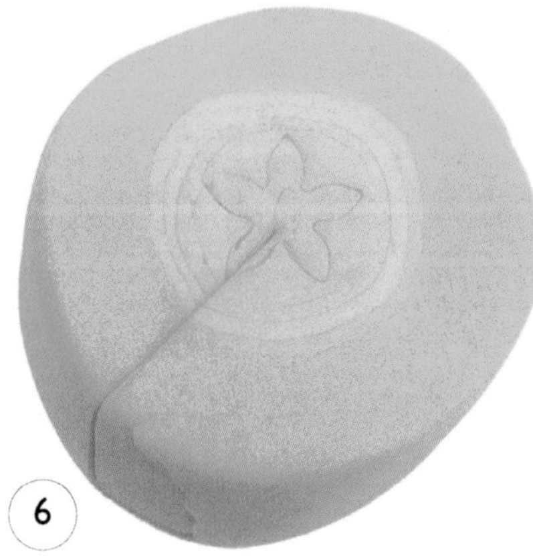

The flowers are quite large and so you can get away with cutting them from slices of a cane.

First I made a cane with lighter colour centre. Then I pressed a 5 pointed flower into it to get the 5 green lines running through it (6) in the right place. This is just like putting the segments into an orange (see my Making Miniature Foods book) or putting the veins into the leaves (see the cabbage leaves project in the allotment garden section on page 50). This isn't very obvious in the final flower but it is subtly slightly better for it. I then sliced thin slices off the cane and used a small (but not tiny) 5 petalled cutter to make the flowers (7) which can be surprisingly big in real life even reaching nearly 15cm (6") across. More if opened right out. That means your miniature can be 1 cm or even more (nearly1/2"). After your cane has cooled for a while slice very thin slices and cut the flowers from these slices using the

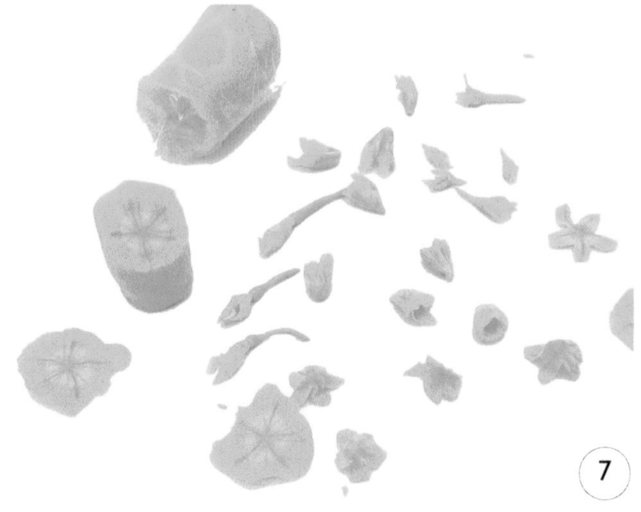

green lines as a guide. Try to get the lines in the middle of each petal on the cutter.

ageing real squash leaf

Flowers

Make sure you do some flowers open, some opening and some lightly closed and twisted as they do when they have been fertilised.

Leaf cane

To replicate the 'turning ochre of the leaves as happens towards the end of the growing season I mix a Skinner-shaded roll from ochre through to brown and then insert a rough half circle into parts of the leaves or on other parts just a tip of ochre and or brown. The rest of the leaf is built up very much like one of my cabbage leaves though a bit more subtle. And in this leaf I also added the first spots of the 'bloom' I mentioned. Of course not all leaves on a plant have the dried edges, so I simply cut out the leaves from leaf slices, a bit smaller. The leaves are veined of course. You'll need to make your own veiner or use a sugarcraft veiner for full size or nearly full size ivy leaves. The leaves are very similar to ivy leaves. There are other members of the cucurbit family with slightly or very different leaves but they all have the ivy style veins fanning out from the base. (10)

Stems

The squash base stems are made by extrusion with a clay gun with a core extruder. I wire the base stems with flower wire in the same way as I did with the sprout stems. Then I bend them and pull one end a little thinner zigzag the whole length leaving the thickest end bent down so it can look as if it grows out of the ground, before attaching the side leaves the base stem with my Goo this has to be supported all the while on folded craft paper.

Tendrils

The tendrils were made by extruding light green clay. Thin at the end to a point, and wrap around sewing pins. Bake them before adding to the plant.

My pre-baked squash, tendrils and squash flowers are also attached with Goo at this stage and the whole thing is baked again.

I have included a photo of a real ageing squash leaf to show the size and colouration. (9)

There are many types of squash, other members of the same Cucurbit family are cucumbers, melons, watermelons, pumpkins etc. They all have different leaf and flower shapes and sizes.

Here's a simple neat little trick. There are some little cutters made by Makins that look like marrow leaves, and you can alter them with pliers to be more of the shape you want. (8) *You can also use sugarcraft ivy leaf shaped cutters.*

Pepper Plants

You will need

Clay: green & spring green, navy blue &/or red, translucent
Core extruder
Ball tools
Leaf cutter
Pasta machine (optional)
Light green flower wire
Single sided blade
Calyx mould (optional)

The Italian green peppers project is already shown in full in my Colour Book so here's just a shortened version for bell peppers, with a little info about extruders and suggesting a different technique for making the delicate leaves.

You will need light green flower wire for this plant and green and red clay both mixed with some translucent.

Using your extruder

A spring green mix mixed down with translucent at a ratio of 4:6 makes a really nice bright vibrant mix for green peppers as they are just popping out in the garden. As they mature they get darker and so, to make a darker pepper you should add a scrap of navy blue, mix, put some to one side and then add just a scrap more. Alternatively if you have already made up a basic summer green colour, add bits of that to 'mature' the colour a bit. This colour does suffer quite badly from a metameric effect so you may need to tweak the blue a bit for different light conditions (for more information on metamerism see my Colour Book.)

Some of the extruders available come with a 'core extruder', (1) I love the effect of actually making an object which is hollow in real life, hollow in miniature. It sounds crazy to do it for a fruit (yes peppers are a fruit) that you aren't going to cut open, but it still does look better when you do. There's a lightness both physically and visually when you do make them hollow.

You can play round with merging your colours in the extruder by using discs of slightly different shades of colour one on top of the other. As this is pushed through the holes and then back through the ring round the central core, it blends the clay somewhat and sometimes a really perfect effect with subtle lines occurs.

For brightly coloured bell peppers you'll need mixes of red/orange and yellow too. Use the widest of the core extruders. Extrude a piece of each of your mixes and cut into short lengths. The shorter the length you cut, the smaller your pepper will be. (2) Carefully join the ends up by nipping them in gently and push the top end slightly inwards with a ball tool. Using your tool shaft press into the sides in a rolling motion from bottom to top (3) to indent lightly in 3 or 4 places and finish at the top centre. (4)

Fill a calyx mould with green clay and press on top of the pepper. As you pull the mould away, the green clay should stay stuck to the pepper. (5) You can accentuate the effect by pressing with your ball tool, then 'twirl' the end to lengthen it and curl it over to form a slightly hooked shape. (6) This will help you attach the peppers to the plant later. If you don't have a calyx mould simply roll a thin stem with a little extra blob of clay at the end. Press this blob on the top of the pepper and press a ball tool several times round the edge of the join.

Pepper plant leaves are fairly even in colour and very delicate so you can use the smearing technique on page 62 to produce really thin leaves. Or you can use the double sided leaf. (7) The leaves are very tiny and so I use the tiny Kemper oval cutter. I vein these with my number 5 small leaf veiner but you don't have to vein too deeply as the texture on a pepper leaf is less pronounced than on, say, a bean leaf or a raspberry leaf. Goo the leaves onto the stems in sets of three (8) and bake before twisting together as in the raspberry plant on page 42 and the tomato plant.

Then add the fruits and any extra leaves. You will need to

stand the plant upright in order to make sure the peppers stay where you put them. Since the fruits often grow in the nodes where branches divide you can hang them in these divisions and it looks quite realistic. Remember usually the lower and nearer to the main stem the fruit is on the plant, the more likely it is to be ripe. The flowers will appear nearer the growing tips, again in the divisions of the branches. The flowers can be made in the same way as the tomato flowers but pepper flowers are usually creamy white *(not shown)*.

Chard

Real chard

You will need

Real chard leaf or similar

Moulding material or bought chard veiner #6

Single sided blade

Clay: summer green, translucent & white

Making a chard leaf veiner

The chard leaf is a very delicate but very undulated leaf. These can be difficult to reproduce in miniature and you definitely need a really good veiner. You also need to take into account that the stem is really thick so you need to leave enough space between the two halves of the mould for a solid enough stem part. If you don't leave a big enough gap you'll find that your mould 'cuts off' the leaf at the stem.

So to make a chard type leaf you need to make a very heavily indented mould but with a full stem rather than making the second part of the mould directly from the first without leaving the leaf in as we did in previous moulds. You can use other types of leaf for example a young basil leaf will make a chard mould but the very best leaf to use is a very young chard leaf from the very centre of the plant. If you are lucky enough to have a chard plant in your garden (also known as perpetual spinach) delve very deep into one of these plants until you get to the growing centre. There you will find the embryonic leaves all curled up ready to grow and open. For twelfth scale you really need a leaf only about 3cm long. (1) You will find that a leaf of this size is very curly indeed. In this case the leaf is curled backwards rather than inwards. When

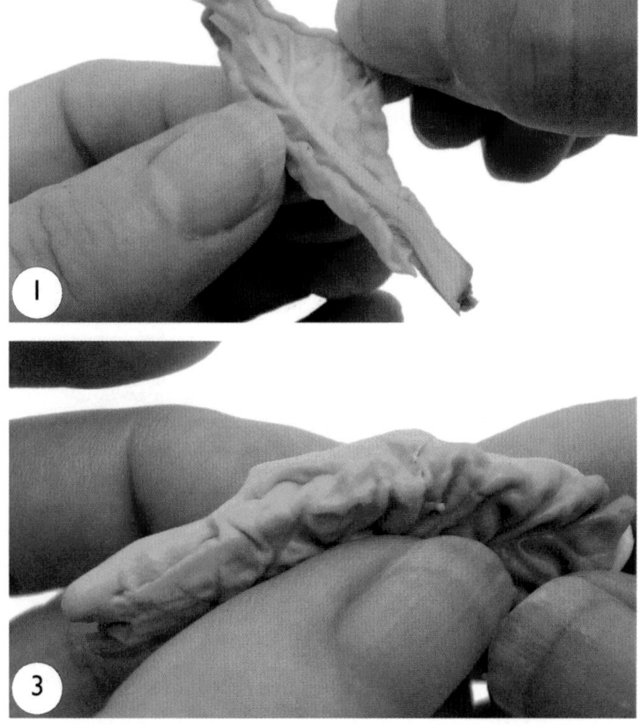

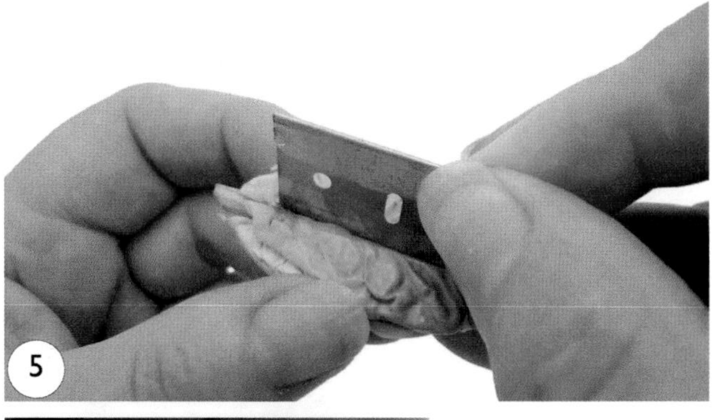

8

10

you have mixed and made a roughly leaf shaped piece of mould making material (2) quickly, but very carefully, uncurl the leaf and press back first onto your mould material. Pushing the material into the centre and allowing the material to help uncurl the leaf as it spreads. You may need to shape and reshape the mould material a couple of times (3) so, if using a fast setting mould material like Minitmold, don't do it in a particularly warm room where the mould material may set too quickly.

The mould material should, as much as possible, fill the indentations in the back of the leaf and go up to, but not over, the curled edges of the leaf. (4)

(5) (6) using a single sided blade very carefully cut along the edge of the leaf where it meets the stem. And peel away all of the leaf leaving the stem in the mould. (7) You can then powder (with talcum powder) the first half of your veiner and form the second half over the first. When it is finished you need to remove the old piece of stem of course.

So this veiner has several deep indentations for the side veins and a really deep central vein. (8)

To make a chard cane

The Chard leaf I've chosen to model from (9) is a strong summer green. However, because it's a delicate leaf, don't forget to add translucent to your mix at 6:4 ratio or 60%. For the veins I use a fairly translucent mix. A porcelain colour (or my foundation mix 2) is a good base for this. You can even add a little more translucent, and then it needs just to be lightly tinted with green to make it an off-white.

As you can see this cane is a sort of rounded off triangle form. (10) This approximates the real shape of the leaf and also makes it easier to cut slices from. In other ways it's just the same process as making a cabbage leaf except I don't make any gradations to the main colour nor do I usually bother with any side veins. Just the main central thick vein and the side ones. Try to match the number of veins and their approximate relative spacing to the veiner that you have made (or bought). Lining them up exactly is not vital but it is nice when you get a lucky break and they do line up. Add a stem to your veined leaf as in the cauliflower on page 54.

9

Grape Vine

real grapes

You will need

Clay: spring green, summer green & translucent
Light green Goo
Burgundy coloured pastels (optional)
A paintbrush
Single sided blade
Vine leaf shaped cutter
Vine leaf veiner or make your own
Flower wire and/or 3D pen

In the Mediterranean, grape vines are often grown to cover patios from the scorching summer sun with two added benefits, one that the leaves die back in winter when the sun is a welcome sight and the second of course is that the sunshade sprouts glorious fruits in the middle of summer. The sight of a heavy crop of grape bunches on the vine is delightful as they start to mature and take on their colour. This happens in late July here. In the early morning light they seem to glow like little jewels in their variety of colours but when you cut a bunch and take it inside to photograph, the bloom on the grapes gives a disappointing photographic result.

Here is an example of what I think is the prettiest of the varieties. I don't know it's name but it gives pink to red fruit and happens to be the one we've successfully grown in our patio. A worthy subject for miniaturisation I think!

Don't be fooled into copying the colours on a photograph of a fully ripe bunch of grapes and replicating that throughout for a garden plant. You should have every level of ripeness on the same plant. Not only is that more realistic but also gives a more attractive result

Grapes

Remember grapes are much more translucent than we imagine and so I don't recommend adding translucency to the colour, rather the other way round and for this grape I've chosen to make a green grape and dust it to get the pinky and reddish tones. Then dust it again for the 'bloom'.

80 to 90% translucent to colour is about right and the colour I've chosen is spring green, very slightly muted with a touch of summer green.

Dusting powder colour in a burgundy colour I used Conte carres 19

Normally to make grape bunches for the table or shop I use a mould because the idea of making hundreds and hundreds

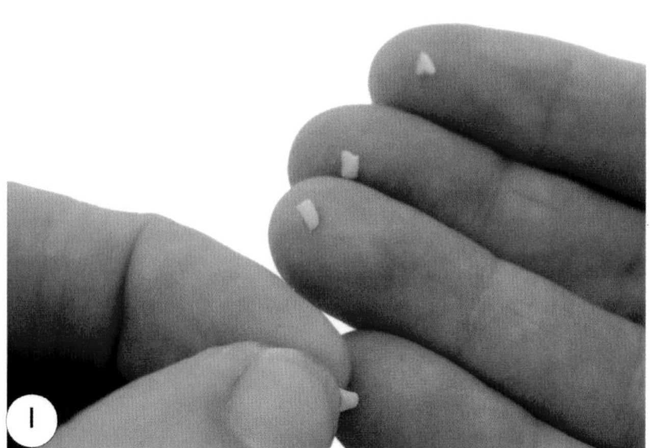

1

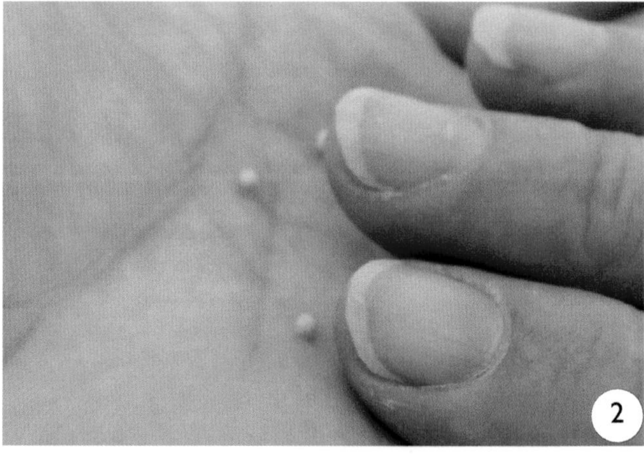

2

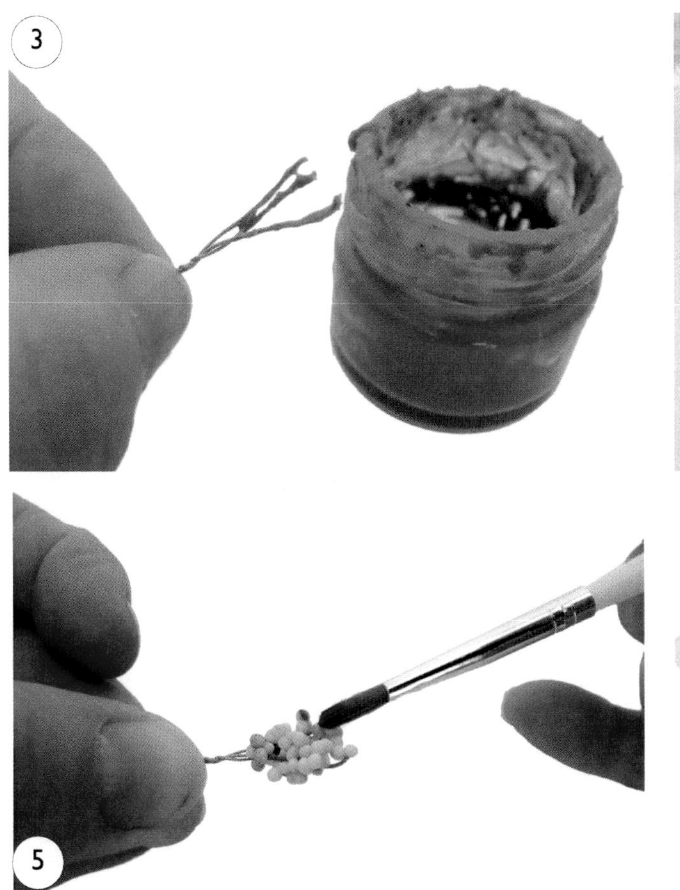

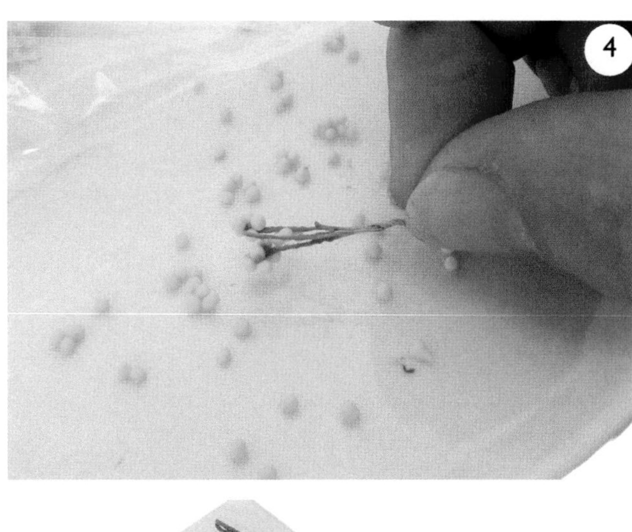

of individual grapes doesn't appeal to me. And you never see the back of a bunch of grapes in a box or bowl. But, because moulded fruits can be too equal and also flat backed I always add a few extra grapes, attaching them using liquid polymer for grapes in a fruit display or Kato Polypaste or a Goo mix. For this project however I went for the full on individual grapes. But I did use my little 3 or 4 at a time trick. ①

② This involves making a thin snake of clay and scraping a tiny amount off onto each of the fingers of the opposite hand and then rolling them all at the same time. At least 3 times as quick! Make as many as you can be bothered to make in one sitting.

Lightly dust the grapes with the reddish dust covering some more than others.

Take some fine paper covered flower wire in mid green. This can be a bit tricky to get hold of but don't use brown or dark green. If you can't get mid green, use white and paint it.

You can either use one strand or three strands twisted together or a combination. If you use twisted wire be careful to cover the ugly twists later with vine leaves. ③ ④ ⑤ ⑥

Dip the end of your wire into mid green Goo. If in doubt with your colour mixes you can opt for a slightly darker goo rather than a lighter one. Then dip the stalks into your pile of grapes and try to encourage them to stick together by using your paintbrush. Don't squash the grapes though as it will be noticeable!

Any grapes that don't stick firmly enough can be used for a second addition after the first bake. Dust lightly again on just a few of the grapes to give a natural ripening look.

Make a zig zag paper cradle to hold your bunches on. This is to avoid flat and shiny spots. Bake your bunches. For your second baking you may want to twist individual wires together, add a few more grapes to cover any bald spots or make a more natural look and perhaps add a leaf and tendril or two. ⑦

To make the leaves:

You will need to source a vine leaf micro cutter. There are several available with slightly different shapes. Don't worry

that your cutter may be simpler than the real leaf. When you have veined the leaf it will look more realistic. (8)

Make a leaf mould from some of the tiniest leaves from either a very small grape vine leaf or another of the vine type leaves. As you can see the grape vine is one of the plants which creates really tiny baby leaves which can be used to mould from for the larger versions.

8

9

Using the smearing method on page 62 to make very fine clay sheets and cut out as many little vine leaves as you have the patience for, remembering to do at least 3 different shades and make the smallest leaves the lighter colour and tinge the tops of these with a little coppery orange and do the same to the upper part of the stem if your vine is the spring or early summer growth.

You can make some leaves together in branches along with tendrils (see page 79) and some single leaves to glue or Goo on later depending on whether you're making an arbor or a covered Patio. Obviously you can't get the whole of a very large plant in your oven in one piece so some parts may have to be glued in place. However I find Goo a much more permanent fix. (9)

Later in the year all the leaves are darker and some may have a small amount of die back. It's well worth considering using a lighter colour and dusting the colours on with pastel chalk powder on some of the leaves.

real leaves

Mediterranean Garden Roundup

For the Mediterranean garden (Spanish 'huerta') base I used a very cheap blackboard in a frame as the simple stable base layer. On top of that I put a thin layer of brown leftover polymer clay, Then added strips of 'raised' polymer clay that I'd pre cooked on a metal safety ruler. The whole of this I covered with another, thin sheet of Polymer clay and I then textured the surface thoroughly with a ball tool.

Next I painted the whole area with brown polymer clay Goo and sprinkled on some scenic stone material from a railway modelling supplier,

Then I pressed on some mossy material from a Chinese store craft department and then blended coconut fibre. You can usually find this, often in dried 'bricks' at plant centres. I bought mine from a German supermarket chain shop.

I asked my friend who is a maker of miniature rustic terracotta pottery for the Spanish 'Belen' market (Xmas scenes) if I could have some broken pots at the same time as I got the pots for my Patio garden. He seemed surprised but was happy to help. Although he's such an experienced artist I don't think he breaks many! I pressed those into the base using Goo to fix them extra well and baked the whole base in the oven.

My husband and I went out walking up our local hill to find the stones for the wall and the well. I formed the well round a thick central roll from some industrial cling film wrapped in paper. I took that out later. The top was made from broken bits of 12th scale bricks from Stacey's.

The wall was built on a cardboard base and later removed. The stones were 'glued' together using flexible tile adhesive.

I wanted a simple 'toldo' as they call a sunshade construction in Spain and I wanted it to look somewhat 'rustic'. So I got my own back on the far east copyists who copied my mum's market stall design off my first book cover, by taking a saw to one of the cheap 'chunky' copies. Very satisfying it was too! I used some craft sticks to put the extra slats on the roof and gave it all a coat of brown acrylic.

In the end I used 3D pen for the main stems. The 3D pen work does slump a bit when baked and I did have to bake it to add the major part of the leaves. I then used plastic from one of the lengths of floral material mentioned on page 107 to make the finer branches and tendril bits. This couldn't be baked because it melts so I glued the leaves on.

Don't use PVA glue for adding extra leaves. I've found this out the hard way. The tiny pieces will come apart fairly easily if you do. A jewellers plastic based glue will work better.

The watering system was made with black 3D pen filament and the little 'drippers' added with the 3D pen.

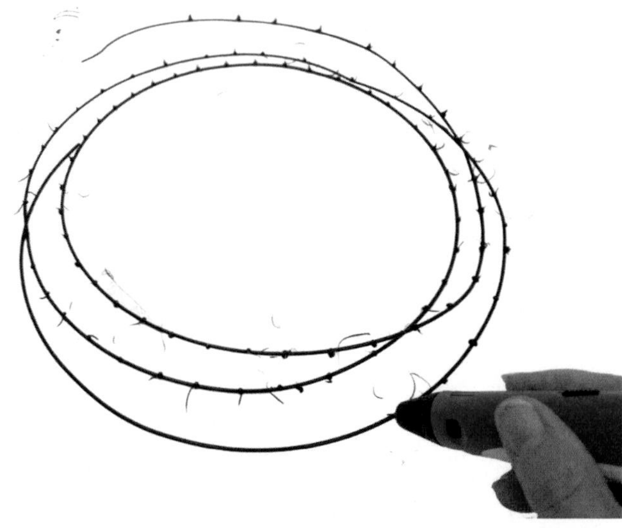

Seville Internal Patio

Introducing The 3D Pen

You will need

A 3D pen and plenty of black filament

A board to work on

Some masking tape.

Faux ironwork using a 3D pen

3D pens are not as expensive as you might imagine! make sure you have a good stock of black ABS 1.75 filament for this project. You might find the quantity which comes with the pen is just not enough. My advice then, for the starter just get a cheap pen. Then buy good quality rolls of filament as you can afford it. You'll need black ABS filament for this project. I recommend you always use ABS filament unless the type of effect you want doesn't come in ABS Wood effect for example. ABS is hotter melting so it's usually stronger. Also, and this is important for users of polymer clay, you can re-bake it in combination with polymer clay and liquid clays. It will 'slump' a little in the oven but won't melt.

If you are buying to use for the projects in this book you can get away with just one of these two greens, some wood effect and a roll of black. You can buy samples of these materials from specialist sample distributors. Or ask me for sources of smaller quantities.

You need to use a surface that the hot plastic will adhere slightly to and if you don't own a specialised board for the purpose then just a print out on paper will do, but you need to tape it down to a solid surface with masking tape because using the plastic will pucker the paper and therefore distort the design if you don't.

You'll also need nail scissors for cutting the ends off the plastic and pliers or tweezers for holding plastic in place or for pulling bits of hot plastic off the tip.

First do a practise piece

So my advice, to get to grips with the pen is start with some black filament and a picture of some simple ironwork and just start practising! Tape your picture to a firm surface so that it doesn't wrinkle.

It's really easy to find attractive ironwork patterns on the internet. Many of them will print out at reasonable scales for 12th and 24th. If they are only for your own use you can use whichever you want. However if you're using them for commercial gain make sure you find a royalty free one.

Make sure you follow the instructions on your pen about loading and unloading the filament. My pen is just a simple version with no extras and it uses the 1.75 ABS filament.

Lets get going

Simply start the feed from your pen and don't worry about lead ins or tail off. When the plastic appears use the pen like a real pen just barely touching the paper. If you touch the paper firmly you will divide the plastic into two and if you don't touch the paper at all it won't stick and may go somewhere you don't want it to. On the scrolls this can be awkward.

Then slowly and patiently fill in as much as you feel comfortable with, letting go of the feed button when you want to pull off. As you pull off you will leave little tails of plastic but don't worry about them you can clean them up later with nail scissors. If you get tired reverse the filament and turn the pen off. Being scrupulous about this will make your pen last longer. A bunged up pen may stop working at all because burnt plastic will clog it up. You can turn the feed faster if you feel comfortable with moving a little more quickly but I think it's best to be patient because the feed can run away with you. However if you're really confident, using a faster feed will result in a thicker stronger line.

When it's cooled which really only takes a few seconds after the last addition, peel your design off the paper. You might be happy that this is strong enough and if you are working in 24th scale it will certainly be thick enough.

If you enjoyed that, get yourself some squared paper, a set of compasses and design your own ironwork. Maybe including your own monogram? Or if you want to get straight on with my design for the patio door. Make several photocopies as you may not be happy with your first attempt.

My first efforts with the pen were a bit clumsy and I kept making mistakes with the angle of the pen or pressing it too heavily or holding it too far away from the surface. There are now several projects on the internet you may wish to watch to help with your technique. For now. Just draw! When you lift the pen from the page you can expect some tail off of plastic. Don't worry you can snip these off later. You can also pull any imperfect lines off the paper fairly soon after making a mistake.

The Patio doorway

When you have built up a little confidence you might like to try photocopying the doorway design at the end of the book. This is the one pictured on my patio and is similar to an authentic Seville Patio door. Or you may wish to design your own! Either way remember to double up on the bits around the door so that it will open. I also added some clear filament to the back of the door hinge and some other weak areas so that it would open and wasn't as fragile. Although I can't claim it actually swings on its hinges. This can undoubtedly be done but would be a more complicated project.

Ivy & vine stems

After the complex ironwork you should find the ivy stems really easy.

The wisteria

Now its time to go just a little more 3 dimensional. For this project I used a wood filament by Ice Inks called Grasshopper Green. You can find drawings of wisteria trees if you go to

Google Images and type "wisteria". Simply print out and use as a template. Make sure to lengthen the trunk if you need a taller plant. Simply draw over it, building up layers over the first design at the trunk part. You can also pull away from the main branches creating a truly three dimensional branch. Sometimes when you try to thicken these branches the heat of the gun can re-melt the filament and it will come away again but its fun. This material can be peeled away or cut away or sanded if you make mistakes. But I don't worry too much about your accuracy I quite like that its knobbly and imperfect.

When you have completed the trunk its time to have a go at the flowers. I found that you can get a simple flower effect

by making a series of tiny loops of filament building one up over another so they almost look like a bunch of grapes. I also played with changing from purple to white filament and back again to get some interesting blends at the changeover.

The leaves were simply tiny light green superfine sliced leaves.

You can also use 3D pen to create a balcony railing and for plant stems such as the jasmine plant and the ivy and trailing ivy plants pictured in the patio. My favourite filaments for plant stems are made my Rigid Ink who make a Khaki and an Olive. It's very difficult to get hold of really good natural greens but these two are lovely natural light greens. Since the 3D pen hobby is expanding I'm sure the colour ranges available will too.

This whole wisteria project is available as a YouTube video on my channel.

A note about 3D pen safety.

The tip of the 3D pen and its extruded filaments can be very hot. Take care when touching recently extruded filaments.

I have never been told to use a face mask when using a 3D pen but I am rather sensitive to the fumes so I use a filtering face mask. I feel pretty sure that if you do a lot of 3D pen work and especially with materials with a lower melt in a machine that runs hot, the fumes could be potentially toxic. Also, and this probably goes without saying for regular polymer clay users, wash your hands after playing with these plastics and especially before eating.

Easy moulded plants for your patio garden

You will need

Silicone mould making material,

Liquid and solid polymer in green and white (Goo)

Flexible thick plastic sheet (I used a kitchen surface protector)

Scissors

Spatula

Flower wire

Drill burrs

3D pen (optional)

'Swiss cheese' plant

Rather than cut these out individually I decided to use a mould and liquid polymer Goo to make these leaves. I cut the masters out of a stiff flexible plastic which was originally a kitchen surface protector. Then I made moulds of the leaf shape with a wire glued to the back for the stem. You can use a slightly larger wire than you will use in the leaf and this will leave space for the Goo to attach to the wire. The Goo, which I made using Cernit Olive colour clay, was put in the moulds and scraped flat with a spatula. You then need to put a wire in. This works best if you lightly coat the wire with Goo first. The leaves are then baked in the mould. For this reason, if you can afford to make a few moulds your task will be quicker and cheaper in electricity!

Because Swiss cheese plants have a shiny waxy surface the Goo which cures shiny on the surface was perfect for this task. If you find your Goo is a bit lumpy, thin the mix out with a little more liquid polymer. Don't forget you can make different sizes of leaf and vary the green you use to make the inner leaves a fresher lighter colour. You can use a centre punch to make holes in the plastic masters if you want the variety which has extra holes in it.

Frond leaf (small palm)

This leaf was taken from a mimosa tree in my local square. Place the leaf into the mould material, with back of the leaf down. Make sure the pieces are perfect and that the tiny sub-leaves are nice and separate and fully in the mould material. When cured you can put a small wire into the stem on the mould and 'squeegee' the Goo into the mould using a spatula

or butter knife. You may need to thin the Goo with more liquid Fimo for this task as the very fine fronds need to be very flexible and the liquid is more flexible than the solid clay.

Leaves can be baked with flower wire in the mould so that they can be bent on their stems later.

The first time you use a mould to bake inside, the polymer clay and/or Goo cures a bit bubbly and therefore not smooth and shiny on the mould side. This can actually make an interesting effect which I'm sure I'll play with more in the future. However it is does make the moulding a bit brittle. The good news is that it does reduce the more often the mould is used and so is probably due to residual oils on the cured silicone. So expect to throw your first couple of mouldings away. It's annoying but just see it as practise!

Jasmine plant

I made a lot of moulds for the jasmine leaves shown in the book from a teeny metal jewellery finding and of course filled and baked them just as I did with the Swiss cheese and fern moulds however I now make stencils for really tiny leaves as I find this much easier and quicker to use.

Moulding the teeny flowers.

Here's a nice little trick I came up with while putting together this patio garden.

I needed tiny flowers for my jasmine plant and had been playing with moulded Goo for the green plants. I was looking for ways to impress tiny flower shapes into the mould when I came up with this lightbulb moment!

I found some drill burrs from my craft drill. You simply impress these into mould material. As with all the moulds intended for baking Goo inside you must clean the mould before using and expect the first use to be unsuccessful. Fill the mould with thin Goo. White for the jasmine flowers but you can use whatever colour you like for other flowers. But here is the very important part. In order to get the Goo to raise up the sides of the mould to form raised 'petals' you have to squeegee material into the mould first (with a butter knife or spatula) then remove most of the material carefully patting to soak up or lift up excess Goo using a finger or better still a kitchen wipe. It's important that some material remains in the mould, clinging to the sides. Bake and then you can attach to the plant using Goo.

To assemble the plant I used my 3d pen to make the stems and just drew loops of material I then attached all the leaves and the tiny white flowers using Goo and re baked before gluing into the pot with some extra pen filament as the support loop. If you don't have a 3d pen simply attach to light coloured flower wire.

Orange / Lemon Tree

You will need

3D pen and wood coloured filament.

Your own colour mixes OR

Cernit olive green and Premo wasabi

Yellow polymer clay

Very fine wire

Very tiny creamy white flowers either made using a calyx mould or you can use the moulded flowers from the jasmine plant project.

Citrus trees are one of the few plants that can have flowers and fruit on at the same time. The smell of orange flowers and of jasmine are the essence of Seville and no Sevillano Patio would be complete without a citrus tree bearing its 'azahares' (orange flowers).

Here we are making leaves with different shades of green in a leaf cane form. This gives a 3 dimensional change to the colour which is a technique I explored a few years ago when making a miniature 50 euro note and when I was making a peacock feather for my colour book. It takes caning and the use of the Skinner shade technique to the next level of dimension and complexity making it possible to create many different colours in the same cane. Appreciating this idea will open your mind to loads of different caning possibilities

The multi-shaded leaf cane

The reason for making a pre baked cane is to use for plants with lots of fairly even leaves without much texture where veining would be too laborious but where you still want a variety of shades of leaf for example the lemon tree but these simple leaves can also be used for many other plants.

You can pre bake and store the canes for use in future projects and just slice them when you want.

Make a Skinner shade of dark through to spring green and fan fold it into a pile. With the dark green on one side and the light on the other. That is to say we are shading through the depth of the cane and not from top to bottom of the leaf as in the lettuce project. (1)

Re-shape the pile into a leaf shape and cut down the centre and add the veins. (2)

As you can see, when lengthened this gives the effect of having leaves of all the natural shades on the same tree. When adding to the tree remember the lightest leaves will be on the ends of the branches/twigs. (3)

I added veins made of a sandwich of Cernit champagne in very dark green. This will leave veins that are so subtle you can barely see them but this is more realistic

**Please note my leaves are machine sliced as I like them really fine. You can learn to slice extremely fine by hand but it does take lots of practise.* (4)

Lemon tree with a 3D pen

You will need a 3D pen (of course) and wood effect filament. An L shaped former.

Also some lemons or oranges and some green and white clay to make flowers.

If you haven't already made the leaves above you can buy my superfine leaves as citrus leaves in a maker size pack.

To make a small 3 dimensional tree without using an armature you can use a 3D pen. However drawing in true 3D is quite difficult because the heat of the second pass over a part can melt the first causing it to droop and so building trees from the ground up can be quite frustrating. The solution is drawing as if drawing in 2d but inside a corner piece and then assembling 3 or 4 parts!

You will need something right angled (or greater) The best thing to use is angled packing board. I have some which has a metal coating which is ideal both sticking the 3D filament to it and releasing it easily but I know this is hard to get hold of. The cardboard type will do but is not as reusable. Cut this to the size of the tree you want. Or just a little longer. If you can't find this material you can just fold cardboard or stick foamcore into a right angle. Or you can get hold of wood

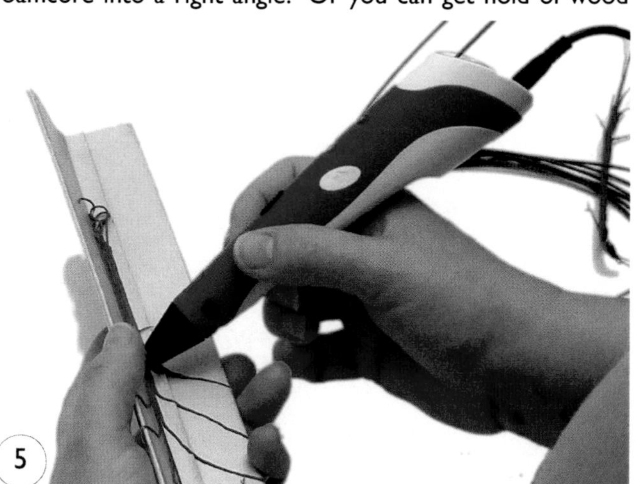
5

6

corner pieces at some DIY stores. I have some packing but a wooden corner piece would do the same trick. First check that your plastic will adhere temporarily to the surface. If not, cover it with paper and tape down.

Set the speed to fast.

Start with the trunk drawing lines inside the angle at the edge. from the bottom to the top stopping the feed and pulling away over the end. (5) Just the same as the wisteria except as you get towards the top pull the pen away from the angle and allow to cool as a thin branch. You can carefully build up this branch but be careful that the heat doesn't melt the first and subsequent layers. Make several of these branches and as you build it up pull away from the branch also to make twigs. Set the speed down to a medium feed (or a slow feed depending on your confidence) and thicken the trunk and the major branches to a nice curve. Add 'twigs to these branches by attaching the filament at the branch and feeding a little then allowing to cool before pulling off. You can expect lots of tail off of the plastic but they can be trimmed off later.

When you are happy with this part, remove this quarter piece from your 'frame' using a palette knife.

Remove the section from the inside of the angle and hold it over the back of the angle allowing it to hang over the end from the start of the branches. (6) Make the major branches 3 dimensional by adding filament (7) *but leave the back of the trunk flat.* This is very important. As you are increasing the thickness of the upper branches allow the branches to bend

7

over due to the heat softening effect and gravity. Add more shortish twigs

I made 2 more pieces like this. I didn't need to make 3 more as the corner angle was a bit opened out and so became more than 90 degrees. (8)

Originally I added the three pieces together before adding the leaves and fruit but if doing it again I would prepare each part individually.

Add citrus leaves to each section with Goo. Do not try to add all the leaves at once but be prepared to bake several times. Add the flowers just before your final bake though as multiple baking can affect the lighter colours of polymer clay. You will need to prop your tree parts off the baking surface when baking as, although the 3D filaments don't fully melt at polymer clay temperatures, they do 'slump'. Use that 'slump' in your favour to make the branches stick outwards. Make yourself a wire prop, or more than one to hold the tree at the best angle so that you don't have to lay it flat on your surface where it would slump causing a flat side.

Oranges/Lemon fruit must be wired on to the parts of the tree as even the thickest Goo won't keep them on for cooking. Pre make your fruits and then drill the top of the fruit. Insert Goo on a wire to glue the wire in. (9) Use fine wire from a wire mesh. The reason I use this is because as it's been woven it is 'wiggly' and that grabs on to the Goo and helps it to stay in where a straight wire wouldn't hold as well. If you can't find a fine wire mesh to disassemble, use fine electrical wire.

When this has been baked you simply tie the fruits on to the tree with wire and trim off excess wire.

Holding the pieces firmly, and using the pen like a glue gun, glue the first 2 parts together in the centre at both the top and the bottom. Don't let go of them until the 'glue' has cooled. Then add the third part and repeat the process.

Draw more filament up the side joins and then fill each trunk piece until it looks rounded.

Trim any 'rubbish' from your tree and if you need a smoother trunk you can sand it down. Make sure you use a mask if sanding. If the colour is not good you can cover it in Goo before baking again, Or you can paint over a wood filament. Some filaments don't take paint well so you would need a spray primer especially for plastics.

Advanced Project: Ivy / Vine Leaf

How to make a leaf cane with shading to produce leaves of subtly different colours all at once!

Following on from the idea of the citrus leaves with the graded colours from dark to light green. You can build a very complex cane where the shape is unusual and the colours vary throughout the leaf. It is important to maintain a strong contrast in leaves like this so that you can still see the veins throughout the leaf and no matter what the colour is. You can of course shade the veins, or you can simply make them very strongly contrasted as I have here. The veins are of very pale green bordered by dark burgundy to provide a very strong contrast.

In the leaf shown here I have made just one very large shaded cane. I realised afterwards that when I cut it I wasn't going to be able to assemble a cane with all the parts of the leaf the same colour and so as you can see the pieces are of varying shades.

The cane can be lengthened without the support of translucent clay in most of the gaps ONLY if you work very quickly and with a very flexible clay as the clay needs to stretch uniformly and without a lot of pressure. This takes some practise. For an introduction to lengthening this kind of shape see the Starfruit project in my Miniature Foods Masterclass book. The area around the stem is supported with translucent. The above pictures show my first attempt however I made a second cane which was made up of 5 individual canes in order to have a more consistent colour across the leaves and a more consistent shade down through the whole cane. The final picture shows slices from the second cane.

If you are interested in this idea and you want to see an example of this very complex shaded caning in action please see page 71 of my Colour Book where every part of the eye of my peacock feather cane changes from one end of the cane to the other. Unfortunately, although the idea was good, the result was dull because there was not enough contrast in the colour values. As I've said before I make all the mistakes!

Cactus Project

Introducing some unusual and advanced mould making tricks including multi stage (generation) mould making.

You will need

Mould making material
Cutters (small leaf shape)
Hockey stick modelling tool
Cutters (star shape)
Tiny beads
Torx screwdriver head

Pale green grey succulent

The nicest thing about this plant is that how chunky it's leaves are. This makes it relatively easy to make for even the most basic modelling skills. The colour mix is somewhat unusual to it's a mix of porcelain coloured clay (or my foundation colour mix 2) and a small quantity of Premo jungle.

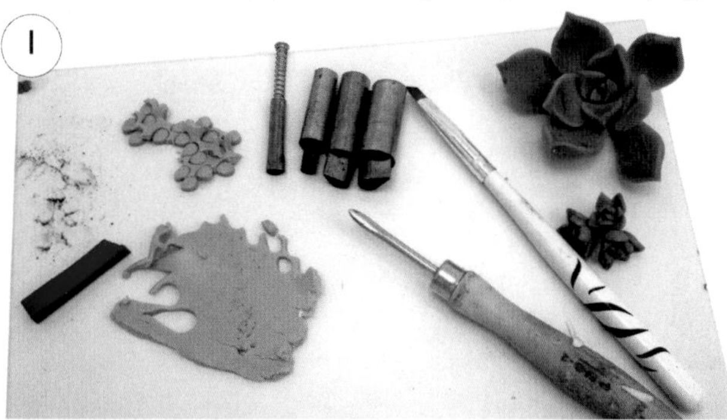

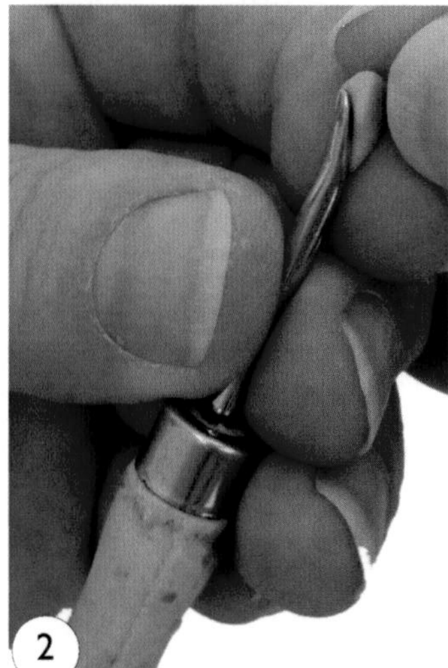

Then use small teardrop or circle cutters of several different sizes to cut out 'petal' shapes. (1)

Then nip the back of each petal to give it a slightly triangular profile and a little tip. (2) Then simply build up a flower shape working your way round getting slightly larger as you go. If you have experience of making cabbages this should be a breeze! Take a paintbrush and a very small amount of red pastel (not a scarlet red, more towards the 'bluer' burgundy red colour) and very subtly dust the edges and tips of each petal. Don't overdo this because less is more on this cactus.

Simple cactus shape - *Prickly pear cactus*

Clay and beads method

Using a tear-drop shaped cutter of two or more sizes (available in a 'petit four' cutter set), cut several pieces from scrap clay rolled out to a moderately thin setting. If too fat

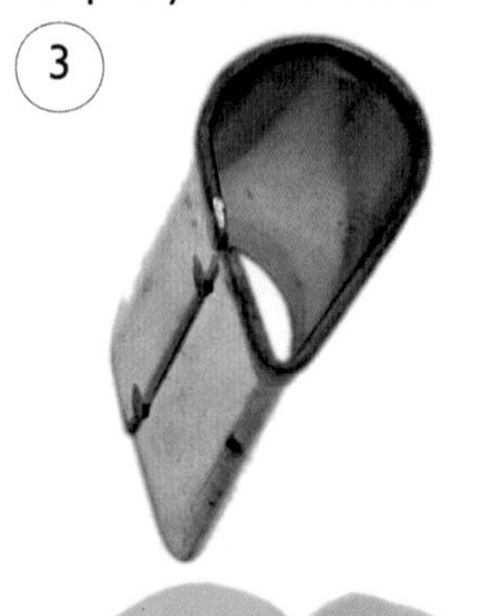

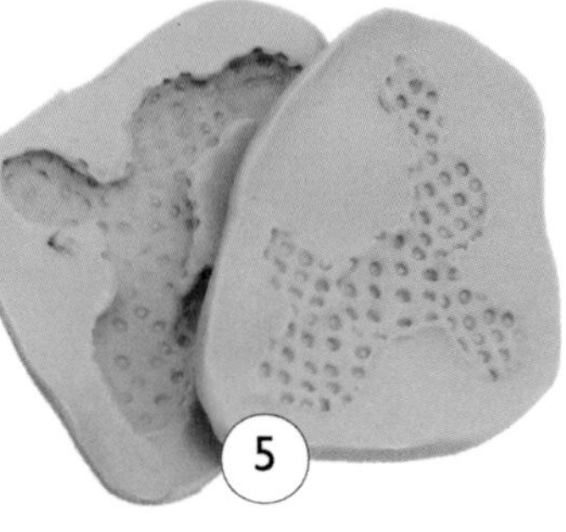

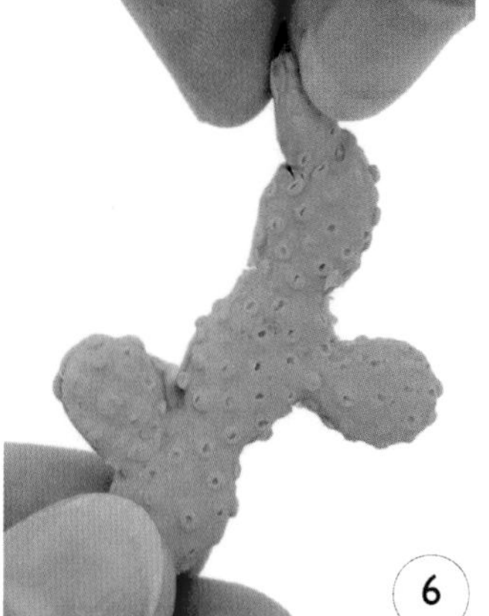

it will look 'cartoonish' ... but that may be the effect you wish to achieve. Smooth the edges to curve them off a little. Put a slight curve on the bottom of each piece and connect them together in fairly random form but flat. Using liquid polymer clay. glue tiny no-hole beads in diagonal lines on the whole surface of each size of piece. (3) (4) (5)

Make a 2 sided mould from this original. You can change the position of the pieces after moulding. (6)

Alternatively you can use pieces from a smaller cactus with a similar shape. Be careful of those little hairs. They can itch for days!

The additional fruit parts for the big cactus (prickly pears) were added simply by making each part with a pointed end and baking, drilling holes into the previously baked main cactus, and pressing the pieces in with Goo to attach. Then re-bake, preferably in it's final pot.

Simple cactus moulds from Torx heads *(from screwdriver kits)*

Some of these kits have small star shaped heads which are ideal for making mini cactus moulds. Just take a mould from the head. (7) Push clay into the mould and then work on the clay to produce a master for the second generation

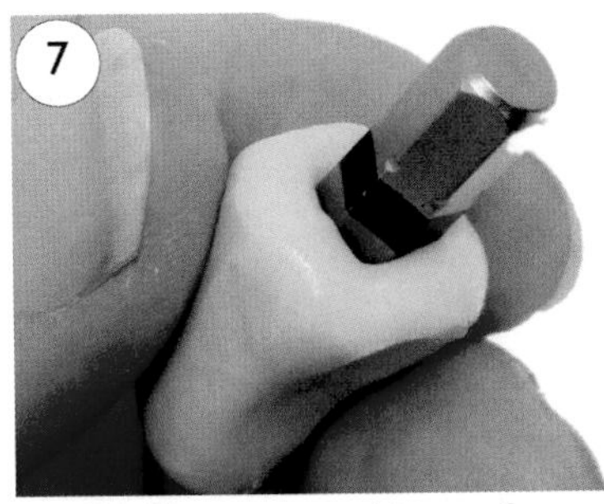

mould. You can try this as often as you like as the first generation of mould will always be there.

Making moulds from star shaped cutters

This is a fairly simple technique you have to cut out the star shape as long as possible and then tweak the points together

The problem is that star shapes only go up to a certain number of points. If you want more points you have to get more creative.

Most of this type of cactus have hairs so when you have made your first generation 'master' (the first moulding). Use a craft drill to make holes in the sides of the cactus. The next generation of moulds will then produce cactus with ready made indentations to glue the hairy prickles in.

Angie's Cutter extrusion for 3D shapes

(advanced ... several stage process)

When requiring a very complex shape which does not exist, or you can't find in 3D, look for a 2D cutter which would have this basic shape if extruded to a 3D shape. I came across this idea of moulding from extrusions when I was looking for a way to produce cactus shapes.

I found some flower cutters which had a greater number of petals. But cutting a long shape is impossible because of the stickiness of most modelling material, so I chose to extrude shapes using the cutter as an extruding nozzle and a fast set silicone mould material as the material to extrude.

Method: Find the shape you want to copy in 3 dimensions. Mix an amount of Minitmold, sufficient to form your shape ... plus a bit to account for errors, feed the mould material into and through the cutter shape before it sets. this takes some judgement as to the timing especially in particularly hot or especially cold environments.

push some right through and pull the extruded end to thinner on the other side of the cutter. Allow the rest to set inside the mould hanging gently from your fingers, and partially supporting the other end to prevent it thinning out too drastically.

You can then produce a first generation mould from this shape simply by powdering the original shape and covering in a thick layer of mould material. Try to mark where the centre will be on the top and bottom of your mould so that when it sets you have a good idea where to cut through. Since this is a self destructive process you'd better get it right first time or you will have to go back to stage 1! The problem with using a fast setting silicone is that in a cold season the material can take too long to set, and in a warm season it can set before you're ready.

Allow the material to drop or pull it through for a smaller shape. Let gravity do as much of the work as you can and gently hold it back from thinning to nothing and just parting.

8

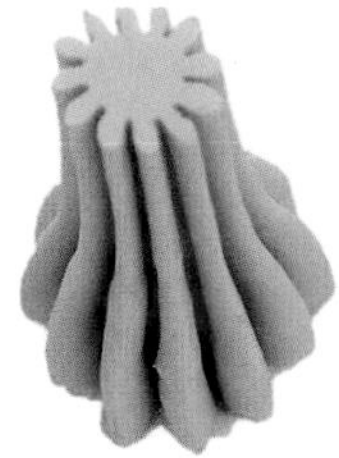
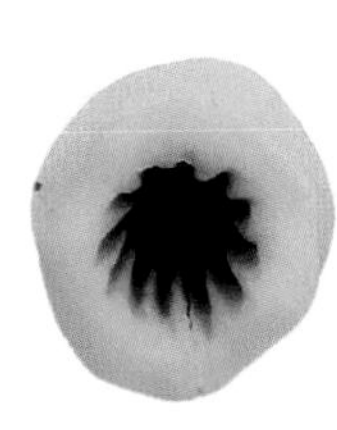

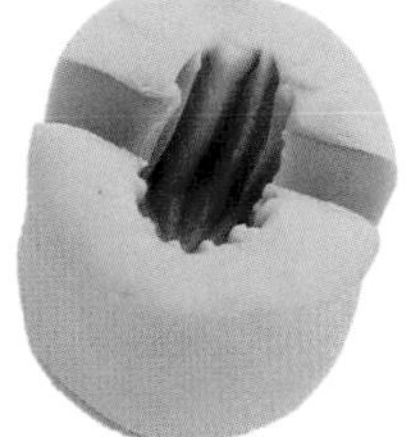
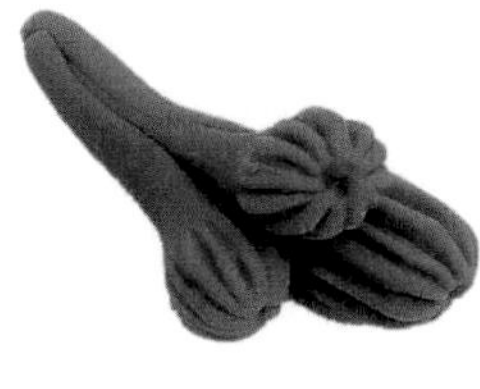

This takes some practise. Do not pull the material right out of the cutter until it has started to set because if you put it down on the surface it will flatten

As with many moulding techniques this just leaves you with a partial design for a mould. You then need to make a mould from this. Take an impression from the mould and improve on it. (8)

From the first flat topped mould you can take a simple impression in clay and work on that to produce the curved top. Starting by pressing in to it with a ball tool to make the clay curve inwards. Then gently using your fingers and modelling tools to produce the curve on the top with the 'fins'

intact. This may require some modelling skill.

When you are happy with this shape you can bake it ready to produce the next generation of mould.

If you wish you can drill or pierce holes into the edges this first model to make spaces to accept spines later. But my advice would always be to make another generation of mould first to preserve each stage of your hard work. The final mould doesn't need to include a stem and therefore you can make a one part mould. Different sizes of cactus can be made from the same mould simply by how you pull the clay out of the mould and how you form the stem.

The dramatic cactus flower was made from porcelain coloured clay using a piece for a stem and simply using the cut and cross method on a larger scale than I use for tomatoes for example. Once again the edges of the petals were very lightly dusted in red pastel. Keep your eyes open for smaller succulents that have the form of larger ones to take impressions of. It can be a lot of fun making your own collection of moulds. I've found the best way to make really small and accurate moulds from real cacti/succulents is to encase the whole plant part and then, when set, simply cut through from bottom to top leaving a teeny bit of the mould uncut. This provides a flexible join to make sure your two parts line up exactly. When reproducing from these moulds make sure you take care mixing colour and translucency. That can make the difference between ugly 'blobs' and beautiful miniature cacti.

Mini Olive

Another plant for the really lazy! However you have to be patient to wait for a weed root to dry.

You will need

Pliers, small with wire cutter

Small scissors

Work surface preferably med large smooth ceramic tile

A small dried out root from a 'woody' weed plant (not sure which I used, so just dry out some of your toughest weeds. A good excuse to go weeding)

Thin light green Goo

1/3rd to half maker bag of superfine olive leaves depending on the size of your plant.

This is the simplest form of tree and because olive leaves are so very tiny you can 'get away with' just dipping. So, go ahead, just dip your weedy root into the light green Goo. Remove the biggest blobs by tapping them on the tile and with a brush. Use the brush to make sure it's properly covered.

Then just dip into the leaves and bake.

You can refine the look by adding a few extra leaves more delicately and plant in a pot permanently by using some gravel with liquid polymer. Bake again.

Patio Garden Round Up

I've chosen to use ready made canvases for the exterior of my patio garden. This provides me with a light weight and the ability to mount and dismount to exhibit.

I was lucky enough to find reasonably priced canvases at a cheap German supermarket chain during their 'art week', which

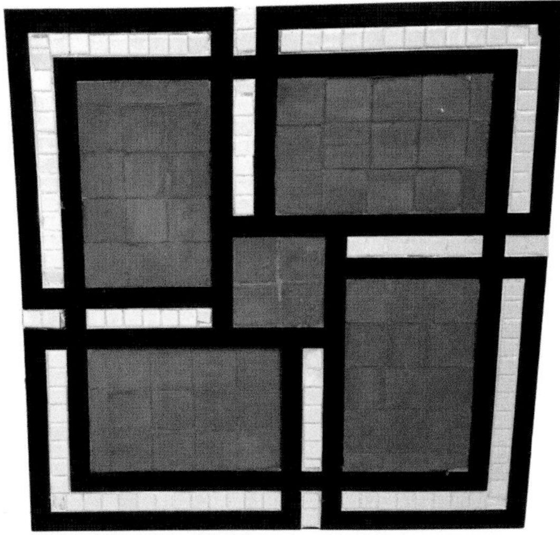

matched perfectly my interior panel which was a flat sectional picture frame from a cheap Asian shop. This was filled with super flexible tile cement and the terracotta tiles and white tiles were simply inset into the sections. The slight extra floor space when the panels were matched together for width is just deep enough for a faux internal arched walkway. I made this with foamcore and used water pipe for the columns. The columns are supported by supports made from polymer clay. Behind the arch I made a little extra terracotta flooring by simply tiling over a small piece of wood battening. Above the arch I folded the foamcore over and attached it to the wall. Tiling directly on to the foamcore. The blue tiling behind the archway is a printout from some Sevillano tiles I found on the internet. I covered this with Liquid Fimo to give it strength and sheen before gluing it on to the wall. I wasn't very happy with the balcony rails as, when I put the plants stems right through them in order to get authentic hanging plants and re-baked the lot together, the railings decided to twist under the heat and gravity pulled them over the pots behind them. Since I was on a deadline to photograph, I left them as they were but its a cautionary tale. You can't re-bake 3D pen filament unsupported!

The front elevation needs the canvas side outwards and the other 3 sides needs it to be pointing in. If you wish to tidy this up on the outside you can use foamcore and coat it with a flexible gritty paint finish. I was only interested in the internal part and the front.

The top can be left open or covered with a clear light well roof or just a safety glass or perspex roof to keep it clean. I sourced plant pots and terracotta jars etc. from a Spanish friend Mibako, listed at the back, and another Spanish miniature

artist friend José Garcia Molano - Miniaturas en Forja provided the authentic ironwork, the plates on the wall are by Elisabeth Causeret. I chose to leave all the terracotta ware fresh and not aged or distressed, for speed of presentation for the book. However the overall look would benefit from a little ageing on these pieces. The water for the fountain was made with a super clear 3D pen filament. Also, when staying recently at a hostal in the city of Seville which had one of the patios I based this idea on, I realised that most of these patios have arched walkways round 2 or 3 sides of the internal light well. That would be a much bigger project!

Making miniature trees with realistic autumn leaves - 'stealing' forms from nature

Warning this is a project which may well require a lot of patience, as you will have to wait for your plant parts to dry out or even to grow first! And the project itself will take the whole of a weekend.

You will need

Some real garden twigs or dried out plants

Some paper coated florist wire. Both thick and fine. Either brown or dark green. Or you can use white and paint it.

A craft drill.

Grey/brown polymer clay Goo (a mix of left over polymer clay and liquid polymer) plus autumn coloured mixes.

You will need a tray to work on, an overall and some cleaning alcohol and wipes to clean up. The polymer clay Goo can be sticky and messy!

'Autumn leaves' (see below)

Real plant 'armature' (see explanation below)

I use some real plant as a base for this tree. Nature is very 'fractal' and can provide very realistic forms in miniature. The trick here is to preserve the forms by using liquid polymer to cover the form so that if the original decays over time, your work remains. I have used a piece of old Tomato plant dried out. I like using hollow forms because I can poke many wires down in to it to add extra small branches.

The birch tree produces seed heads which, when they fall off and disintegrate fall into 'bits' some of which resemble autumn leaves. The best time to collect these is midsummer so you may have to wait some time. I found these in Denmark but there are several different trees which produce different shaped 'leaves' in their flower/seed parts. Apparently you can also source them from a company called 'Green Scene' in the UK. (1)

In order to separate the useful bits from the other ones (to save time) make yourself a small 'riddle', that is to say a sieve. I find that a wire pen holder has a size of mesh which sieves the tiny seeds and smaller bits through leaving the leaf like pieces If you can find some netting of a similar size (I used netting from a potato sack) you can attach it with an elastic band and simply sieve the tiny bits out through the net. Otherwise you can top off the holder, and allow the bits to fall out of the sides as you shake it. You are left with the larger leaf shaped bits in the mesh holder. Save the little bits as they will make a scenic scatter for bases, very small leaves or for autumn leaf piles in a smaller scale. (2) (3)

Alternatively you can use my superfine autumn leaves which are produced in polymer clay and machine cut to be really fine.

Now you need to make up some mixes of Goo. I suggest you make a really thick mix of the colour you have decided to use for your tree bark. You also need to make a slightly thinner version of this mix for sticking 'leaves' on to the branches and twigs. The leaves have to dip easily into it. Not too thin or the leaves won't have enough stickyness to stay put. Put this to one side while you prepare your tree.

To make a tree trunk and branches with dried out tomato stems

I collect stems of certain of my annual vegetable plants and find pieces with pleasing shapes. When the plants cease to be green they will also have useful hollow centres which you can use to poke flower wires down. For this you need a thicker flower wire. Push pieces of wire either singly or bent into pairs into the holes in the 'branches' where you have cut them off. Before pushing in, dip the wires into some polymer clay Goo. This means that when you bake your work the wires will both stick in, and reinforce your 'tree'. (4) (5) (6) If you use a dried hollow plant you have the option of adding

1

2

3

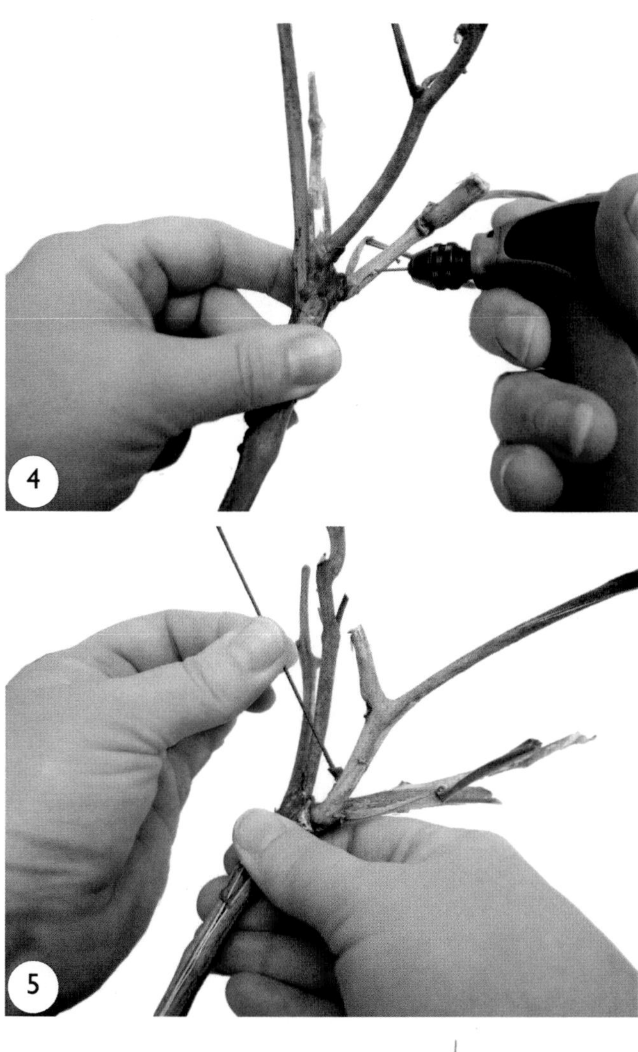

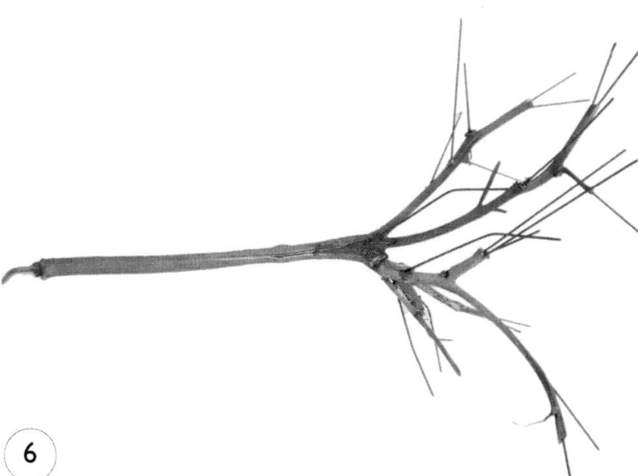

different sizes of branches easily, but they are more fragile and you will need to use a lot of Goo to build up your tree shape. This means a lot more work and baking but leaves you plenty of chance to make the work your own. This makes you the artist. In case you think it's 'cheating remember you are only using nature to provide an armature.

At this stage it is quite sensible to add a hook to the bottom of the tree this allows you to hold it, hang it upside down and even to wire it into the base. I like to drill into the base and add a little threaded bolt to take a hook which can be replaced at any time with a nut for attaching the tree to the base.

As an alternative to the hollow form you can choose to select a more solid piece from a fruit tree. The downsides of this are that you may have to twist your wires round the existing twigs. It may shrink as it dries so that the 'twigs' are shrugged off and you don't have so much chance to build up your shape since adding Goo and baking doesn't work very well as the plastic gets shrugged off the surface by the oils and moisture in the living plant as it dries and can crack badly. In this case I would only use Goo where it's absolutely necessary for the joints and on the flower wire.

At some point you will feel the need to do your first baking of your work. At this time you might add one layer or at least a part layer of Goo to the whole of the surface of your work.

Whenever you are going for a bake, it's worth paying extra attention to any joins between real plant and wire and to any cracks which may have appeared in/after a previous baking. Don't worry about cracks. These are natural as the plant material may shrink, expand or give off water during baking. A few cracks in a tree, filled in with more Goo can look even more natural and where they look good can even be accented using paint or alcohol inks.

At any time you can start to add a few of the really fine branches but don't put too many on at the first stage or you will find them difficult to work round when adding layers of polymer clay to the tree.

While your tree is baking you can start adding leaves to the fine flower wire 'twigs'.

Making the leafy twigs

I attach my flower wire to a combi-oven metal turntable rack but you can use any kind of method for raising your wires off the surface. Make sure whatever you use can be put in the oven. You need to bend your wires over to have them

Baking instructions and safety warnings

If you are using a large oven you can either hang the tree from a rack placed at the top of the oven or lay it on a baking tray. You may find some 'goo' can pool to one side of the trunk and will bake shiny. You can sand this down afterwards. N.B. if you are using a combi oven with a rotating base please make sure you don't exceed the dimensions of the plate or the height of the oven. When I'm working with one of these ovens in class I draw round the base plate on a piece of kitchen paper and tape it to my work table with masking tape. I also draw the vertical dimensions on to this paper so that I can check as I work.

It is very dangerous to allow the wire to exceed this dimension as it can get caught in the vents of the oven. Always protect the base of your oven from spills and smears of polymer clay.

horizontal. This is so that the leaves appear to hang off the twigs of the tree. (7) Using tweezers pick up each leaf and dip into the Goo and then attach to the flower wire. You can prepare the flower wire by painting on a layer of Goo to help it stick. You can only attach leaves to one side of the wire because of gravity. To add more leaves you can bake and then turn the wire. Or you can simply add lots of leaves and twist the wire later with pliers. I prefer the first method as the wire doesn't always twist as you want it and can snap. This is a very long winded process of course. Expect to spend a whole day doing this and my advice is to think of it as a meditative relaxation rather than a chore! If you can't do this, perhaps this project is not for you!

Between each bake add more layers of Goo to the stem and branches and add more of the smaller twigs which you have already prepared with leaves on. Twist these round the slightly thicker branches or drill and poke into the holes. Cover the joins with thick Goo. Add extra autumn leaves dipped in Goo. You can also add some leaves to the smaller of the branches. (8)

At the final baking which could be number 3, 4 or even 5 depending on how methodical and perfectionist you are, paint the autumn leaves with a wash of coloured Liquid Fimo. You can colour the Liquid Fimo with oil colours or thin out your pre made Goo.

I've chosen to colour mine with a quite deep red look but obviously the colours are mellower on some parts of the tree. Don't try to paint all your leaves the same colour.

I don't just use paint for this because paint isn't protective enough of the very fragile 'leaves'. The liquid polymer sets them permanently and even if some mites etc. eat away at the real leaf over many decades, or it gets damp, the 'image' will be left in polymer. Again, nature is just being used as an armature.

I finished my tree off by hanging a few leaves on an extremely fine invisible thread so they look as if they're in mid fall and even blowing away in the wind. I thank my friend Steve for this little magicians 'prop'. You should be able to find this material on the internet.

To assemble the tree on to the base, remove the hook and push it back up through the base and simply 'screw' the tree to the base. If your tree is 'wonky and doesn't hold well you can add extra wire underneath and as a last resort you can glue the tree to the screw thread of the hook if you want it to be permanent. If you have any real problems with cracking in the 'trunk' of the tree, glue a metal nut into the stem to hold a bolt and re Goo any cracks, not forgetting to bake again afterwards. Don't worry about a few cracks in the Goo on the tree trunk from the constant re-baking. This can actually make the tree look older and more realistic!

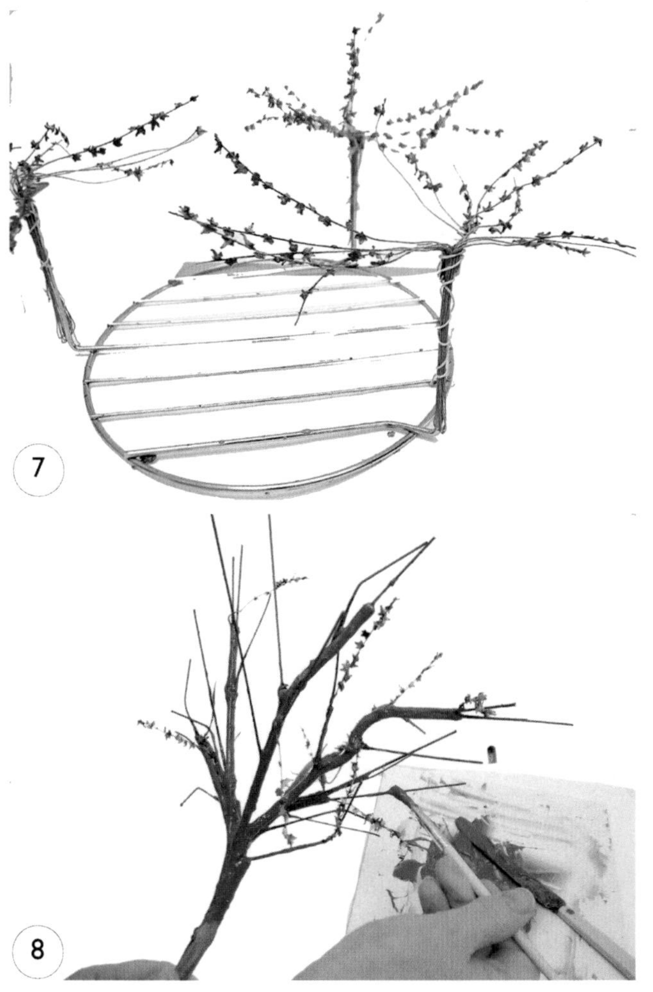
7

8

Ancient Olive Tree

You will need

The roots of 2 tomato plants, very dry. These roots upside down simulate the growth of an old heavily pruned Olive tree far better than building a tree from wire ever could.

Tomato or other plant roots. Dried out! (1)

Leave the tomato roots to dry as long as possible. Months is best. Then shake off or brush off any mud. If the mud still doesn't come off rinse under a fast hose and dry again. OK you may well be impatient about this but respect the ancient olive tree. Even the miniature one takes months. A real one can be millennia old!

You will need to wear old clothes or an overall as this can be very sticky

You will be baking the project several times over and depending on the age of your roots the clay may crack a little on the surface. Don't worry, this can make your tree look even more ancient and so even more realistic!

Fine flower wire to bind tree parts together and a bolt with a long nut or similar to attach to the base.

A craft drill.

An easily cleaned tray or lap tray to work on or masking tape paper to your table top.

Heavy gauge paper coated flower wire brown or white.

Medium weight paper coated flower wire Brown or white.

A nut and bolt or nut and hook shaped bolt

A large oven unless you are making a particularly small tree, and you will also need to cover an oven tray in silver foil to catch any stray drips of polymer Goo.

Polymer clay Goo in dark grey brown

Goo in light grey brown. The Rhino colour in Premo clay is perfect. (2)

Black & white acrylic paint (or dark grey) or ink stains.

Cleaning or surgical alcohol and lots of kitchen roll/rags for clean up.

Soil substitute.

A lot of olive superfine leaves or very small cut paper leaves in long 'lozenge' shape. If you are able to cut these out yourself you will be able to colour one side of the paper dark green and one side silvery green - before cutting the leaves of course!

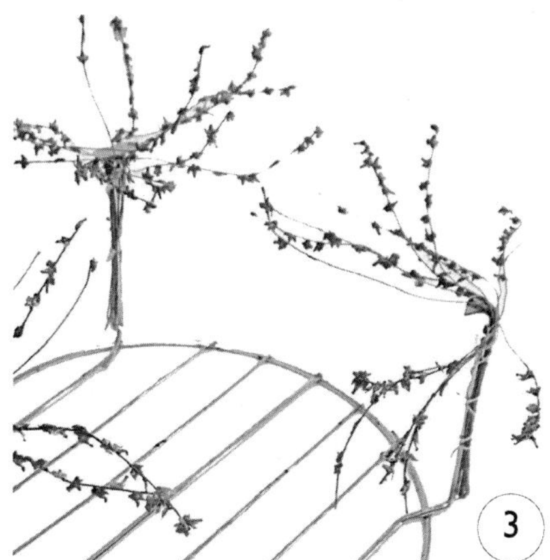

To make the main tree trunk

Select one, two or three plant roots and bind them together using floral wire. It is important to check the size of your oven first. The entire tree must sit within it comfortably with no chance of the branches touching the sides of the oven or getting too close to the elements or gas jets. If the tree is too large you should cut across the bound stems diagonally and work on the two parts separately so you can re-glue them later.

Thickly Goo (with a grey / brown colour) the two stems together making the 'branches' stick outwards and wrap with very fine wire, but don't lose the impression of there being two or three stems. Insert a screw in bolt in the base and wire tightly adding plenty of Goo to make sure it stays in place. Insert a hook shaped bolt and bake the tree by hanging upside down in a full size oven or you can lay the tree down in the oven but you may have to clean up baked Goo and disguise 'shiny bits'

Before a second and following bakes add layers of the lighter grey Goo. Dragging a cocktail stick through it to make quite a strong texture non the trunk but leaving the 'branches' fairly smooth. And bake again Repeat this stage until you are happy that your 'armature' is fully covered. Any naked bits will be weak and liable to break.

Olives

During baking time on the previous stages you can make a good quantity of olives by the same method as the grapes on page 84. If your tree has just green olives just make that colour which, while on the tree is a pale spring green and not the colour you would imagine from a jar of olives. If it has black olives remember these are quite a purplish colour and some of them will be green tinged with red/purple. You can either choose to bake these in advance or attach them unbaked to the twigs at the end of the next stage.

To make small branches and twigs

Attach medium thin paper coated flower wire with more wire, to a support for baking in the oven. I find the rotating metal stand out of a combi microwave/grill ovens works really well to make one tree (3) (used in a big oven of course) but you can use any support which you can use in your work-shop and then transfer directly to the oven. I have also used skewers attached to silver foil baking dishes with the wire passed through the loops of the skewers when I needed more 'props' for a big class.

Bend the wire over so it's parallel or pointing very slightly downwards towards the base.

Coat the wires with a light coating of the light grey-brown Goo using a paintbrush, a cocktail stick, or if you enjoy getting messy, use your fingers.

Add the leaves one by one from one end of the leaf with tweezers. Gravity will make them point downwards. If you have trouble getting the leaves to stick, dip each one in a little more Goo. Don't worry a few will fall off but they will tend to be the heavier thicker cut ones, leaving only the finest and best still attached. If they fall off really easily your Goo is too liquid.

Bake these wires for 10 minutes and then take them out of the oven and re-position the wires by bending them in another direction so that the first set of attached leaves are now upwards.

Repeat the process adding more Goo to one side and sticking more leaves on. (4)

Repeat a third time. But this time you can add olives in twos and threes just above some of the leaves.

You will also want to add leaves to the thinner branches on your tree. Don't put leaves on the thicker parts as nature wouldn't do that.

Bake again.

Add branches to the tree wherever needed

Drill small holes into the tree branches and add both medium and fine wires with leaves and fruit on. Hide the joins with more Goo and if necessary a few extra leaves. Don't worry if this join looks a little 'blobby' because this is quite realistic for a tree which has been pruned harshly over the years, which many of them have. You will then give the tree a final bake for the full 20 minutes.

Using paint or alcohol ink in very dark brown or black coat the main trunk and any large branches (but not the thin ones with leaves on). Rub away any excess just leaving ink in the cracks.

Attach the tree to your garden or base.

Cheap Tricks

Old Apple tree

Of course all of the hand making is time consuming. Even the caning or stencilling and assembly of leaves takes quite a bit of time. We can't possibly make every leaf in a stuffed garden by hand. So how to fill in the empty bits? Well here is where the cheating comes in. Once again it's the cheap end of the miniatures shop and even the pound shops and the import shops. Train your eyes to look for tiny leaves and flowers. I can

only say where I got things from but those items may not now be available and in any case your garden is your garden and shouldn't look exactly like any of mine.

For the apple tree I used a strip of wired green silk leaves off a length of flowers and leaves which I bought from Skala Minimal in Sweden. The material had a label which said Creal on it but so far I haven't found other worldwide suppliers. I bought 4 lengths but only used 3 here.

I added apples on wires in the same way as with the lemons in the project in the Patio Garden.

When I'd used the the green silk leaf length, the other parts were used to cheat other parts of the garden

The small plastic leaves were used as infill around the base of the apple tree in the Kitchen garden and in other spaces where disguise of extra 'green' were needed. And for the leaves on a blackberry bush, see page 43.

The green and orangey twiggy bits were used as Grape vine in the Mediterranean garden. And for some little pea plants. I still have a box full of orange flowers which I'll find a use for I'm sure.

Other cheap tree forms

Some plants were used to simulate trees in the background of the Kitchen Garden. One was just some greenery which already looked like a tree. One of these was originally a herb pot of some unnamed herb. I took it apart and pushed the individual pieces on to a branching stem from another plastic posy I'd taken to pieces to use as a small tree/shrub.

Appendix 1:
The Potting Shed

1:12 Scale Plan Set.

Length - 150mm
Width - 112mm
Height - 205mm

Designed in England by Treacle Lane.
(c) Treacle Lane - 2016

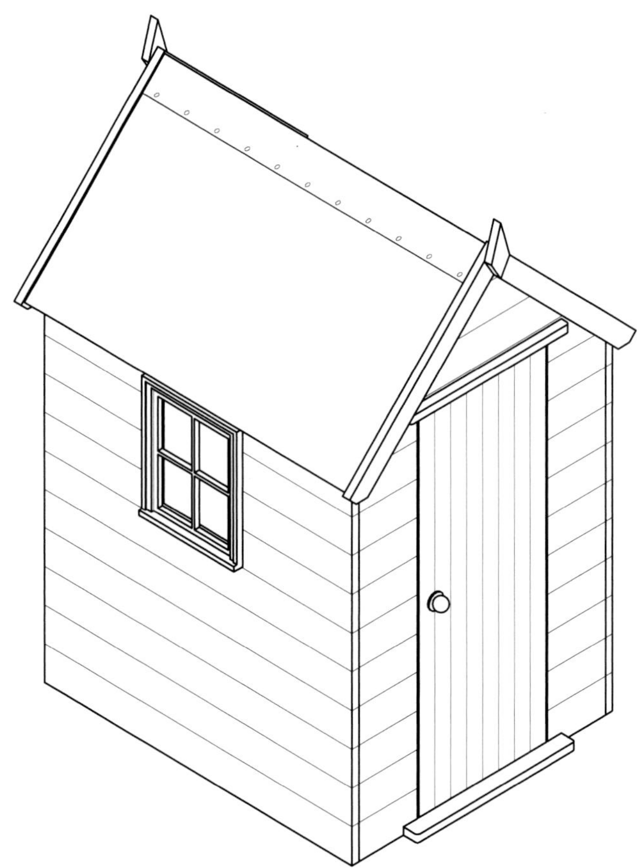

Tools Required:

PVA Wood Glue.
(always follow the manufacturers instructions).
Masking Tape
Craft Knife & Cutting Mat
(always take care when using a knife).
Double Sided Tape
Brace & Bit
(always take care when drilling).
Ruler & Black Biro
Brushes & Paints for Finishing.
(always follow the manufacturers instructions).
Abrasive Paper
(always wear a dust mask when sanding)
Fret or Coping Saw
(always take care when using a saw).
Mitre Box
Fine Blade Wood Saw
(always take care when using a saw).

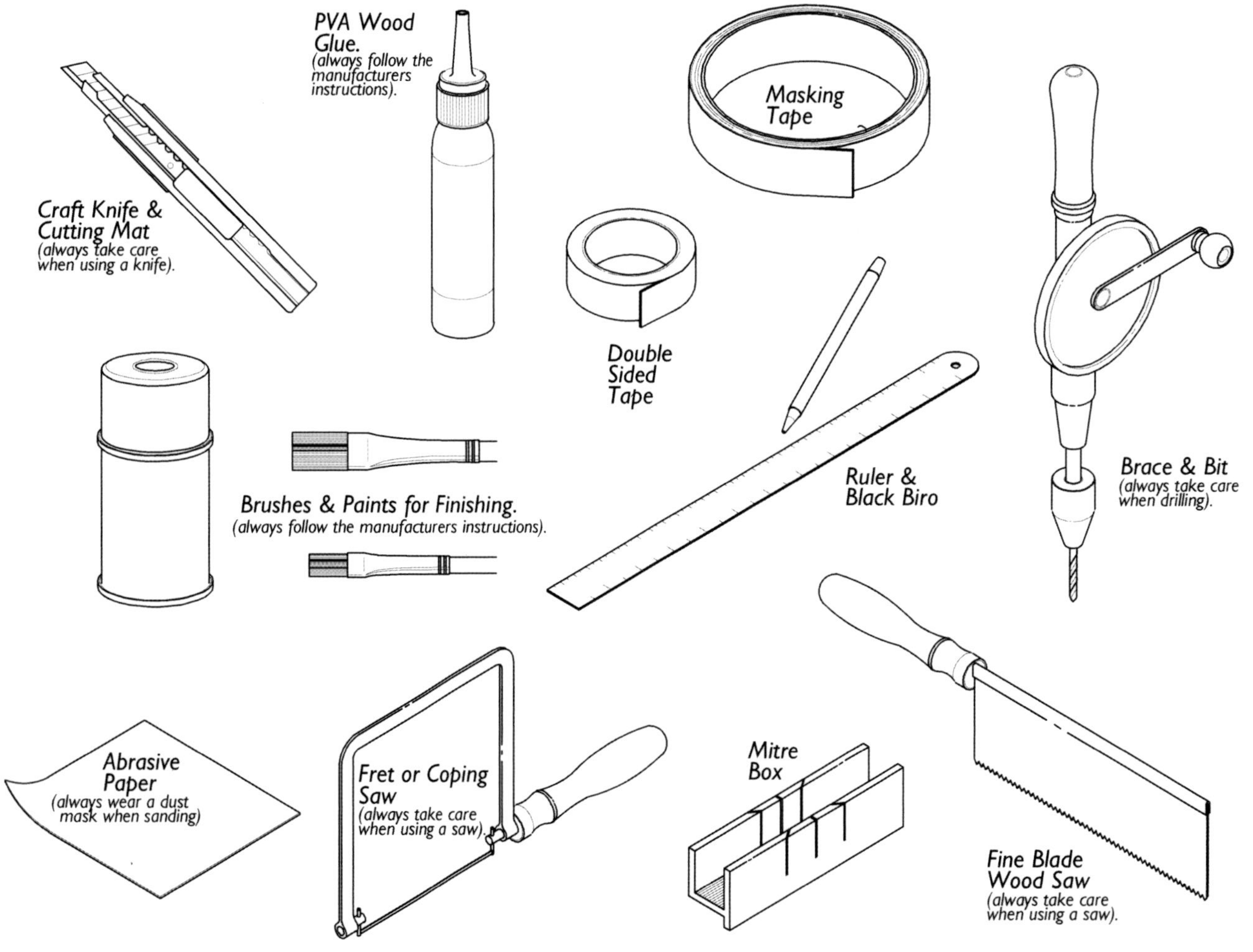

Materials Required:

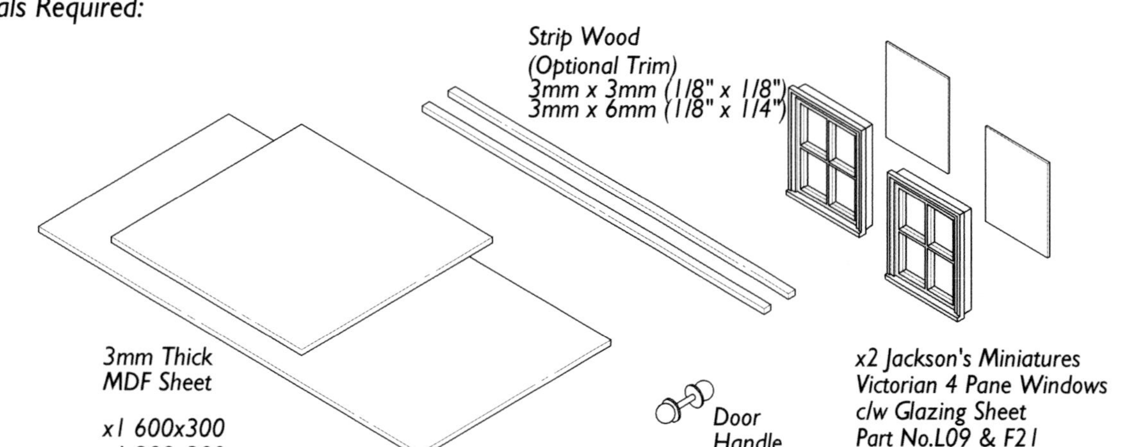

Assembly Instructions:

Read the instructions carefully before starting and familiarise yourself with all of the components required.

Prepare the required tools and adhesive for the construction of your model as shown on page 1.

Photo copy pages 5 to 9 (note that you need two copies of page 5) of this plan set - do not scale the copies.

Apply double sided tape to the 3mm MDF board that forms the main body of the potting shed and apply the photocopied patterns onto the board. Apply the pattern to the wood by matching up the bottom corner of the pattern first. Press diagonally up and out to ensure that the pattern does not wrinkle as it is applied.

You can now cut the board roughly around the individual parts to make each piece more manageable.

The individual pieces can now be accurately cut out, following the lines of the pattern.

Use a handsaw for all of the external cuts - a saw with a fine blade will give the best results. To produce the window apertures use a drill to form a pilot hole inside the window opening - then using a coping saw or fretsaw - pass the blade through the pilot hole and cutout the window aperture.

Each completed part can now be lightly sanded to remove any burrs and imperfections (always wear a dust mask when sanding MDF) - don't forget to remove the paper patterns.

Now that you have completed making the individual parts you can start to assemble your potting shed.

Follow the recommended build sequence on pages 3 and 4. Each part shown is numbered and referenced back to the patterns.

Where you see this symbol allow the glue to dry before moving on to the next stage.

External planking detail can now be marked onto each piece. The size and design of planking (vertical or horizontal - straight planks or waney edged) is all down to personal taste. Use black biro to draw the lines - push down hard so that the surface of the board becomes indented - the detail will then show through once the potting shed is painted. Add the board detail to both the outside and inside faces.

The completed structure can now be customised with additional detail if you wish. Using 3mm x 3mm strip wood replicate the internal frame that all small potting sheds have. Cut each piece to suit your preferred design (a razor saw and mitre box are perfect for cutting neat accurate joints).

Add beam and brace detail to the back of the door using 6mm x 3mm strip wood.

The finished model should be finished with a suitable primer and then can be either spray or brush painted in the colours of your choice.

Complete the shed roof by applying a piece of course grade wet and dry paper to represent roofing felt. Don't forget to add the nail detail along the roof line.

We would love to receive a photo of your finished model - you never know it may appear on our website gallery.

Mark all of the panels on both the inner and outer faces with your preferred planking detail (don't forget the floor panel) before you glue the parts together.

The grey shaded areas indicate where the parts join together. Apply glue to these faces and then assemble the parts. Wrap the main body in a couple of bands of masking tape to hold the parts in position whilst the glue sets.

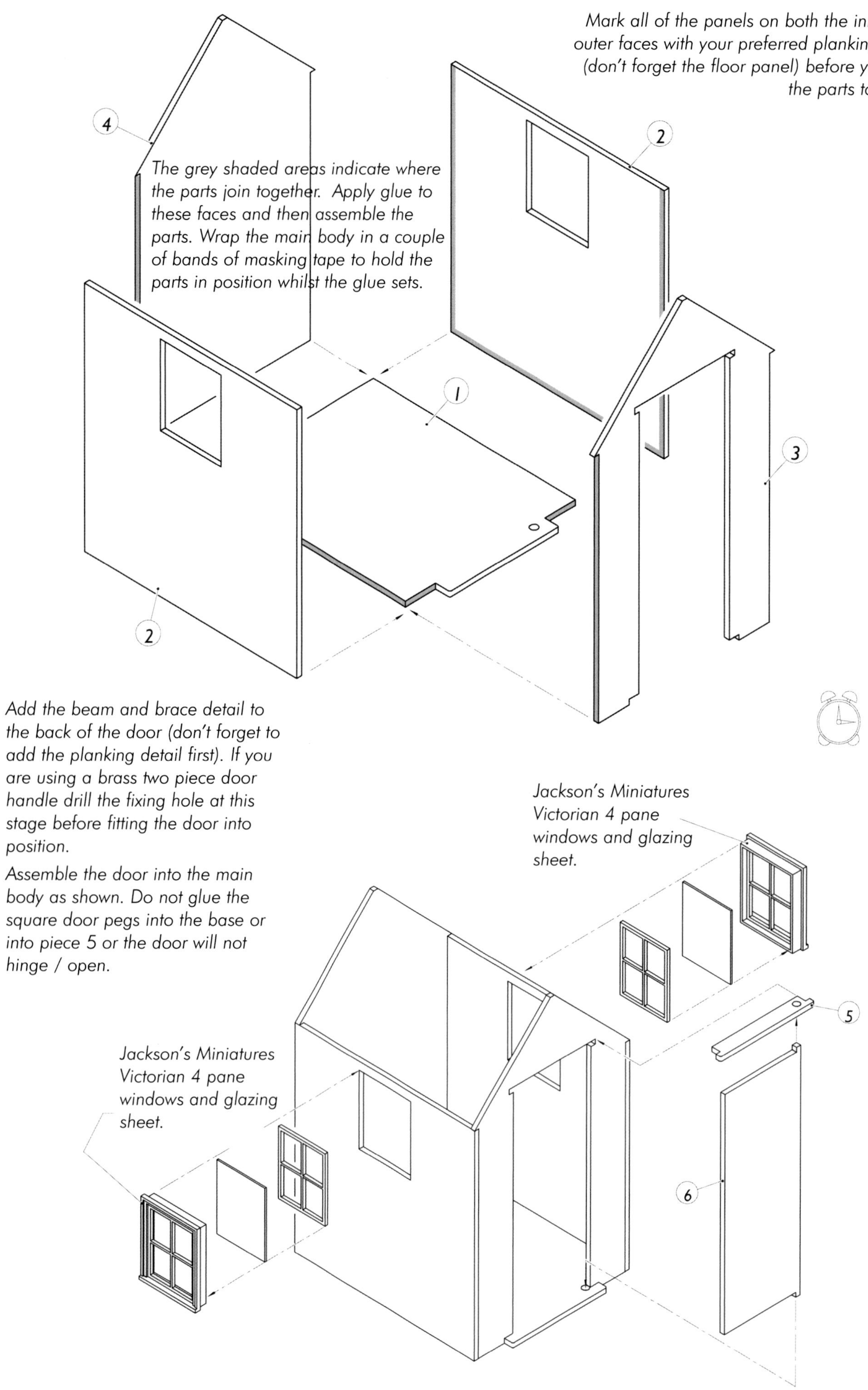

Add the beam and brace detail to the back of the door (don't forget to add the planking detail first). If you are using a brass two piece door handle drill the fixing hole at this stage before fitting the door into position.

Assemble the door into the main body as shown. Do not glue the square door pegs into the base or into piece 5 or the door will not hinge / open.

Assemble the roof panels as shown. Note the locations for the roof braces (9) are shown on the patterns. It is important that the outer braces are in the correct location - these position the roof when fitted to the shed. Fix the barge boards (10) into position. Dotted lines are shown on the patterns to ensure that the parts are fitted in the correct locations.

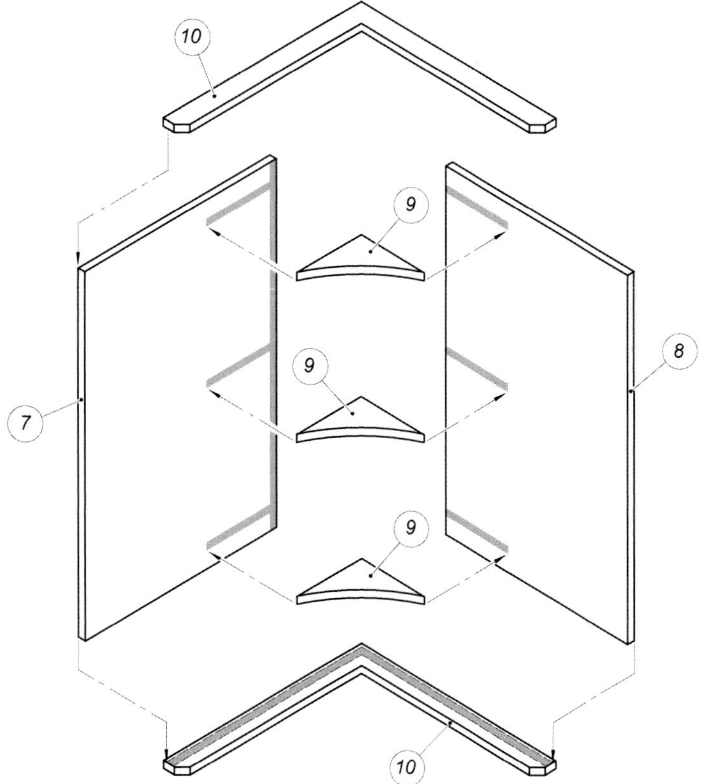

11

For the final touch glue the roof finial's (11) into position on the barge boards.

Do not glue the roof into position. It is designed to be removable for access.

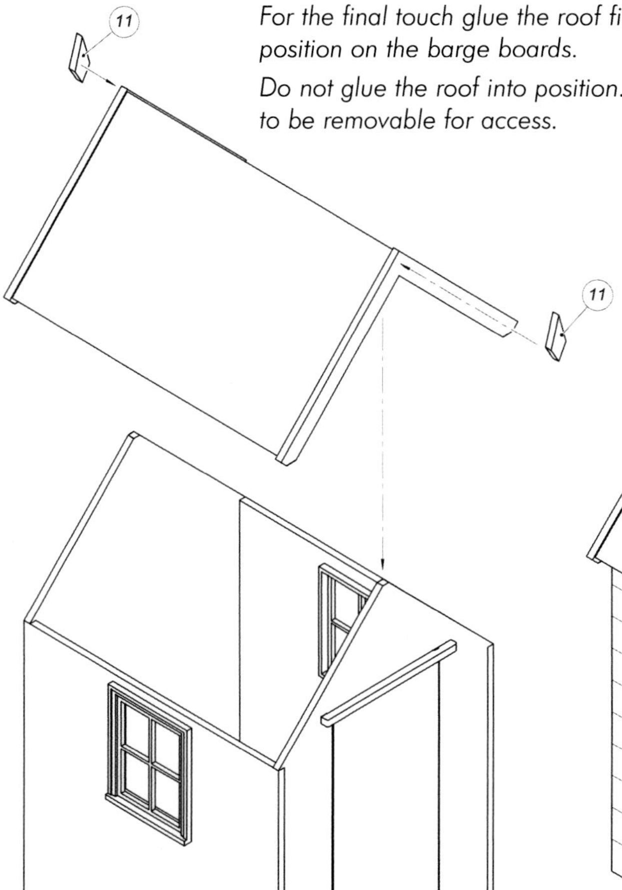

11

Your completed Potting Shed can now be fully decorated and fitted out to suit your final design.

1
Ø4.5 hole.

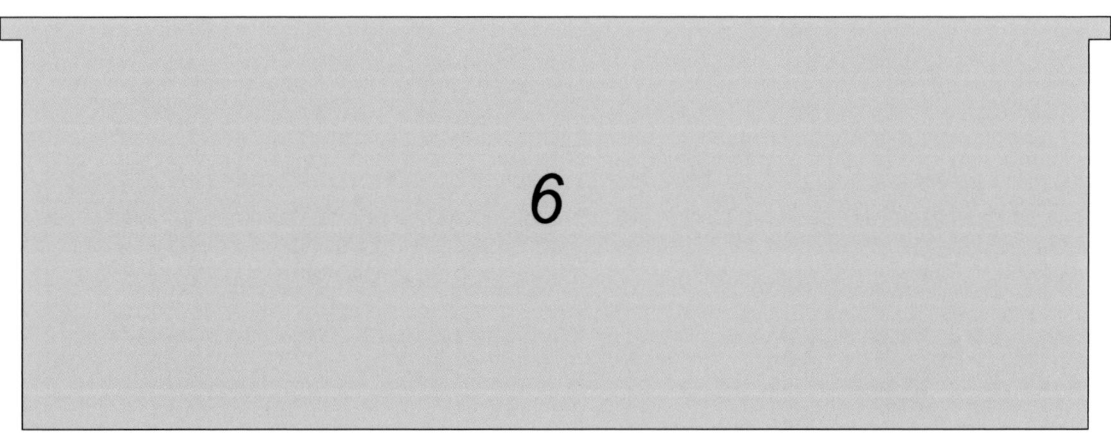
6

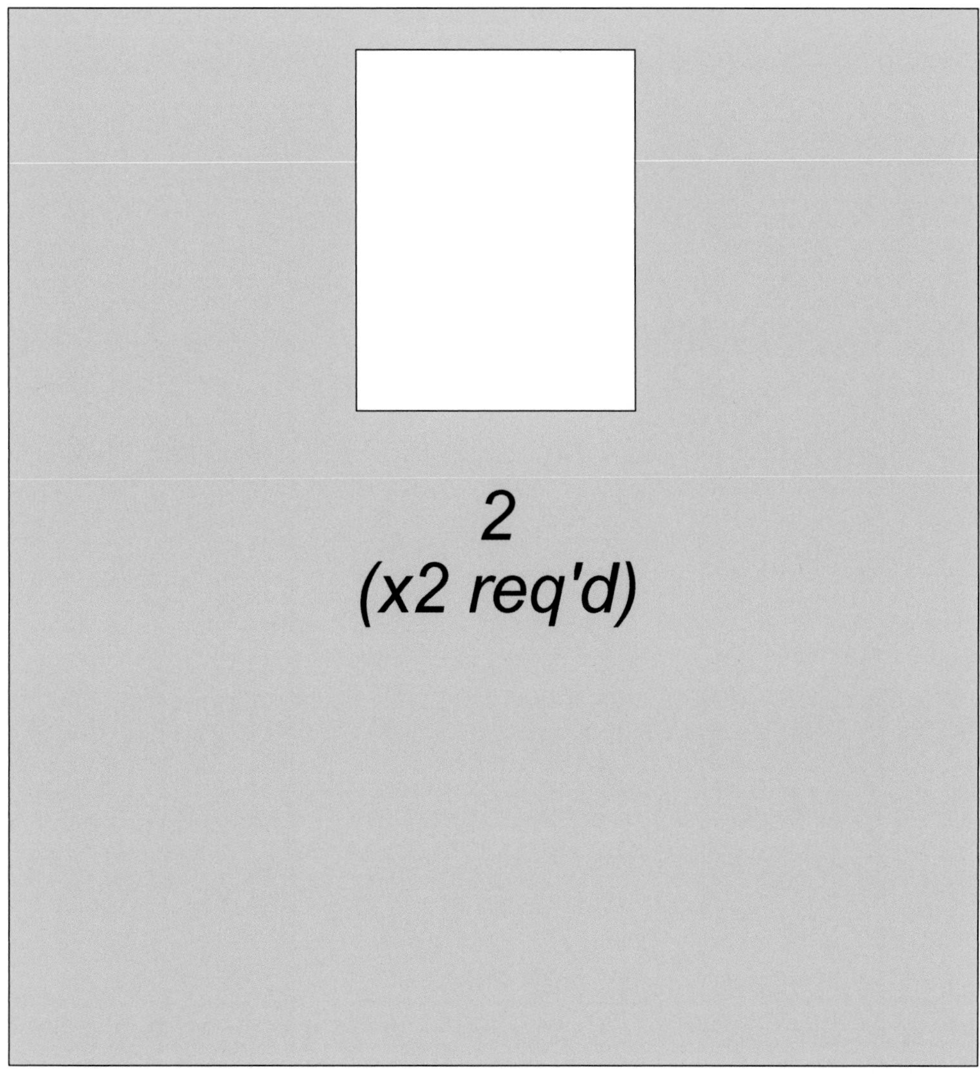
2
(x2 req'd)

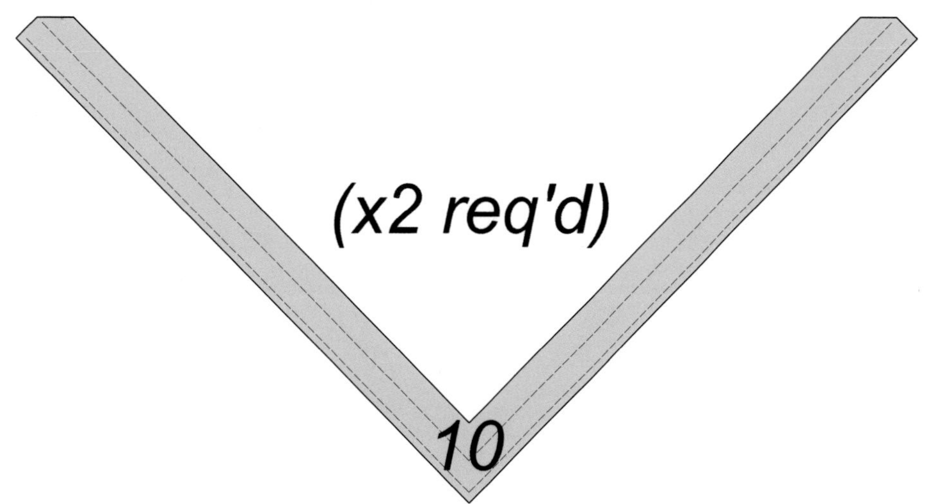
(x2 req'd)
10

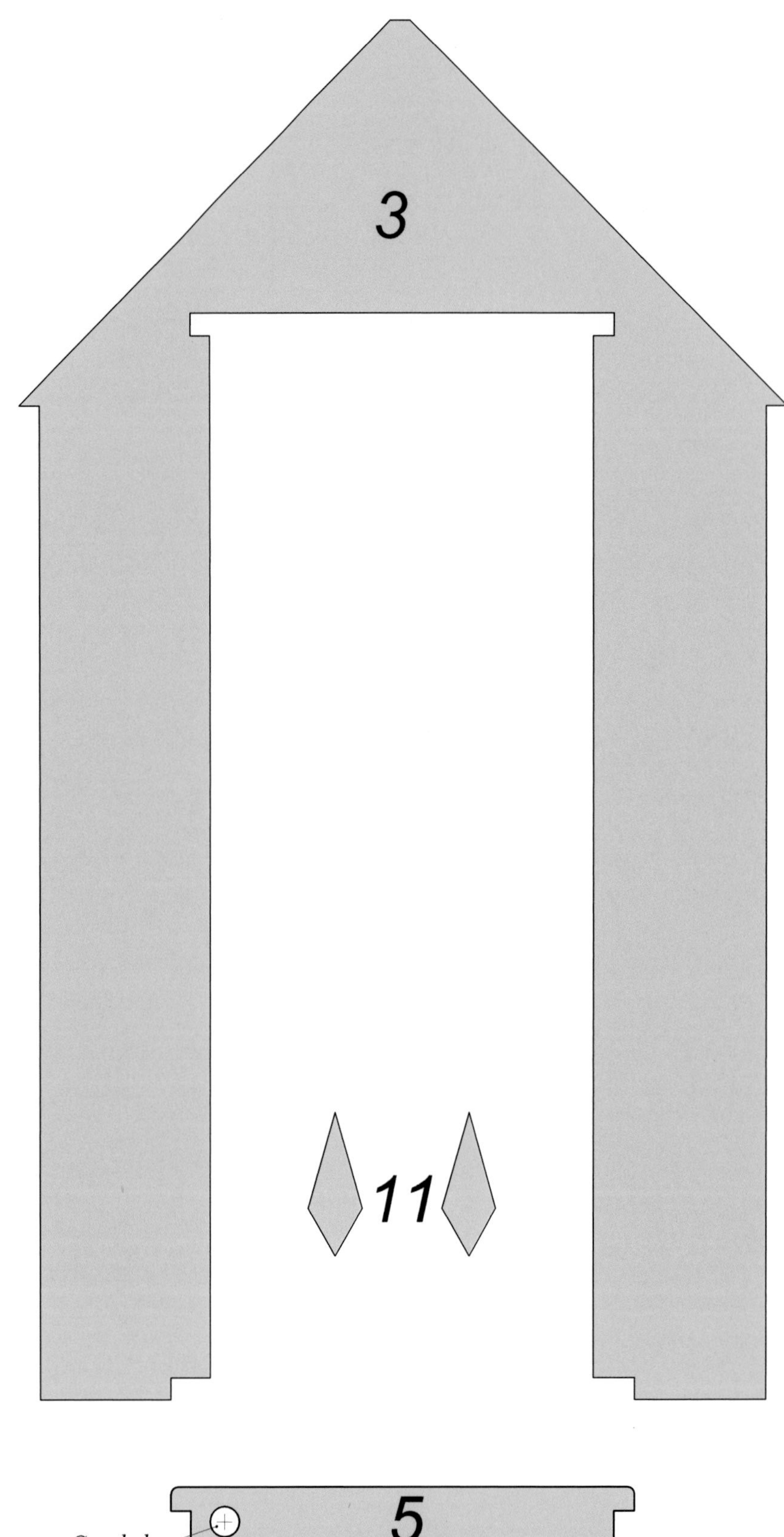
3
11
5
Ø4.5 hole.

4

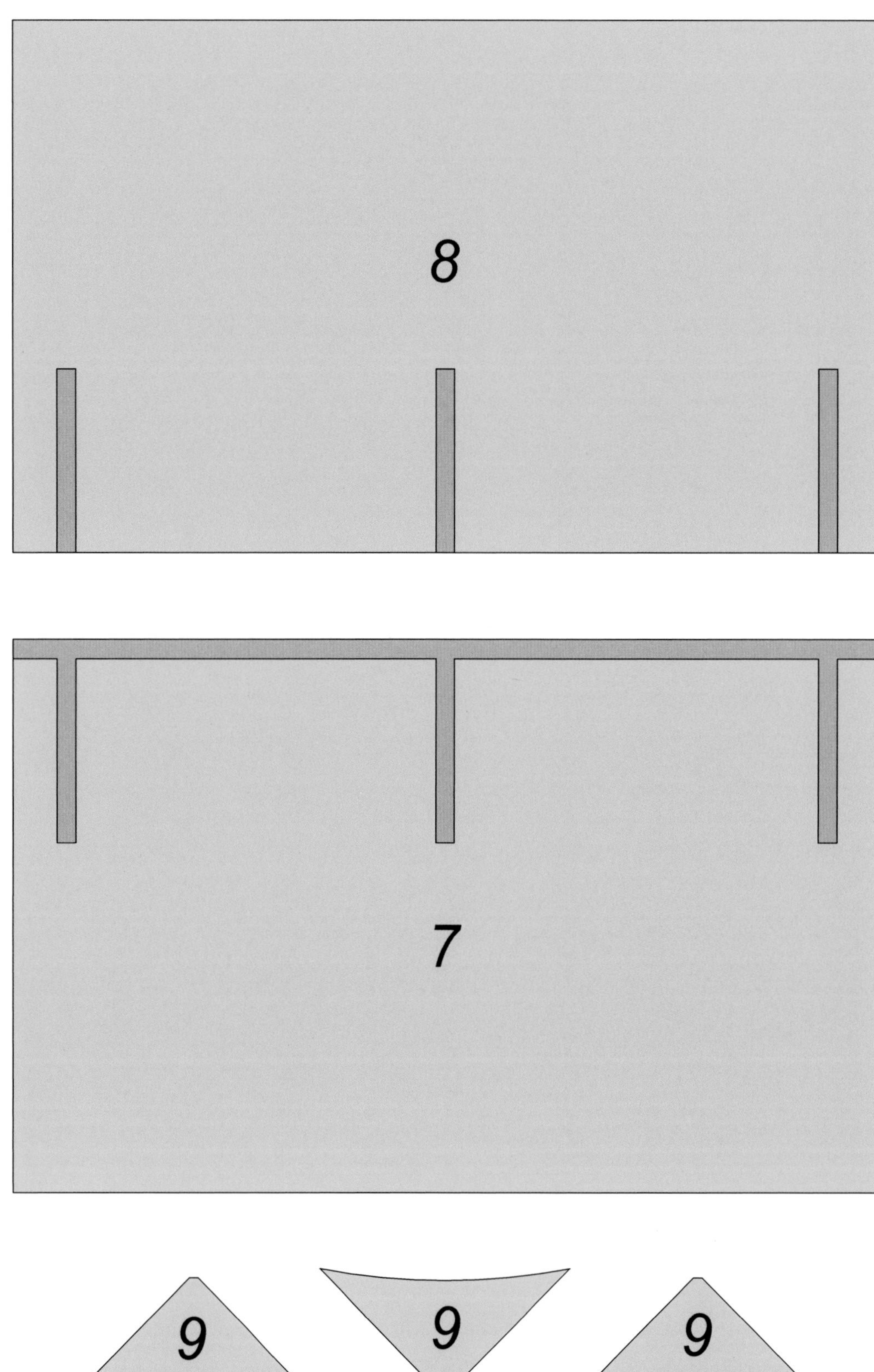
8
7
9
9
9

Appendix 2: Iron Gate Pattern

Resources, Information, Further Reading and Watching

My YouTube channelvideos from archive material made back in the days when the internet was newborn and YouTube wasn't even thought of, to up to date projects & some further explanations on projects in this book.

www.youtube.com/user/angiescarr

My Facebook page

www.facebook.com/angiescarr.miniatures/

Miniatures Magazines

UK

www.hobbies-and-crafts.co.uk/dolls-houses-miniatures
www.dollshouseworld.com

USA

scottpublications.com/mcmag
www.americanminiaturist.com

Germany

1zu12 www.1zu12.com/Magazin_Start_Grau.htm

Spain

Miniaturas www.miniaturasrevista.com

Information on polymer clays and some lovely tutorials (Not Miniatures specific)

thebluebottletree.com
www.glassattic.com

The Polymer Clay Artists guide (book) Marie Segal. A near encyclopaedic collection of polymer clay ideas.

Check out the work of of these artists who make beautiful flowers and plants in many materials:-

My friend Anja Van den Doel (Netherlands) now sadly deceased made wonderful paper plants.

Diane Harfield (UK) works with Cold Porcelain

Gosia Suchudolska (Poland)

Pia Becker (Germany)

Pascale Garnier (France)

Loredana Tonetti (Italy)

Mary McGrath (USA)

Donna Greenberg - not a miniaturist as such but makes wonderful natural forms (USA)

Suppliers

3d pen & accessories

A search on Amazon is the best place for the cheap Chinese pens

Natural green filaments

rigidink www.rigid.ink

Wood filaments

ice filaments www.icefilaments.com

Stone filaments

Treed treedfilaments.com/3d-printing-filaments/architectural-dark-stone

Polymer clays and liquid clays, cutters, tools

Clayaround – UK www.clayaround.com

ConAdearte – Spain www.conadearte.com/catalog/en

Potting shed kit

Treacle lane www.treaclelane.co.uk

Leaf and flower Cutters and stencils

Stencils, Moulds, flower and leaf canes and superfine slices and Minitmold Franks Craft Shop www.angiescarr.co.uk

Coronet Porcelain (micro size) www.coronetporcelainpaste.co.uk

Celcraft (micro size) www.celcrafts.com/?product_cat=celcutters-micro

Makin's nature set for frogs contains leaf for squash www.makins-usa.com/products.jsp?prod_catg_id=6

Miniseum www.miniseumwebshop.dk/shop/frontpage.html

Skala Minimal theswedishcorner.com/?lang=en

Flower wires

Vanilla valley www.thevanillavalley.co.uk/florist_wire_accessories.html

Metal stands etc. in Patios section

Miniaturas en Forja www.facebook.com/MiniaturasenForja

Teracotta pottery in Patio section

Mibako mibako.galeon.com/Index_archivos/inicio.html

Miniature Bricks etc.

Stacey's Miniature Masonry www.miniaturebricks.com

Scenic grass on sheets

Imthurn www.imthurn.com

Biography

Angie Scarr started playing with polymer clay in the mid 1980s when she was in her 20s but it was in 1989 after her daughter was born and she quit a job as a social work assistant that she took it up more seriously, initially making miniature foods as a complement to the work of her Mum, who was a dolls house enthusiast and miniature woodworker. Frustrated by the lumpen miniatures available at the time from all but a very few miniaturists, and inspired by the sight of a millefiori lemon slice, Angie accidentally made an orange cane by a different method than the one she'd seen. This design allowed her to re-enclose the cane into a full orange, and peel the skin back to make a realistic peeled fruit. And it was from this simple mistake and the addition of the Skinner Shade technique that she drew the inspiration which helped her to develop many ideas which, though innovative at the time are now part of the way miniatures are routinely made. Her work is now often copied, and as Angie herself readily admits, regularly equalled and often improved upon. Angie however, now with her 60s just starting, carries on innovating, solving three dimensional problems, finding short cuts and sharing inspirations and continues to have an influence on a new generation of miniature artists.

Thanks & Acknowledgements

Thanks for the inspiration to write this book, Ahmed Al Thani, who encouraged me to make my first large 12th scale garden after seeing a small version. I enjoyed it so much at the time, but now having reviewed all my methods I wish I could go back and do it all again.

For all my students in classes who enjoy my ideas and contribute theirs. My work is always a combination of my own inspiration (otherwise known as 'mad ideas') and their little tweaks. So many that I can't always pin down who it was that shared some little improvement. So to represent them all I thank Grethe Holme Jantzen who very often, and very politely and respectfully, shows me where I'm going wrong!

I'd like to thank all the polymer clay and liquid clay manufacturers for their wonderful products which constantly inspire me to find new ways to use and abuse them!

For support of many kinds I'd also like to thank Hazel Dowd and John Dowd of Minis4all, Cilla and Par, Sanne (Mus) Lundby and Keld (Yellow) Hansen, Leea Lehelma, Angie Grace, Rachel Taylor, Andrea Currie, Agneta and Frederik Lokranz (Ekeberg), Claire Scarr, Miguel Angel of Mibako, Jose Garcia Molano of Miniaturas en Forja. And my Brothers Derek for supplying inspiration and photographs from his wonderful allotment, and Howard for sending me my Mum's miniature cold frame. And while I'm at it those family, friends and neighbours who, sometimes totally unexpectedly helped out during the year off I was forced, by ill health, to take from this project. You know who you are!

As always I'd like to thank the innovative miniature artists who've inspired me along the way including Sue Heaser and Alex Blythe. Apologies for any I've missed.

Index

Made in the USA
Middletown, DE
13 February 2020

84766960R00069